THE ANCIENT
GIANTS
WHO RULED
AMERICA

"This is the most comprehensive and level approach to the subject of giant humanoids in Earth's past to have ever been published. The most appealing aspect is that Dewhurst has collected a vast array of primary sources and presents them here. Reading one newspaper discovery after another of giant skeletons and artifacts is perhaps the most compelling reason to question the standard lines we are given about humanity's origins. When coupled with his persuasive theories explaining why the Smithsonian would actively cover up such discoveries, you have one valuable and entertaining read! Highly recommended."

ROBERT R. HIERONIMUS, PH.D., AUTHOR OF
FOUNDING FATHERS, SECRET SOCIETIES
AND HOST OF 21ST CENTURY RADIO

"Giants in ancient America? You bet! It's all here in Richard Dewhurst's fabulous book. Extensively illustrated and chronicled with firsthand accounts from early 19th- and 20th-century news clippings, this book will shatter the mainstream academic teachings that continue to ignore and cover up the role giants played in early American history."

XAVIANT HAZE, AUTHOR OF *ALIENS IN ANCIENT EGYPT*
AND COAUTHOR OF *THE SUPPRESSED HISTORY OF AMERICA*

"At last, a comprehensive sourcebook that demystifies the giants of ancient America. Lavishly illustrated, this goliath and gutsy book delivers an unprecedented wealth of information on the great mound builders. Dewhurst digs deeper than the rest. Don't miss it."

SUSAN B. MARTINEZ, PH.D., AUTHOR OF
LOST HISTORY OF THE LITTLE PEOPLE
AND *THE MYSTERIOUS ORIGINS OF HYBRID MAN*

THE ANCIENT
GIANTS
WHO RULED
AMERICA

The Missing Skeletons and
the Great Smithsonian Cover-Up

RICHARD J. DEWHURST

Bear & Company
Rochester, Vermont • Toronto, Canada

Bear & Company
One Park Street
Rochester, Vermont 05767
www.BearandCompanyBooks.com

Text stock is SFI certified

Bear & Company is a division of Inner Traditions International

Library of Congress Cataloging-in-Publication Data
Dewhurst, Richard J.
  The ancient giants who ruled America : the missing skeletons and the great Smithsonian cover-up / Richard J Dewhurst.
      p. cm.
  "A study of the substantial evidence for a former race of giants in North America and its 150-year suppression by the Smithsonian Institute" — Provided by publisher.
  Includes bibliographical references and index.
  ISBN 978-1-59143-171-8 (pbk.) — ISBN 978-1-59143-752-9 (e-book)
  1. Giants—North America. 2. Human remains (Archaeology)—North America.
3. Paleoanthropology—North America. 4. Civilization, Ancient. I. Title.
  GN69.D49 2013
  930.1—dc23

                                                                      2013019220

Printed and bound in the United States by Lake Book Manufacturing, Inc. The text stock is SFI certified. The Sustainable Forestry Initiative® program promotes sustainable forest management.

10   9

Text design and layout by Brian Boynton
This book was typeset in Garamond Premier Pro with Trajan Pro and Cambria as the display typefaces

To send correspondence to the author of this book, mail a first-class letter to the author c/o Inner Traditions • Bear & Company, One Park Street, Rochester, VT 05767, and we will forward the communication.

CONTENTS

Part II

SOPHISTICATED CULTURES OF THE ANCIENT GIANTS

Part III

PRE-COLUMBIAN FOREIGN CONTACT

ACKNOWLEDGMENTS

Giant gratitude to my wife, Maxine, and son, Charles, for their continued love and support, without which this book would have been impossible. Giant bro' love to Doug Grant, Ben Edmonds, Tom McGowan, Jay Kriss, Derek Crockett, Bruce Marshall, and Ehud Sperling, president of Inner Traditions, for their friendship and inspiration along life's often perilous and bizarre journey. Giant respect to all the wonderful people at Inner Traditions who made this book possible: Jon Graham, for his great eye and greater mind; Mindy Branstetter, for her admirable patience and meticulous editing; Jeanie Levitan, for her wise guidance; Nancy Yeilding, for shaping the manuscript into its final form; and Cyndi Marcotte, for keeping it all together. And finally, giant thanks to the Quarry Hill community for providing me with shelter from the storm.

The eyes of that species of extinct Giants, whose bones fill the mounds of America, have gazed on Niagara, as ours do now.

ABRAHAM LINCOLN, 1848

ON BEING TALL AND MY FASCINATION WITH GIANTS

I discovered that I was going to be tall one fateful year between the seventh and eighth grades when I grew eight inches. My unnatural growth spurt so alarmed my mother that she set up an appointment with our family physician to see if there was "something wrong with me." Needless to say, I found all this extremely upsetting. The thought that there was something wrong with me had never occurred to me before, and the prospect of suddenly looming over my once "peer-friendly" classmates was also deeply unsettling.

Before my growth spurt, my best friend was Phil Whitcomb, who was shorter than me, but no one ever commented on it. After my growth spurt, we were immediately dubbed Mutt and Jeff. Phil hated being called Mutt in my presence, and it eventually led to a cooling of our lifelong friendship. From this I learned that being tall has its consequences, and being called a freak was one of them.

Another component of being tall was an immediate interest in giant stories. Thus the kernel for this book was born. Over the years, I took an immediate interest in various reports of giants, and when they were referenced in a newspaper account, I always gave them more credence. The only problem was that every time I tried to chase such articles down to their full-length, original newspaper nubs, I mostly came up with a shortened blurb or nothing at all.

In order to finally get to the bottom of the mystery of the giants, I subscribed to several online newspaper archive services that covered over four hundred years of newspaper accounts from the United States. I then tried to search out the cross-referenced articles I had compiled over the years. When I was able to specifically search with date and publication, I got results, but on average I only found about 25 percent of the articles I was searching for. Lacking dates and publications, how was I going to crack this thing?

Then one day, out of sheer frustration, I put on my old *Miami Herald* editor's hat and began thinking about how a typical sensationalistic newspaper headline would read. My reasoning was that if dates couldn't crack it, then word search could. My first headline search was for "Giant Skeletons Unearthed." No dates, no publications, just pure sensationalism and the hope that the word search would come up with something. Almost immediately the search engine spit back more than thirty hits, and I was off to the races. More headlines were fed in: "Amazing Giants," "Giant Skulls Found," "Secret Cave Reveals Startling Discovery," "Smithsonian Discovers Giant Skeletons," and so on. Within a month I had archived several hundred articles on various giant finds across the entire country. What I found changed my thinking about myth and history forever.

I sincerely hope that reading this book will change your thinking as much as it did mine.

INTRODUCTION

Uncovering the Real History of America

Writing this book has been the most exciting voyage of discovery I have ever taken. What started as a somewhat idle inquiry into clouded reports of giants—in and of itself not that groundbreaking—ended with my having to rethink everything I ever learned in school. After all, we've all heard of giants before. What we have not heard is that these people were as real as you and me.

But the most important thing about this book for me was not discovering that giants were real, although in these pages we will most definitely see the historical evidence of that fact. What really surprised me was discovering something very much more shocking: the truth about the early history of America and the people who lived here.

Long before the so-called "discovery of America," this land was populated by very ancient peoples, some of whom were of enormous size, as attested to by the numerous reports of giant finds, a sampling of which is presented in the first two chapters. Those reports make it clear that in the nineteenth century such finds were common knowledge around the country. When carbon dating became available in the twentieth century, earlier estimates of the age of the remains were increased by many magnitudes: with ranges from five thousand to fourteen thousand years! I examine the reports of these extraordinary results in chapter 3, in addition to finds linking some of those early, magnificent humans with mastodons (which became extinct some twenty thousand years ago). Not surprisingly, many finds indicate that the giants were royal beings, as the reports of copper crowns and pearl robes in chapter 4 make clear.

While certain monuments and parks in various parts of the country offer silent testimony to the creative efforts of these early peoples, few of us are aware of the true scope of the mounds and cities that once revealed advanced ancient civilizations. In chapter 5 we take a closer look at studies and reports about pyramids and pictorial mounds, while in chapter 6 we learn of discoveries of once-thriving cities most of us have never heard of.

When we learn of the importance of the copper mines in upper Michigan at Isle Royale and the mica mines of North Carolina, reported on in chapter 7, we must necessarily take a deep breath and think, What are the mines telling us? They are telling us that as early as 10,000 BCE, Americans were mining mica for ornaments as well as mining and refining copper into weapons, jewelry, and exquisite grave goods. Along with the "buried treasures" spoken of in chapter 8 and later chapters, reports and studies of the mines make it clear that this land was home to very ancient, fully developed, sophisticated cultures capable of fine weaving, mummification, beautiful artworks, and even duck decoys so expertly crafted you'd think a New England decoy maker had made them in his workshop today.

Discrepancies between the amount of copper estimated to have been mined and findings of copper in the country hint at world-wide trade in those very ancient times. In fact, a long history of pre-Columbian European and Asian contact is evidenced all over the continent, as seen in artifacts like the Roman coins and engraved tablets examined in reports in chapter 9 or the existence of red-haired, blue-eyed Mandans of North Dakota or the nine-thousand-year-old Caucasian mummies of Spirit Cave in Nevada, reported on in chapter 10. Some still argue that there was no European contact; even when confronted with the evidence of the Florida bog mummies—hundreds of red-haired corpses so perfectly preserved that their hair and brain tissue can be seen and tested—they still refuse to give up the old historical canards. The reports given in chapter 10 give rise to questions about whether these were the red-haired ancestors of the later Europeans and not the other way around. Added to this are the startling reports of finds of seven-thousand-year-old skeletons of a race of blond-haired giants along with the remains of a megalithic "Stonehenge-era" temple on Catalina Island in California given in chapter 11. The suggestions about possible far-flung genetic and cultural connections shared in chapter 12 provide fascinating material for musing on, offering insights regarding very ancient travel and cultures, north and south, east and west. Only true historical inquiry, unclouded by prejudice, will eventually tell us the answer.

But what we have instead is a perfect storm of wrong-headed thinking in order to protect current scientific theory. And central to the promotion of wrong-headed thinking has been the Smithsonian Institution, an institution originally intended to "increase the diffusion of knowledge among men." Although scant official papers exist to attest to its purpose beyond that statement, its true mission to unearth the real history of America is evidenced by its first commissioned and published book, *Ancient Monuments of the Mississippi Valley,* written in 1848 by Ephraim G. Squier and Edwin H. Davis. This lavishly illustrated work is an invaluable and open-minded study of the huge number of earthworks found along the Mississippi River.

But something happened after that promising beginning. What my research has revealed is that the Smithsonian has been at the center of a vast cover-up of America's true history since the 1880s. The Smithsonian was originally founded in 1829 with a $500,000

ANCIENT WORKS , MARIETTA , OHIO ,

Fig. I.1. This Library of Congress image was used as the frontispiece for the 150th-anniversary reissue of *Ancient Monuments of the Mississippi Valley* by Squier and Davis.

grant from the British mineralogist James Smithson, who never visited the United States, died without heirs, and was buried in Genoa, Italy. A sign of the Smithsonian's utter disregard for history is that Smithson's body was reburied at the Smithsonian Castle in the twentieth century in a sarcophagus that lists his age at death as seventy-five, when it is common knowledge that he was closer to sixty-five when he died.

After the Civil War the Smithsonian began to adopt a policy of excluding any evidence of direct foreign influence in the Americas prior to Columbus. Some have argued that it was an attempt by the fractured post–Civil War government to downplay any regional and ethnic conflicts in the still fragile national rebuilding after the war. Others have pointed to the expansionist policies incorporated in the doctrine of manifest destiny and the desire to obscure the origins of the tribes being displaced and annihilated by westward expansion. Still others have alleged that it was a direct religious policy adapted to counter the growing problem with the Mormon religion and its assertions that the lost tribes of Israel were to be found in America.

All of these policies can be directly traced to Major John Wesley Powell and his tenure at the Smithsonian from 1879 to 1902. Powell was a geologist and explorer who led expeditions and conducted surveys of the American West. In 1869 he set out by boat to explore the Colorado River from the Green River, Wyoming Territory to the foot of the Grand Canyon.

When Congress created the Bureau of Ethnology in 1879 Powell was named its first director, a post he held until his death in 1902. Placed under the auspices of the Smithsonian Institution, the bureau, whose name was changed to the Bureau of American Ethnology, was to be the repository of the archives, records, and material relating to the Indians of North America. Because of his experience as a Western explorer, Powell was considered an expert on the geography of the American West, and he was asked to write a report on the history of the ancient tribes and their probable origins, which was to become the official policy of the Smithsonian for the next hundred-plus years.

The title of Powell's first report to the secretary of the Smithsonian in 1879, "On Limitations to the Use of Some Anthropologic Data," is revealing and shows the ulterior policy at work within the nascent institution. The following is taken from that report.

Investigations in this department are of great interest, and have attracted to the field a host of workers; but a general review of the mass of published matter exhibits the fact that the uses to which the material has been put have not always been wise.

In the monuments of antiquity found throughout North America, in camp and village sites, graves, mounds, ruins, and scattered works of art, the origin and development of art in savage and barbaric life may be satisfactorily studied. Incidentally, too, hints of customs may be discovered, but outside of this, the discoveries made have often been illegitimately used, especially for the purpose of connecting the tribes of North America with peoples of so-called races of antiquity in other portions of the world. A brief review of some conclusions that must be accepted in the present status of the science will exhibit the futility of these attempts.*

In the study of these antiquities, there has been much unnecessary speculation in respect to the relation existing between the people to whose existence they attest, and the tribes of Indians inhabiting the country during the historic period. It may be said that in the Pueblos discovered in the southwestern portion of the United States and farther south through Mexico and perhaps into Central America tribes are known having a culture quite as far advanced as any exhibited in the discovered ruins. In this respect, then, there is no need to search for extra-limital origin through lost tribes for any art there exhibited. With regard to the mounds so widely scattered between the two oceans, it may also be said that mound-building tribes were known in the early history of discovery of this continent, and that the vestiges of art discovered do not excel in any respect the arts of the Indian tribes known to history. There is, therefore, no reason for us to search for an extra-limital origin through lost tribes for the arts discovered in the mounds of North America.

---

*Powell then goes on to definitively state that there are no foreign influences to be seen or studied in relation to the pueblo- and mound-building cultures of the Americas that are believed to precede the American Indians. In relation to his dismissive comments regarding any connections to the "lost tribes" from the Old World, it is interesting to note that Powell was the son of a preacher in Palmyra, New York, who lost his flock to Mormon missionaries.

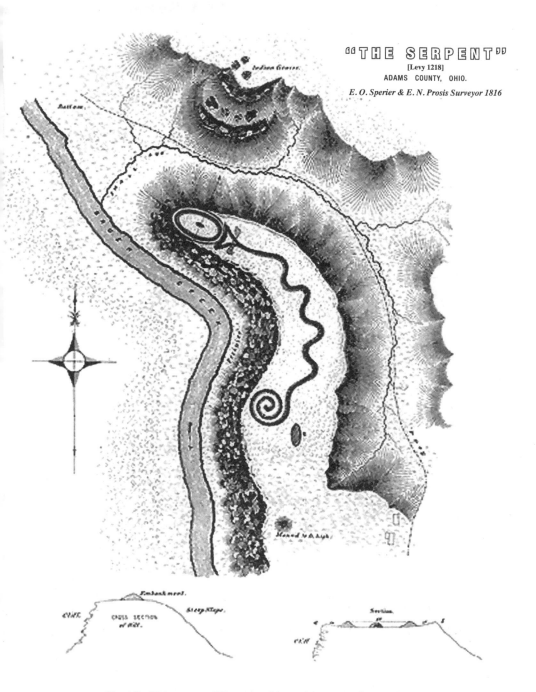

"THE SERPENT"
[Levy 1218]
ADAMS COUNTY, OHIO.
E. O. Sperier & E. N. Prosis Surveyor 1816

Fig. 1.2. This map of Serpent Mound is one of many in
Ancient Monuments of the Mississippi Valley that were surveyed and sketched
by Squier and Davis.

Fig. I.3. The Kincaid Site, a Mississippian settlement in southern Illinois
(courtesy of Herb Roe)

Foremost among the wrong-headed theories Powell championed is
evolution. We are shown charts of man becoming bipedal and each "new"
man being bigger and smarter than the last. This is in direct contradic-
tion to the charts we use for every other animal we study. We have only to
look at a bird and be told that it was once a dinosaur to know how false
this paradigm of man's growth is. Look at the evolution of most animals,
and the record says they got smaller over time, not bigger. However, with
all the modern edifices of education built on the theory of evolution and
the growing stature of humanity, we can't very well have the Smithsonian
running around telling people that we have degenerated from an ancient
race of giants who once ruled America, now can we?

The second theory current at the time was called uniform gradual
history, a benign theory that says Earth goes along for huge spans of
time with no catastrophes. The opposite of this theory is the more modern school of thought called catastrophism, based on the provable fact
that disasters happen frequently and often. The record here in America

speaks clearly on the subject. It relates not only to the disappearance of the Western inland civilizations dating back before 5000 BCE, which were wiped out by volcanoes, but also to the sudden cessation of the copper trade around 1500 BCE. Why is this significant? Because Cretan culture was wiped out in a series of catastrophes brought on by the massive explosion of the Santorini volcano on one of the Cretan Empire's islands. I do not think it a coincidence that in 1500 BCE the volcano wiped out the Cretan Empire (the Exodus in Egypt factors into this as well), and shut down the copper trade in America for almost two thousand years.

The third major contributing factor to the extant historical myopia is the land bridge theory, which states that all the Indian tribes reached America from Asia across the Alaskan land bridge. The man who came up with this absurd and unprovable theory is none other than Dr. Ales Hrdlicka, the first curator (in 1903) of physical anthropology of the U.S. National Museum, now the Smithsonian Institution National Museum of Natural History. No boats for him. They walked—even though we know they would have had to walk

Fig. I.4. The Nodena Site, possibly in the Province of Pacaha, encountered by Hernando de Soto (courtesy of Herbert Roe)

around or through the extensive glaciers still blocking Canada. Were they not capable of slowly sailing from one island to another, as we know the Polynesians and Australians did for forty thousand years? The theory is absurd, but the Smithsonian told us to believe it, and we did. When academics get caught in such a perfect storm of wrong theories, they have a very hard time wriggling out of it. Reputations and careers are at stake. Books have been written and published and promotions garnered on the weight of their verity, so the fix was in from the beginning, so to speak.

Then there is the thorny question of racism and manifest destiny (which, decoded, reads like this: America is inhabited by inferior races of people whom "civilized man" has a God-given right to exterminate so that he can exploit the country he now considers his domain). One has only to read Powell's 1879 theories about the aborigines and their inherent lack of intelligence to get an unpleasant whiff of what we are dealing with here. Powell finishes his "proof" of no European or Asiatic influences by boldly asserting, without a shred of supporting evidence, that all pictographic writing found anywhere in the Americas is evidence of nothing more than the most rudimentary picture making, despite having no working knowledge of any of the ancient writing systems to which he alludes. He continues in his report to explain:

> Many of these pictographs are simply pictures, rude etchings, or paintings delineating natural objects, especially animals, and illustrate simply the beginning of pictorial art; others we know were intended to commemorate events or to represent other ideas entertained by their authors; but to a large extent these were simply mnemonic—not conveying ideas of themselves, but designed more thoroughly to retain in memory certain events or thoughts by persons who were already cognizant of the same through current hearsay or tradition. If once the memory of the thought to be preserved has passed from the minds of men, the record is powerless to restore its own subject-matter to the understanding.

The great body of picture-writings is thus described; yet to some slight extent pictographs are found with characters more or less conventional, and the number of such is quite large in Mexico and Central America. Yet even these conventional characters are used with others less conventional in such a manner that perfect records were never made. Hence it will be seen that it is illegitimate to use any pictographic matter of a date anterior to the discovery of the continent by Columbus for historic purposes.

When you step back for a moment from the pseudo-scientific double-talk, what he is saying is this: these are essentially dumb savages with the minds of children. Other pictures and trinkets that we have found that hint at intelligence, language, or higher knowledge are simply the scribbling of children trying to leave a garbled record of their childish view of history and religion.

It is bad enough that these biased and unsupported claims were the policy of the Smithsonian in the nineteenth century, but to make matters worse, Charles Doolittle Walcott, secretary (chief executive officer)

Fig. I.5. Major Paleo-Indian sites in North America

of the Smithsonian from 1907 to 1927, made the "Powell Doctrine" the official dogma of the museum for the entire twentieth century as well. In fact, the Powell Doctrine is still the official policy of the Smithsonian as of this writing, despite the fact that some scholars associated with the museum are finally starting to speak out in support of evidence of early European settlement of the Americas.

The great crime and tragedy of this policy is hard to compute. One glaring result has been the suppression of hundreds of "out-of-context" finds, all submitted to the museum in naive ignorance of the museum's official policy of suppression of alternative perspectives. To compound the problem, all major universities in the United States also adopted this policy in conjunction with the official position of the Smithsonian, thus making it impossible to study alternative American history and receive any grants or funding for pursuits of this nature. A giant problem for the giants and a giant problem for history.

It is the express intent of this book to bring to light the many discoveries about the ancient history of this land that have all but disappeared from public awareness over the last hundred years.

Fig. I.6. Beanstalk giant, *Jack and the Beanstalk* by John D. Batten

ONE

Findings on Ancient American Giants

1

HOW BIG WERE THEY?

What makes us call a person a *giant?* Here are some ways to place the term in context:

- Typically, the height of Americans today ranges between five feet, four inches, and five feet, ten inches (National Health Statistics Report No. 10, October 22, 2008).
- Only twenty players in National Basketball Association history have exceeded a listed height of seven feet, three inches, with only a few reaching as tall as seven feet, seven inches. Some, but not all, of the tallest players have the condition known as gigantism or giantism, a condition usually caused by a tumor on the pituitary gland of the brain. These terms are typically applied to those whose height is not just in the upper 1 percent of the population but also several standard deviations above the mean for people of the same sex, age, and ethnic ancestry.
- The tallest person in recorded history was Robert Pershing Wadlow (February 22, 1918–July 15, 1940). He was sometimes called the Alton Giant or the Giant of Illinois because that's where he was born and raised. His height was eight feet, eleven inches, and he weighed 490 pounds at his time of death.

Fig. 1.1. Robert Wadlow (right) pictured here with his father, Harold Wadlow (left), who was five feet, eleven inches tall (www.sciencekids.co.nz).

With these facts in mind, let's review a sampling of the many reports of finds of very-tall human remains on this continent.

THE BONES TELL THE TALE

Extremely ancient human remains have been found throughout New York State and New England that date back to at least 9000 BCE. A report from the *Syracuse Herald American* in 1983 (see pages 78–79) said that anthropologists from the Buffalo Museum of Science dug up 1,400 artifacts from a site called Phoenix Hilltop. The following county historical report published in 1824 reported that in 1811 "rude medals, a pipe and other articles" were uncovered at an Indian mound on Mount Morris in New York State, in association with the remains of a giant "of enormous size."

A History of Livingston County, New York, 1824

When Jesse Stanley came to Mount Morris in 1811 an Indian Mound nearly 100 feet in diameter and from 8 to 10 feet high covered the site of the late General Mills' residence. The mound had long been crowned by a great tree, which had recently fallen under the axe. Deacon Stanley was told that when freshly cut, it disclosed 130 concentric circles or yearly growths.

About the year 1820, the mound was removed, and in its removal arrowheads, a brass kettle, and knives were thrown out. A number of skeletons were also disinterred. Among the bones was a human skeleton of enormous size, the jawbone of which was so large that Adam Holslander placed it, mask-like, over his own chin and jaw. He was the largest man in the settlement, and his face was in proportion to the rest of his body.

Metal in the form of rude medals, a pipe and other articles were picked out of the earth thrown from the excavation.

A History of Western New York, 1804

Human bones of gigantic proportion were discovered in such a state of preservation as to be accurately described and measured. The cavities of the skulls were large enough in their dimensions to receive the entire head of a man of modern times, and could be put on one's head with as much ease as a hat or cap. The jawbones were sufficiently large to admit to being placed so as to match or fit outside of a modern man's face. The other bones so far discovered appear to be of equal proportions with the skulls and jawbones, several of which have been preserved in the cabinets of antiquarians, where they still may be seen.

NEW HAMPSHIRE GIANT NINE FEET TALL

PORTSMOUTH HERALD, AUGUST 17, 1899

Relics of a prehistoric age have been brought to light in Noble County. The find is in York Township where workmen excavating for a public highway found the skeleton of an inhabitant of early days.

The bones indicate that the person was fully nine feet tall.

The bones are unusually large and the position of the skeleton when found indicated that the person had been buried in a sitting position. The belief is advanced that the remains are those of a mound builder.

History of the Town of Rockingham, Vermont, 1907

When the earth was removed from the top of the ledges east of the falls a remarkable human skeleton, unmistakably that of an Indian, was found. Those who saw it tell the writer the jaw bone was of such size that a large man could easily slip it over his face and the teeth, which were all double, were perfect. . . . This skeleton was kept for many years deposited in the attic of a small building on the north side of the Square. This building was then occupied by Dr. John H. Wells' office and drug store and stood where the Italian fruit store now does. When the building was rebuilt a decade ago or more the bones disappeared.

BONES OF GIANT INDIANS FOUND IN MARYLAND

PREHISTORIC MEN SEVEN FEET TALL WHO ONCE LIVED IN WHAT IS MARYLAND

BALTIMORE AMERICAN, NOVEMBER 15, 1897

There has just been received at the Maryland Academy of Sciences, the skeleton of an Indian seven feet tall. It was discovered near Antietam. There are now skeletons of three powerful Indians at the Academy who at one time in their wildness roamed over the state of Maryland armed with such instruments as nature gave them or that their limited skill taught them to make.

Two of these skeletons belonged to individuals evidently of gigantic size. The vertebrae and bones of the legs are nearly as thick as those of a horse and the length of the long bones exceptional.

The skulls are of fine proportions, ample and with walls of moderate thickness and of great strength and stiffened beyond with a powerful occipital ridge. The curves of the forehead are moderate and not retreating, suggesting intelligence and connected with jaws of moderate development.

The locality from which these skeletons came is in Frederick County, near Antietam Creek. It was formerly supposed to have been the battleground of two tribes of Indians: the Catawbas and the Delawares.

Before the coming of the white man, this site was occupied as a village by Indians of great stature, some of them six-and-a-half to seven feet in height.

POTOMAC RIVER GIANT

MORNING HERALD, MAY 14, 1956

The skeleton of a giant Indian, maybe seven or more feet in height, who died and was buried about the time Christ was born, has been unearthed from prehistoric burial grounds along the Potomac River near Point of Rocks recently.

Nicholas Yinger, who has been excavating at this and other sites of early Indian villages along the Potomac River in recent years, discovered the skeleton of the giant Indian, along with the other artifacts buried with the body, on Saturday, April 28, just a few weeks ago. Mr. Yinger said that apart from the huge size of the Algonquian Indian, the next most interesting thing about the remains is that the bow and quiver of five arrows were buried with the body. Two elk-antlers and three-and-one-half-inch arrow points in the center of the tibias are part of the quiver of arrows. Near the point of the antler-arrows is a perfect boiled-bone fishhook revealing his fishing line was also placed with the body. Three large white-flint triangular arrow heads were found at the side of the left tibia.

"This aborigine must have been a hunter with great strength as is indicated by the broad-shank flint points used in a powerful bow," explained Yinger.

ANCIENT BURIAL GROUND AT BLACK CREEK

CHARLEROI MAIL, MAY 7, 1953

Along the Susquehanna River in Indiana County, Pennsylvania a major Indian burial site was uncovered. All together, forty-nine skeletons were exhumed, the tallest being eight feet tall. These skeletons were reportedly taken to the Harrisburg Museum for reassembly and then shipped to the Smithsonian for further study. However, the Smithsonian denies any knowledge of them.

On the site of the William H. Rhea farm (circa 1871–1880) in Conemaugh Township just west of the mouth of Black Legs Creek, skeletons of men, probably Indians, were found. Noted local historian Clarence Stephenson says, "One of the skeletons is of a giant nearly eight feet tall. The giant's skeleton measured 89 inches from the top of the skull to the phalanges of the feet. It was covered with small stones, lay on the back, and measured 26 inches across the chest."

The following report from 1916 is of the discovery of skeletons found in the area of Sayre, Pennsylvania.

REPORT OF SIXTY-EIGHT SKELETONS AVERAGING
SEVEN-FEET TALL

CHARLESTON DAILY MAIL, SEPTEMBER 20, 1916

On July 13, Professor Skinner of the American Indian Museum, excavating the mound at Tioga Point, near Sayre, Pennsylvania, uncovered the bones of 68 men, which he estimates had been buried at least seven or eight hundred years. The average height indicated by the skeletons was seven feet, but many were taller. Evidence of the gigantic size of these men was seen in huge axes found beside the bones.

GIANT EIGHT FEET, SEVEN INCHES TALL
UNEARTHED

OHIO SCIENCE ANNUAL, 1898

A rare archaeological discovery has been made near Reinersville in Morgan County, Ohio. A small knoll, which had always been supposed to be the result of an uprooted tree, was opened recently and discovered to be the work of mound builders.

Just below the surrounding surface, a layer of boulders and pebbles was found. Directly underneath this was found the skeleton of a giant 8 feet, 7 inches in height. Surrounding the skeleton were bone and stone implements, stone hatchets, and other characteristics of the mound builders.

The discovery is considered by the scientists as one of the most important ever made in Ohio. The skeleton is now in the possession of a Reinersville collector.

THE BIG WHOPPER: EIGHTEEN FEET AND COUNTING?

The following newspaper account from an 1870 edition of the *Ohio Democrat* postulates that the giant, whose skeleton was found with a nine-foot-long sword, must have stood eighteen feet tall "in his stockings." It then alleges that the skeleton was shipped to New York. Since this account is highly speculative to say the least, let's just say this was one big skeleton and leave it at that.

CARDIFF GIANT UNDONE WITH AN ENORMOUS IRON HELMET

OHIO DEMOCRAT, JANUARY 14, 1870

On Tuesday morning last, while Mr. William Thompson, assisted by Mr. Robert R. Smith, was engaged in making an excavation near the house of the former, about half a mile north of West Hickory, preparatory to erecting a derrick, they exhumed an enormous helmet of iron, which was corroded with rust.

Further digging brought to light a sword, which measured nine feet in length. Curiosity incited them to enlarge the hole, and after some little time they discovered the bones of two enormous feet. Following up the "lead" they had so unexpectedly struck, in a few hours' time they had unearthed the well-preserved remains of an enormous giant, belonging to a species of the human family, which probably inhabited this and other parts of the world, at the time of which the Bible speaks when it says: "And there were giants in those days."

The helmet is said to be of the shape of those among the ruins of Nineveh. The bones of the skeleton are a remarkable white. The teeth are all in their places and all of extraordinary size. These relics have been taken to Tionesta where they are visited by large numbers of people daily.

When his "giantship" was in the flesh he must have stood eighteen feet tall in his stockings. These remarkable relics will be shipped to New York early next week. The joints of the skeleton are now being glued together. These remains were found about twelve feet under the surface of a mound, which had been thrown up probably centuries ago, and which was not more than three feet above the level of the ground around it.

SKELETONS SEVEN FEET LONG

NEW YORK TIMES, MAY 5, 1885

Centerburg, Ohio: Licking County has been for years a favorite field for students of Indian history. Last week a small mound near Homer was opened by some school boys. Today further search was made and several feet below the surface of the earth, in a large vault with stone floor and bark covering, were found four huge skeletons, three being over seven feet in length, and the other a full eight feet.

The skeletons lay with their feet to the east on a bed of charcoal in which were numerous burned bones. About the neck of the largest skeleton were a lot of stone beads. The grave contained about 30 stone vessels and implements, the most striking being a curiously-wrought pipe. It is said to be the only engraved stone pipe ever found. A stone kettle, holding about a gallon in which was a residue of saline matter, bears evidence of much skill. Their bows, a number of arrows, stone hatchets, and a stone knife are among the implements that were found at the site.

ANOTHER OHIO GIANT NOW SEEMS SMALL AT ONLY EIGHT FEET

OHIO MORNING SUN NEWS HERALD, APRIL 14, 1904.

A giant skeleton of a man has been unearthed at the Woolverton farm, a short distance from Tippecanoe City, Ohio. It measures eight feet from the top of the head to the ankles, the feet being missing, says this newspaper reporter.

The skull is large enough to fit as a helmet over the average man's head. This skeleton was one of seven, buried in a circle, the feet of all being towards the center. Rude implements were near. The skeletons are thought to be those of mound builders.

GIANT BURIED WITH A PANTHER

This is one of several accounts that I ran across in my research of a giant skeleton being buried with a panther. The ritual context of these animal burials has never been properly studied or understood. In this account, the contents of eleven mounds were said to have been shipped to the Smithsonian for study.

GIGANTIC MAN BURIED NEXT TO FEROCIOUS PANTHER

CINCINNATI COMMERCIAL GAZETTE, SEPTEMBER 26, 1889

Soon after the 1st of March relics were collected to be placed on loan to the Smithsonian Institution at Washington D.C. During the last two months eleven mounds have been opened and their contents taken to the museum and placed on exhibition. These mounds vary in height from eight to thirty feet, are generally conical in shape, and contain all the way from 300 to 10,000 square yards of dirt. They were built by the aborigines of this country hundreds of years ago to serve as burial places for the distinguished dead. They are generally placed near some stream in a valley and not infrequently on high points of land, which command a good view of the country, but the larger ones are in the valleys. These mounds are usually composed of clay, sometimes of sand, and often have layers of charcoal or burnt clay in them. These layers are often as brightly colored as if they had been painted. . . .

About five feet above this layer, or nine feet from the summit of the mound, was a skeleton of a very large individual who had buried by the side of it the bones of a panther. Whether the person had killed the panther and it was buried with him as an honor, or whether the panther had killed the individual, one cannot say.

FORTY-THREE MOUNDS OPENED

This much, however, can be said— That in 43 mounds opened no find of this nature has been made. It is therefore quite interesting and important. The skull of this panther was very large, teeth very long and sharp. It would take a mound builder of a great deal of nerve to attack a beast of this size if he had nothing but a stone hatchet and bow and arrows to defend himself with.

REGULAR SKELETON FOUND NEXT TO GIANT

Just below this skeleton and lying on the layer of buried bones was a medium-sized personage who had buried around his neck in the manner of a necklace, between his upper and lower jaw, 147 bone and shell beads. The shell beads were made from the thick part of Conch and Pyrula shells. These shells must have been carried from the Atlantic Ocean, as they are ocean shells, and not found inland, or the tribe to which the man belonged may have traded with tribes near the ocean and thereby got the beads.

THE GIANTS OF CONNEAUT

This is only one of many accounts of ancient burial fields containing multiple giant burials. In this case the burial site was said to have been three to four acres in size and to have contained several thousand burials, including a magnificent eight-foot-tall queen bedecked in elaborate copper jewelry.

Ashtabula County Historical Record, 1878

In 1798 the first permanent settlers from the east arrived in the Western Reserve of Ohio. They began to clear the forests along the southern shore of Lake Erie, and in the process found numerous ancient earthen structures and almost everywhere the finely made spear points and other artifacts of a long forgotten and once populous native society, a people obviously quite different from the Massasauga Indians then living in that country. A generation before the first immigrant explorers of western Pennsylvania and southern Ohio had made similar discoveries: the extensive earthworks of Circleville and Marietta, Ohio, were already well publicized by the time that settler Aaron Wright and his companions began to stake out their new homes along Conneaut Creek, in what would become Ashtabula County, Ohio.

The Discoveries of Aaron Wright in 1800

Perhaps it was because he was a single young man with plenty of energy, or perhaps it was because his choice for a homestead included a large "mound builder" burial ground. Whatever the reasons may have been, Aaron Wright has gone down in the history books as the discoverer of the "Conneaut Giants," the unusually large-boned ancient inhabitants of Ashtabula County, Ohio. In an 1844 account, Harvey Nettleton reported that this "ancient burying grounds of about four acres" was situated in what soon became the village of New Salem (later renamed Conneaut), "extending northward from the bank of the creek . . . to Main Street, in an oblong square" tract that "appeared to have been accurately surveyed into lots, running from the north to the south." Nettleton also said that the ancient graves "were distinguished by slight depressions in the surface of the earth disposed in straight rows, with the intervening spaces, or alleys, cover[ing] the whole area . . . estimated to contain from two to three thousand graves. These depressions, on a thorough examination made by Esq. Aaron Wright, as early as 1800, were found invariably to contain human bones, blackened with time, which on exposure to the air soon crumbled to dust."

The prehistoric cemetery on Aaron Wright's land was remarkable enough, just in its size and the configuration of the graves; but it was what was in those graves and in the adjacent burial mounds that captured Nettleton's attention.

The mounds that were situated in the eastern part of what is now the village of Conneaut and the extensive burying ground near the Presbyterian Church appear to have had no connection with the burying places of the Indians. They doubtless refer to a more remote period and are the relics of an extinct race, of whom the Indians had no knowledge. These mounds were of comparatively small size, and of the same general character of those that are widely scattered over the country. What is most remarkable concerning them is that among the quantity of human bones they contain, there are found specimens belonging to men of large stature, and who must have been nearly allied to a race of giants. Skulls were taken from these mounds, the cavities of which were of sufficient capacity to admit the head of an ordinary man, and jaw-bones that might be fitted on over the face with equal facility. The bones of the arms and lower limbs were of the same proportions, exhibiting ocular proof of the degeneracy of the human race since the period in which these men occupied the soil which we now inhabit. Circleville, Ohio, antiquarian Caleb Atwater was the known first person to comment upon the earthworks at Conneaut (then New Salem) in a published text. In his 1820 report, "Description of the Antiquities Discovered in the State of Ohio" Atwater describes the "work at Salem . . . on a hill near Coneaught river . . . having two parallel circular walls and a ditch between them." Atwater says practically nothing about the burial mounds in the vicinity of this pre-Columbian fort "on a hill," but he does provide the following information on page 125 of his report: "My informant says, within this work are sometimes found skeletons of a people of small stature, which, if true, sufficiently identifies it to have belonged to that race of men who erected our tumuli." Thus, it was Caleb Atwater's opinion that the builders of the ancient mounds were a "people of small stature," and that reports of larger skeletons uncovered among their ruins were the exception, not the rule. To the above summary of Atwater's investigations it might also be added that many of the earthworks he described he never saw himself, relying upon information supplied by untrained observers living in the vicinity of these ancient remains.

What Nehemiah King Found in 1829

Nettleton's account was widely circulated when it was summarized in Henry Howe's *Historical Collections of Ohio,* 1847. Howe writes of Thomas Montgomery and Aaron Wright coming to Ohio in the spring of 1798, and of the subsequent discovery of the "extensive burying ground" and of "the human bones found in the mounds" nearby. Howe repeats the report that among these uncovered bones, "were some belonging to men of gigantic structure." He also tells how, in 1829, a tree was cut down next to the ancient "Fort Hill in Conneaut" and that the local land owner, "The Hon. Nehemiah King, with a magnifying glass, counted 350 annualer rings" beyond some cut marks near the tree's center. Howe concludes: "Deducting 350 from 1829 leaves 1479, which must have been the year when these cuts were made. This was thirteen years before the discovery of America by Columbus. It perhaps was done by the race of the mounds, with an axe of copper, as that people had the art of hardening that metal so as to cut like steel."

The same year that Henry Howe's history of Ohio appeared another interesting book was published by the Smithsonian Institution, entitled, *Ancient Monuments of the Mississippi Valley*. On page 38 of that seminal report by E. G. Squier and E. H. Davis appears the first known published description of "Fort Hill," that strange pre-Columbian landmark situated on the property of Aaron Wright's neighbor, Nehemiah King.

Ancient Work near Conneaut, Ashtabula County, Ohio

This work is at present very slight, but distinctly traceable. The sketch is a mere coup d'oeil, without measurements. The elevation on the bluff upon which it stands is about seventy feet; and the banks of the aluminous state are, upon the north, very precipitous. . . . Upon the south side . . . the wall, which skirts the brow of the hill, is accompanied by an outer ditch, while upon the north there is a simple embankment. The ascent (marked C-C in the cut), is gradual and easy. Within the enclosure the earth is very black and rich; outside of the wall it is stiff clay. The adjacent bottoms are very fertile, and the creek is everywhere fordable. There can be no doubt that this was a fortified position. Near the village of Conneaut are a number of mounds, and other traces of an ancient population, among which is an aboriginal cemetery regularly laid out, and of great extent.

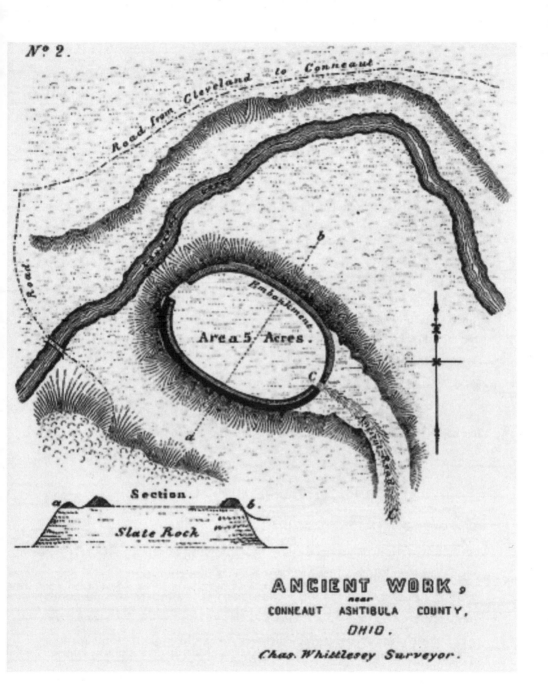

Fig. 1.2. An 1847 sketch of Fort Hill by Chas. Whittlesey, surveyor

OHIO ACCOUNT OF NINE-FOOT GIANTS

STEVENS POINT DAILY JOURNAL, MAY 1, 1886

It is very evident that at an early day in the history of this country, this section of Ohio was an important camping ground for the American Indian. And, indeed, discoveries are frequently made, which lead people interested in the matter of prehistoric America to believe that a race of mankind, superior in size, strength, and intelligence to the common red man of the forest, flourished not only along the coasts East and South, but right here in southern Ohio. There are in this county several burying grounds, and two of them are located five miles west of this city, near Jasper, one on the farm of Mr. William Bush and one on Mr. Matthew Mark's farm. In a conversation with a gentleman who has seen [skeletons] unearthed at the Mark bank, we were told that many dozens of human skeletons have been exhumed since the bank was first opened.

Some of these skeletons have been measured, and the largest have been found to be nine feet long and over.

At one time ten skeletons were exhumed. They had been buried in a circle, standing in an erect position, and were in a comparatively well-preserved condition. One remarkable fact about all the skeletons unearthed at these places is the perfect state of preservation in which their teeth are found to be. Not a decayed tooth has been discovered, and this would seem to indicate that these people naturally had excellent teeth or some extraordinary manner of preserving them.

GIANTS FOUND IN GEORGIA

The find of a giant race averaging six and a half to seven feet tall electrified the nation, as attested to by the following Sunday photo feature, which appeared in prominent newspapers across the country on August 2, 1936. This article appeared complete with comparative photos of giant skulls and photos of an entire skeleton laid out on its back at the site. Beneath one of the photos of the main archaeologist pointing to a giant skull was this caption: "Dr. Preston Holder (above photo), who is directing archaeological study and excavation on Sea Island, Georgia, points out the unusual characteristics of one of his amazing finds. The skeletons of these hitherto unknown American aborigines showed they all ranged in height from six-and-one half to seven feet in height."

GEORGIA'S SAND DUNES YIELD STARTLING PROOF
OF A PREHISTORIC RACE OF GIANTS

ARCHAEOLOGISTS MYSTIFIED AT FINDING SKELETONS OF
MEN WHO WERE SEVEN FEET TALL

SALT LAKE TRIBUNE, AUGUST 2, 1936

Perhaps the discovery of the first dinosaur bones on the North American continent created no more sensation in scientific circles than the recent revelations of prehistoric man lately developed off the coast of Georgia. Excavating in the sand dunes of the sun-sprayed Golden Isles, Georgia, archaeologists have gouged out the strange record of an amazing prehistoric race of giants.

With pick ax and spade, these searchers into the past have burrowed their way beneath the surface of the palm-clad dunes of Georgia's semi-tropical coastal islands, to delve into the mysteries of a previously unsuspected race of mankind. The question uppermost in their mind today is: What manner of men were these, the members of whose tribe all averaged between six and one half and seven feet tall?

Preston Holder, archaeologist, is directing the excavation work, which has been sponsored by the Smithsonian Institution. Slowly, painstakingly, Holder is endeavoring to piece together the slender threads that will lead him into the past. He has expressed the opinion that the Smithsonian enterprise will throw important light upon a thus far unrecorded tribe, and perhaps establish a new link in the history of mankind in North America.

The Golden Isles extend in a chain from Savannah as far south as Fernandina. They are today inhabited mostly by wealthy Americans whose luxurious summer homes dot the landscape. The Golden Isles are romantic in the extreme. The known history of these islands fairly reeks with pirate lore, tales of mystery and violence, and lost treasures.

NEW AIRPORT, OLD GIANTS

But today only one of all the islands still remains open to the public. It is called Saint Simons and Sea Island. And had it not been for the never-ceasing strides of modern civilization, it might well be that the new proof of America's prehistoric giants might never have been found. For it was the ground-breaking for Georgia's new Glynn County airport—which will be constructed on Sea Island—that revealed the first evidences of the find that has since brought archaeologists fairly tumbling over one another.

Workers on the proposed new airport hadn't set off more than two or three charges of dynamite when they were amazed to find a number of shattered skulls and skeletons scattered about. One of the nation's leading archaeologists, Dr. F. M. Setzler, of the United States National Museum, was dispatched to the scene. One look, and Dr. Setzler was convinced that the earth beneath the sand dunes would bear importantly upon the history and habits of southern coast aborigines.

SMITHSONIAN FIRST TO TEST GIANT SKELETON

So the systematic work began. Some of the first skulls to be disinterred by Preston Holder have already been examined at the Smithsonian Institution by Dr. Ales Hrdlicka (to appear at another site as well), foremost authority on North American types.

One mound located at the airport site was composed by at least three layers of shell, each six inches to a foot thick. Very little midden, or garbage, was found in the shell. The mound was fifty feet in diameter, with a six foot rise. Burials were found to have been made immediately beneath the layers of shell.

It was in this mound that archaeologists made the important discovery of a complete skeleton of a young man, believed to have been in his teens at the time of his death. From tip to tip it exactly measured six and one half feet. Every detail of the burial of this skeleton indicated that he had been an important member of the tribe—

probably a chieftain—or at least the son of a chieftain.

His bones were arranged with exceeding care. And between his right arm and his side were found three small bone awls, three large deer bone awls, and three split and worked bones in the process of being made into implements or weapons. Over his left shoulder were four mussel-shell pendants and a chipped-stone spear point, while fastened about his left knee was a string of sea snail shell beads, numbering about 80 beads in all.

AN APRON WOVEN OF SHELLS

Of the first four interments made in this mound, all were of the full-flexed type or curled up with knees close to the chins. Two of these were children, buried close together in "spoon fashion." They were heavily covered with hematite paint, a red pigment used by these Indians. One of the skeletons still wore an apron woven of 225 olivella shell beads. Other burials yielded by the mound were all prone or fully extended. Skulls were missing from these.

THOUSANDS OF ARTIFACTS DISCOVERED BY THE SMITHSONIAN

At the village under the airport site, Holder and his workers recovered approximately 4,000 shards, or pieces of tribal pottery and cooking utensils. While a great deal of the pottery was plain ware and quite crude, there were a few pieces that were somewhat decorative. Colors ranged from black, through gray and red, to buff. The decorated ware showed at least five types of stamped design, including the "check" stamp, the "delta" stamp, and a "herringbone" stamp. In addition there was discovered three distinct types of cord-marked ware, three types of thong-marked ware, and examples of rare incised and punctuaic sherds (connection to Stonehenge cord-marked pottery).

Aside from pottery, numerous examples of implements and burial offerings have been found, both in the village and the burial mound. They include a conch hoe, a conch abrader, a conch bowl, and an unidentified piece of polished conch. Pendants carved from turtle shells and the teeth of bears are among the invaluable archaeological finds which have been made.

SACRED POOLS, SECRET CAVES, AND THE HALLS OF THE MOUNTAIN KINGS

In all my extensive research into the hidden history of giants in America, the most detailed, wide-ranging, and colorful account I came across was *The Natural and Aboriginal History of Tennessee: Up to the First Settlements Therein by the White People, in the Year 1768* by John Haywood. Haywood combines an exhaustive first-person account of his many astonishing discoveries with an excellent overview of the previous historical finds in the area. Among his many amazing discoveries are accounts of giants found in a walled spring; caves with stones that rolled away, containing more giants; and four upright standing stones that formed a square box, inside of which was the body of another giant.

ON THE TENNESSEE GIANTS

The Natural and Aboriginal History of Tennessee, 1823

By John Haywood

The length and dimensions of the skeletons . . . found in East and West Tennessee . . . prove demonstratively, that the ancient inhabitants of this country, either the primitive or secondary settlers, were of gigantic stature compared with the present races of Lydians.

On the farm of Mr. John Miller of White county are a number of small graves and also many large ones, the bones in which show that the bodies to which they belonged, when alive, must have been, seven feet high and upwards.

THE HIDDEN ROOMS FILLED WITH GIANTS

I am always particularly fascinated with reports of hidden caves and giant burials. In this account, the cave in question is located near Sparta, Kentucky. In 1814, giant bones were found in this cave, as well as in a grave burial in the same area. Later in the report, more giant bones are found along the Tennessee River below Kingston and at another site two miles from Nashville. John Haywood continues:

About the year 1814, Mr. Lawrence found in Scarborough's cave, which is on the Calf-killer River, a branch of the Cany Fork, about 12 or 15 miles from Sparta, in a little room in the cave, many human bones of a monstrous size. He took a jaw bone and applied it to his own face, and when his chin touched the concave of the chin bone, the hinder ends of the jaw bone did not touch the skin of his face on either side. He took a thigh bone, and applied the upper end of it to his own hip joint, and the lower end reached four inches below the knee joint.

Mr. Andrew Bryan saw a grave opened about 4 miles northwardly from Sparta, on the Calf- killer Fork. He took a thigh bone and raising up his knee, he applied the knee joint of the bone to the extreme length of his own knee, and the upper end of the bone passed out behind his as far as the full width of his body. Mr. Lawrence is about 5 feet, 10 inches high, and Mr. Bryan about 5 feet, 9. Mr. Sharp Whitley was in a cave near the place where Mr. Bryan saw the graves opened. In it were many of these bones. The skulls lie plentifully in it, and all the other bones of the human body; all in proportion, and of monstrous size.

Human bones were taken out of a mound on the Tennessee River below Kingston, which Mr. Brown saw measured by Mr. Simms. The thigh bones of those skeletons, when applied to Mr. Simms's thigh, were an inch and a half longer than his, from the point of his hip to his knee: supposing the whole frame to have been in the same proportion, the body it belonged to must have been seven feet high or upwards. Many bones in the mounds there are of equal size. Suppose a man seven or eight feet high, that is from 10 inches to 2 feet taller than men of the common size; suppose the body broader in the same proportion, also his arms and legs; would he not be entitled to the name of giant?

Col. William Sheppard, late of North-Carolina, in the year 1807, dug up, on the plantation of Col. Joel Lewis, 2 miles from Nashville, the jaw bones of a man, which easily covered the whole chin and jaw of Col. Lewis, a man of large size. Some years afterwards, Mr. Cassady dug up a skeleton from under a small mound near the large one at Bledsoe's lick, in Sumner County, which measured little short of seven feet in length.

SQUARE WALLS ENCLOSE SPRING, MORE GIANTS

While a cellar was being dug at a plantation four miles outside Nashville, giant burials were found in association with a walled and enclosed sacred spring.

Human bones have been dug up in the cellar at the plantation where Judge Overton now lives, in Havidbon County, four miles southwestwardly from Nashville. These bones were of extraordinary size. The under jaw bone of one skeleton very easily slipped over the jaw of Mr. Childress, a stout man, full fleshed, very robust, and considerably over the common size.

These bones were dug up within the traces of ancient walls, in the form of a square of two or three hundred yards in length, situated near an excellent, never failing spring of pure and well-tasted water. The spring was enclosed within the walls. A great number of skeletons were found within the enclosure, a few feet below the surface of the earth. On the outer side were the traces of an old ditch and rampart, thrown up on the inside. Some small mounds were also within the enclosure.

ROLL AWAY THE STONE—MORE SECRET CAVE ROOMS

This part of Haywood's report is of the discovery of a cave with several secret rooms, located seven and a half miles north of Pulaski, Kentucky. The entrances to the cave and to an interior secret passageway were both covered by flat stones that could be rolled away. Inside, the bones of giants were found laid out over a paved floor.

At the plantation of Col. William Sheppard, in the county of Giles, seven and a half miles north of Pulaski, on the east side of the creek, is a cave with several rooms. The first is 45 feet wide, and 27 long; 4 feet deep; the upper part is formed of solid and even rock. Into this cave was a passage, which had been so artfully covered, that it escaped detection until lately. A flat stone, three feet wide and four feet long, rested upon the ground, and inclining against the cave, closing part of the mouth. At the end of this, and on the side of the mouth that is left open is another stone rolled, which filling this also, closed the whole mouth.

When these rocks were removed, and the cave opened, on the inside of the cave were found several bones—the jawbone of a child, the arm bone of a man, the skulls and thigh-bones of men. The whole bottom of the cave was covered with flat stones of a bluish hue, being closely joined together, and of different forms and sizes. They formed the floor of the cave. Upon the floor the bones were laid. The hat of Mr. Egbert Sheppard, seven inches wide and eight inches long, just covered and slipped over one of the skulls.

At the mouth of Obed's river, on the point between it and the Cumberland river, which is high ground, certain persons, in digging, struck a little below the surface, four stones standing upright, and so placed in relation to each other, as to form a square or box, which enclosed a skeleton, placed on its feet in an erect posture. The skull was large enough to go over the head of a man of common size. The thigh bones applied to those of a man of ordinary stature, reached from the joint of his hip to the calf of his leg.

The article below is one of the first articles to lament the destruction of the mounds, with these florid words, which bring an ironic Victorian smile to my face when I read them.

PLOWED UP AN INDIAN

KEWANNA HERALD, AUGUST 18, 1898

For two centuries, at least, the body has lain crumbling away to mother earth. Who can speak the weal and woe, the heart ache and joy thus represented? It is like a breeze from another world, and life seems fleeting faster still as one gazes on the remains of a once glorious union, now silent evermore.

SKELETON OF INDIAN BRAVE FOUND NEAR SHADY DELL

The finding of arrowheads and stone axes that were used by the roaming Indians of other days is a common enough occurrence, but this week there was disinterred the bones of one of these ancient inhabitants, which has made it the talk of the community. Charley Dukes, on the old family farm near Shady Dell School House, while plowing near a large, old oak stump, the tree of which was cut down over forty years ago, turned up the skeleton of a giant of the Indian occupation of this country.

For years, two large rocks in the field, which had the appearance of being perfectly placed, have been the wonder of the Dukes family, but now they find that the mound in which the bones were found is directly on the line between these stones, designating, therefore, the place of burial like our tombstones of today.

The bones are those of a large person, although the two centuries of summer and winter have dealt severely with them. The remains show parts of the femur, tibia, innominate, phalanges, and several face bones including some very well-preserved teeth.

MANY SKELETONS OF AN EXTINCT INDIAN RACE UNEARTHED IN THE HOOSIER STATE

A huge gravel pit has been opened at Whitlock, Indiana. Soon after the excavating began a skeleton was found and as the pit widened other skeletons were unearthed until at least thirty graves had been opened and many skeletons brought to light, evidently the remains of an Indian tribe.

One skeleton was found beneath a large stump, and another was found twelve feet underground. The graves appear in regular order, and the occupants were buried in a sitting posture. In one grave three skeletons, supposed to be those of a woman and two children, were found.

The other day the largest specimen was unearthed, the body of a person who in life must have been a giant.

A peculiarity of the skeletons is that the teeth are nearly all in a perfect state of preservation. In one grave beside the human skeletons was that of a dog, a copper spearhead, an earthen pot, and numerous beads proving that some important personage had been put to rest there.

A NINE-FOOT GIANT BURIED NEXT TO A FAIR-SKINNED INFANT GIRL

Here is a case of the burial of a white-haired child and a nine-foot-tall giant with a chain of mica around his neck. Other finds in Indiana include giants clad in copper armor.

A History of Jennings County, Indiana, 1885

Years ago, when Mr. Robinson's father began digging a cellar out of the hillside, he found there the skeleton of a little child. The hair was white and there were many indications that the child was not an Indian, but belonged to a fair-complexioned race of people.

Again in 1881, the skeleton of a human of unusual size was found in the mound. From comparative measurements of bones of this skeleton, it was thought to have been about nine feet in length. Cedar sticks were found around his waist, probably a symbol of some religious rite. A chain of mica was around his neck.

DOUBLE DENTITIONS

LOGANSPORT PHAROS TRIBUNE, JUNE 19, 1912

Charles Milton found a skeleton that is thought to be that of an Indian while digging sand near Lake Cleott yesterday. The bones are well preserved and very large. The jaw bone is almost twice as large as that of the ordinary person.

One peculiarity about the jaw is the fact that the teeth are double both front and back. The sandpit where the bones were found is supposed to be an old Indian mound. Several arrow heads were excavated and other like utensils were found. Among these was a peculiarly shaped flint supposed to have been a fish scaler. About two or three bushels of charcoal was found along the side of the skeleton.

A History of Clay County, Missouri, 1888

In his researches among the forests of western Missouri, Judge E. P. West has discovered a number of conical-shaped mounds similar in construction to those found in Ohio and Kentucky.

As yet only one of these mounds has been opened. Judge West discovered a skeleton about two weeks ago and made a report to other members of the society. They accompanied him to the mound, and not far from the surface excavated and took out the remains of two skeletons.

The bones were very large—so large, in fact, that when compared with an ordinary skeleton of modern date, they appear to have formed part of a giant.

The head bones, such as have not rotted away, are monstrous in size. The lower jaw of one skeleton is in a state of preservation, and is double the size of the jaw of a civilized person. The thigh bone, when compared to that of an ordinary modern skeleton, looks like that of a horse. The length, thickness, and muscular development are remarkable.

The bodies were discovered in a sitting posture in the mounds, and among the bones were found stone weapons different in shape from the tools and weapons known to be in use by the aboriginal Indians of this land.

SCIENTISTS FIND GIANT SKELETONS: IN LIFE THEY AVERAGED TWELVE FEET HIGH

MONROE COUNTY MAIL, JUNE 18, 1914

Skeletons of a race of giants who averaged twelve feet in height were found by workmen engaged on a drainage project in Crowville, near here.

There are several score at least of the skeletons, and they lie in various positions. It is believed they were killed in a prehistoric fight and that the bodies lay where they fell until covered with alluvial deposits due to the flooding of the Mississippi River. No weapons of any sort were found at the site, and it is believed the Titans must have struggled with wooden clubs. The skulls are in a perfect state of preservation, and some of the jawbones are large enough to surround a baby's body.

"GIANT ON THE BEACH" IN TEXAS

In Texas, where everything is big, it would be to the state's everlasting horror if it turned out that its giants were smaller than the other giants who once ruled over the rest of America in ancient times. In 1931, the *San Antonio Express* announced that a federal Works Progress Administration (WPA) archaeological team digging in association with the University of Texas discovered what at that time was called "the largest human skull found in the world in Victoria County Texas," and its owner was dubbed the "giant on the beach." Photographs reveal that this skull was "twice the size of the skull of a normal man." This find was held at the University of Texas, where Dr. Ales Hrdlicka of the Smithsonian examined it and related discoveries, and in a joint press release it was said that "these finds in Texas are beginning to give weight to the theory that man lived in Texas 40,000 to 45,000 years ago."

A close-up photo shows three skulls in comparison with the Giant Skull. The caption under the giant skull reads: "Believed to be possibly the largest found in the world, the human skull shown on the right was recently unearthed in Victoria County by the University of Texas anthropologists. The other two skulls are of normal size."

SAN ANTONIO EXPRESS

Beach Giant's Skull Unearthed By WPA Workers Near Victoria

Believed to Be Largest Ever Found in World; Normal Head Also Found

That Texas "had a giant on the beach" in the long ago appears probable from the large skull recently unearthed in a mound in Victoria County, believed to be the largest human skull ever found in the United States and possibly in the world.

Twice the size of the skull of normal man, the fragments were dug up by W. Duffen, archaeologist, who is excavating the mound in Victoria County under a WPA project sponsored by the University of Texas. In the same mound and at the same level, a normal sized skull was found. The pieces taken from the mound were reconstructed in the WPA laboratory under supervision of physical anthropologists.

A study is being made to determine whether the huge skull was that of a man belonging to a tribe of extraordinary large men or whether the skull was that of an abnormal member of a tribe, a case of giantism. Several large human body bones also have been unearned at the site.

Marcus B. Goldstein, physical anthropologist employed on the WPA project, formerly was an aide of Ales Hdrlicken, curator of the National Museum of Physical Anthropolgy.

Finds made through excavations in Texas are beginning to give weight to the theory that man lived in Texas 40,000 to 45,000 years ago, it is said.

STAMP SOCIETY MEETS

San Antonio Philatelic Society will hold its first meeting of 1940 at the Y. M. C. A. at 8:30 p. m.

GIANT SKULL—Believed to be possibly the largest found in the world, the human skull shown on the right was recently unearthed in Victoria County by Texas University anthropologists. The other two are of normal size.

Monday, when a hourse of rare stamps will be shown by collectors in this vicinity. New officers of the society are Norman H. Brock, president; B. A. Tur-ner, vice president; L. F. Fields, secretary and treasurer, and Edward Albach, reporter. Both the president and vice president were re-elected.

Fig. 1.3. This 1931 article documents the WPA find of the largest skull ever discovered. Scientists from the University of Texas posited inhabitation of Texas 40,000 years ago (*San Antonio Express*).

THE SMITHSONIAN AND THE DR. HRDLICKA CONNECTION

Earlier we learned about Hrdlicka in connection with the finds of giants off Georgia's coast (see page 30). Now we find that Hrdlicka was also involved with the Texas beach giant, in a special consultation for the Smithsonian.

SMITHSONIAN SAYS THE SKULL SIZE OF ARIZONA GIANT IS "BEYOND COMPREHENSION"

For anyone doubting the immediate and immense reach of the Smithsonian, here is an amusing article about a rancher who refused to sell his giant to the Smithsonian representatives, who had traveled from Washington D.C., reaching Arizona within an incredible two weeks of the discovery.

RANCHER REFUSES TO SELL SKELETON OF GIANT

ARIZONA JOURNAL-MINER, OCTOBER 13, 1911

Peter Marx of Walnut Creek, discoverer of a prehistoric human giant on his farm several weeks ago, while in the city yesterday, stated that the curiosity is attracting such deep interest in scientific circles that he is almost delayed with his letters and during the past two weeks he has been visited by Mr. and Mrs. Shoup, the former an attaché of the Smithsonian Institution at Washington, who made the long journey for the express purpose of viewing the frame of the giant of other days. Mr. Shoup was provided with photographic instruments and took several pictures.

Mr. Shoup, of the Smithsonian, also desired to take it (the giant skeleton) back to Washington, but this request was held up by Mr. Marx stating that as the subject was found in the territory it should be kept there.

Mr. Shoup was very much interested in those portions of the human frame that were unusually large, particularly the skull, which indicated that the giant was of such abnormal size as to be beyond comprehension as that of a human being. Mr. Marx has uncovered another burying ground near the point where the skeleton was found.

IRRIGATION DITCHES ARE A SIGN OF ANCIENT HIGH INTELLIGENCE

An old irrigating ditch has also been partly recovered, and it is Mr. Shoup's (of the Smithsonian) belief that the place was intelligently cultivated in some past age by an industrious people. Mr. Marx has uncovered many implements, some of which are unique in construction and for what purposes they were utilized is problematical.

FROM SEA TO SHINING SEA

When looked at in its entirety, it seems fitting that our trip west across the United States in search of the ancient giants who once ruled this land should end at the Pacific Ocean. In 1911, it was reported that William Altmann, assistant curator of the Golden Gate Park Memorial

Museum, found skeletons, pottery, and artifacts in Port Costa, California, including the skeleton of a giant more than seven feet tall. Later the same year, Altmann reported finding more giants on an island in the Santa Barbara Channel, including one skeleton that measured in at seven feet, four inches tall.

BONES OF SEVEN FOOT CALIFORNIAN GIANT FOUND IN SOUTH

OAKLAND TRIBUNE, JULY 25, 1911

Ethnologists will be interested in a discovery made by Assistant Curator William Altmann of Golden Gate Park Memorial Museum—namely, the fact hitherto denied that the Digger Indians of California were acquainted with at least the rudiments of pottery making. "Until now, no pottery of Digger Indian manufacture has ever been found," says Altmann, and therefore he highly values the find he made in an Indian Burial Mound at Concord, in Contra Costa County.

From an excavation made by workmen in the employ of the Port Costa Water Company has been found a large number of Indian relics of great age, including the specimens of crude pottery already mentioned and the skeleton of an Indian giant more than seven feet tall. The skeleton is in the possession of Dr. Neff of Concord, who is mounting it for exhibition. The pottery specimens consist of charm stones of baked clay of spindle shape and pierced so that they may be suspended from the neck by cords.

In addition, there are a large number of knives and arrowheads of obsidian or volcanic glass, which is extremely rare in this part of the state, and leads to the belief they were brought down by the Shasta or Modoc Indians and traded for other things with the Diggers of Contra Costa.

A striking peculiarity about these arrowheads is their shape and pattern. They are notched in a very painstaking way with jagged division and resemble very much some of the weapons Filipino warriors use. A stone mortar and several phallic pestles carved with considerable skill and precision, stone sinkers for fishing, and artistic pipes made of soapstone, together with a quantity of wampum, are among the souvenirs secured by Assistant Curator Altmann, the donor being Joseph Hittman of Concord.

The mound from which these relics were taken is close to the railroad depot at Concord. The work of excavation is still going on and more interesting finds are looked for.

Fig. 1.3. Indian cemetery, Santa Rosa Island, containing abalone shells carbon dated at seven thousand years old. The tops of the skulls were painted red; several skeletons measured over seven feet tall (photo courtesy of Santa Barbara Museum of Natural History, 1959).

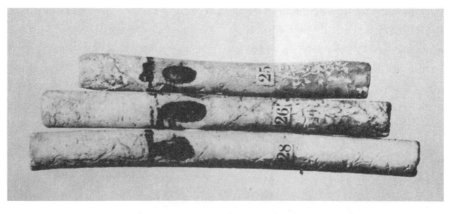

Fig. 1.4. Bone whistles from Santa Rosa Island, early to mid-1900s

BEST-PRESERVED SKELETON OF
EXTINCT TRIBE HAULED FROM CHANNEL

OAKLAND TRIBUNE, JUNE 10, 1912

Up to about three hundred years ago, a giant race inhabited the coastal regions of California. Remains of these people have been discovered in the islands of the Santa Barbara Channel. To William Altmann, assistant curator of the Golden Gate Park Memorial Museum, belongs the honor of discovering one of the tallest and best preserved skeletons of this extinct tribe. Altmann utilized his vacation a week ago in excavating an old Indian burial mound in the nursery of Thomas S. Duane, two miles from Concord, in Contra Costa County.

The giant skeleton found was ten feet from the surface and around it were a large number of mortars and pestles, charm stones, and obsidian arrow heads. The giant skeleton has been laid and reconstructed in the Curator's office and placed on private exhibition yesterday. The bones are in a good state of preservation, being hard and firm, although brown with age. Two or three of the vertebrae are missing and the skull is broken into three parts.

The skeleton is seven feet four inches. The skull is in great contrast to that of the Indian today. The under-jaw is square and massive, being remarkably thick and strong.

PHALLIC CARVINGS

The artifacts are ornamented with phallic carvings, whereas the marks made by the former and present-day Diggers are not carved or ornamented in any way. The charm stones are of baked clay, a beginning of the more advanced works of pottery, which are not found with Digger remains. This interesting find was made on the Salvadore Pacheen Ranch, part of which is occupied by Duane's nursery. It is Altmann's intention to make a further exploration of the mound at an early [date] for other relics of this by-gone era.

A SUPERIOR RACE OF
GIANTS ADMITTED IN
CALIFORNIA

The find is of the greatest importance to anthropologists the world over, confirming as it does, the theory originally advanced when the giants were unearthed in the Santa Barbara Islands, that a superior race of Indians, both physically and mentally, preceded the Digger and other native races of the present day. This is evidenced also in the burial posture and the charm stones found near the body.

Fig. 1.5. Bones of a giant found in southern California (*The World*, 1895)

2

NORTH AMERICA

Land of the Giants

While the idea of prehistoric giants inhabiting the United States may seem strange to us today or the result of some fantastic hoax, in the nineteenth century, reports of archaeological evidence regarding giants were commonplace. In addition, one must remember that America was an agrarian society at this time and its citizens were in regular contact with their fields, as well as the mounds and the remains they found while plowing. Knowledge of the giants was part of the current thinking, as was a heightened awareness of who the mound builders really were. As this chapter demonstrates, highly credible reports of skeletons and artifacts, from the eastern states to the Pacific Ocean, appeared in newspapers across the country with surprising frequency. The fact that this idea seems so strange to us today can be directly attributed, at least in part, to the role the Smithsonian played in suppressing the evidence, as attested by several of the reports documented here.

Fig. 2.1. Giant skeleton from Serpent Mound of Adams County, Ohio

THE LENNI LENAPE GIANTS OF THE EASTERN UNITED STATES

The Lenni Lenape Indians were often referred to as a tribe of giants. Technically, their name translates as "the real people," or "the human beings" in the Unami language. Their principle area of inhabitation encompassed much of southeastern New York State, including the lower Hudson River Valley and most of Long Island and Staten Island, as well as eastern Pennsylvania around the Delaware and Lehigh Valleys, in addition to the coastal regions that extend south to the north shore of Delaware. Another designation of the tribe was the "original people," which is similar to the appellation of the Copper culture tribes of Michigan, which were called the "Old People," and the Anasazi of the Southwest, who were called "The Ancient Ones." Since their legends state that they originally migrated from the west, this is not surprising.

Lenni Lenape legend relates what is no less than a mass exodus that began west of the Mississippi and involved the use of scouting parties

Fig. 2.2. Lappawinsa, chief of the Lenni Lenape
(*Lappawinsa*, painted by Gustavus Hesselius in 1735, Library of Congress
Rare Book and Special Division Collection)

Fig. 2.3. Benjamin West's painting (in 1771) of William Penn's 1682 treaty with the Lenni Lenape Indians. Notice that the seated warrior is taller and whiter than anyone else present.

that went out in search of suitable land. Although the legends are thought to be several hundred years old, research in chapter 10 indicates that this migration may have happened as long ago as 5000 BCE as a result of the cataclysmic explosion of the Lassen Volcano in California.

An Account of the History, Manners, and Customs of the Indian Nations Who Once Inhabited Pennsylvania and the Neighboring States, 1819

BY REV. JOHN GOTTLIEB ERNESTUS HECKEWELDER

The Lenni Lenape, according to the legends handed down to them by their ancestors, resided many hundreds of years ago in a very distant country in the western part of the American continent.

For some reason I do not find accounted for, they determined on migrating to the eastward, and accordingly set out together in a body. After a very long journey, they fell in with the Mengwe (Iroquois), who likewise emigrated from a distant country. Their object was the same as with that of the Delawares. They were proceeding along to the eastward until they should find a country that pleased them.

The spies, which the Lenape had sent forward for the purpose of reconnoitering, had discovered that the country east of the Mississippi was inhabited by a very powerful nation who had many large towns built on the great rivers flowing through their land. These people (as I was told) called themselves "Talligew" or "Talligewi." Colonel John Gibson, however, a gentleman who has a thorough knowledge of the Indians and speaks several of [the languages], is of the opinion that they were not called Talligewi, but Alligewi. And it would seem that he is right, from the traces of their name which still remain in the country, the Allegheny River and mountains having indubitably been named after them.

The Delawares still call the former the Alligewi Sipu, the River of the Alligewi.

MANY WONDERFUL THINGS ARE TOLD OF THIS FAMOUS PEOPLE

The Lenni Lenape eventually came in contact with the ancestor race of the Allegheny or Alligewi people, a race even greater in stature than the Lenni Lenape and known for their massive earthworks throughout the regions of Lake Erie and Lake Huron. Heckewelder continues:

They are said to have been remarkably tall and stout, and there is a tradition that there were giants among them, people of a much larger size than the Lenape. It is related that they had built regular fortifications or entrenchments. I have seen many of the fortifications said to be built by them, two of which in particular were remarkable. One of them was near the mouth of the river Huron, which empties itself into the lake St. Claire, on the north side of that lake at a distance of about twenty miles northeast of Detroit.

Fig. 2.4. Teedyuscung (1700–1763) was known as king of the Delawares. He worked to establish a Lenni Lenape (Delaware) home in eastern Pennsylvania in the Lehigh, Susquehanna, and Delaware River Valleys (*King of the Delawares: Teedyuscung 1700–1763,* courtesy of the Pennsylvania Historical and Museum Commission).

The other works, properly entrenchments, being walls or banks of earth regularly thrown up with a deep ditch on the outside, were on the Huron River east of Sandusky, about six or eight miles from Lake Erie.

Outside of the gateways of these entrenchments were a number of large flat mounds, in which the Indian pilot said, were buried hundreds of slain Alligewi.

When the Lenape arrived on the banks of the Mississippi, they sent a message to the Alligewi to request permission to settle themselves in their neighborhood. This was refused them but they obtained leave to pass through the country and seek settlement further to the eastward. They accordingly began to cross, when the Alligewi, seeing that their numbers were so very great, and, in fact, they consisted of many thousands, made a furious attack on those who had crossed, threatening them all with destruction if they dared to persist in coming over to their side of the river. Fired at the treachery of these people and the great loss of men they sustained, the Lenape consulted on what was to be done. Whether to retreat in the best manner they could, or try their strength and let the enemy see they were not cowards but men, and too high-minded to suffer themselves to be driven off before they had made a trial of their strength and were convinced that the enemy was too powerful for them.

THE MENGWE JOIN IN THE WAR

When the Mengwe, or Iroquois Indians, saw that the Lenni Lenape were losing the battle, they agreed to fight on their side in exchange for a promise that they would have a part in jointly ruling the conquered lands east of the Mississippi. The Alligewi were finally defeated, and it was said that they fled south down the Mississippi River, never to be seen again. Again, Heckewelder continues:

Fig. 2.5. The giants Fafner and Fasolt seize Freya in Arthur Rackham's illustration of *Der Ring des Nibelungen* by composer Richard Wagner.

The Mengwe, who hitherto had been satisfied with being spectators from a distance, offered to join them on the condition that, after conquering the country, they should be entitled to share it with them. Their proposal was accepted and the resolution was taken by the two nations to conquer or die.

Having thus united forces, the Lenape and Mengwe declared war against the Alligewi, and great battles were fought in which many warriors fell on both sides. The enemy fortified their large towns and erected fortifications, especially on large rivers and near lakes, where they were successively attacked and sometimes stormed by the allies.

An engagement took place in which hundreds fell, who were afterward buried in holes or laid together in heaps and covered over with earth. No quarter was given, so that the Allegewi, at last finding that their destruction was inevitable if they persisted in their obstinacy, abandoned the country to the conquerors and fled down the Mississippi River from whence they never returned.

PIGEON CREEK VALLEY, PENNSYLVANIA

CHARLEROI MAIL, MAY 7, 1953

The name "Monongahela" derives from the Indian river title, it being the name by which the Indian described the falling banks of the river as soil erosion loosened the earth on its sides and caused it to slip into the stream. The other two bodies of water also derive their name from the Indian: Mingo Creek (and the entire Mingo section) and Pigeon Creek.

The Mingoes, with Chicka-Mingo as their Chief, inhabited the section to the north of what is now Monongahela, while Pigeon was the Chief of the great tribe which occupied for many seasons the waters of what is now called Pigeon Creek.

Earlier Indians in this section of the county were "Mound Builders," evidences of such still being apparent from the surface in several places. The "Mounds," embracing the section surrounding Decker Street and the old Crall greenhouse property, took its name from the huge mound at the southern end of Decker Street. Mounds also have been discovered on the Van Voorhis farm and at a site near Elrama.

The Elrama mound revealed 45

skeletons, giving proof that the Mound Builders lived here 10,000 years ago.

The late George S. Fisher, Finleyville archaeologist, made excavations at the site and reported that the largest skeleton was seven feet five inches in length. The bones, unearthed in pieces, were put together and sent to the museum at Harrisburg. At a distance of 29 feet behind the mound, another terrace was apparently a place of sacrifice to the Diety. Here were found beads, knives, bear tusks, arrow points and clay ovens.

Fisher, during his years as an Indian authority, excavated more than one thousand skeletons, claims this 1953 article in the local Pennsylvania newspaper. There were more than one hundred campsites marked in the immediate district and a number were not yet listed.

GIANT SKELETON FOUND IN PETERSBURG, KENTUCKY

DAILY NORTHWESTERN, OSHKOSH, WISCONSIN, JULY 8, 1886

At Petersburg, Kentucky, twenty-five miles below here, an excavation for a new building has brought to light a peculiar find; it being a strange-looking Indian grave, the receptacle of which has been made of stone and clay, formed into a kind of cement, about three feet in height, and fully nine feet in length.

Within the rude vault lay a giant human skeleton that measured seven feet, two inches, in length. The bones were all of large proportions, and the monstrous skull, with teeth perfect and intact, was more than half an inch thick at the base.

A number of copper pieces, evidently worn for ornaments, a stone pipe, and a quantity of arrowheads were found with the decaying bones.

AMAZING FINDS FROM EARLY AMERICAN HISTORY

In the diary entry below, written in 1792, General John Payne reports uncovering an ancient burial ground along the banks of the Ohio River in Kentucky. A total of 110 skeletons were removed, the tallest measuring in at seven feet tall.

Diary of General John Payne, 1792

FROM *THE NATURAL AND ABORIGINAL HISTORY OF TENNESSEE*
BY DR. JOHN HAYWOOD

The bottom on which Augusta is situated is a large burying ground of the ancients. They have been found in great number and of all sizes. From the cellar under my dwelling, over 110 skeletons were taken. I measured them by skulls, and there might have been more whose skulls had crumbled into dust. The skeletons were in all sizes, from 7 feet to infant. Dave Kilgour, who was a tall and very large man, passed our village at the time I was excavating my cellar, and we took him down and applied a thigh bone to his. The man, if well-proportioned, must have been 10 to 12 inches taller than Kilgour. The lower jawbone would slip over his skin and all.

A Survey of Archaeological Activity in Tennessee, 1835

In the county of Williamson, on the north side of Little Harpeth, in the lands owned by Captain Stocket northwardly from Franklin, are walls of dirt running north from the river and east and west.

In 1821 they were four or five feet high, and in length from the river between 490 and 300 yards. There is a ditch on the out-side all around, four or five feet in width, partly filled up. Upon the soil, which has partly filled it up, are black oaks two feet or more in diameter. A spring of excellent water is in the middle of the enclosure and a branch runs from it into the river through the interval left by the wall of its passage. The enclosure contains 40 or 30 acres.

Three mounds are in the inside, standing in a row north to south, and near the wall and ditch on the north side of the area. All these mounds are of nearly the same size. Within the enclosure are a vast amount of graves, all of them enclosed within rocks, and the bones are very large. James McGlaughlin, who is seven feet high, applied one of the thigh bones found there to his thigh, and it was three or four inches longer than his thigh.

OHIO STATE GETS IN THE ACT

The tight-lipped account below concerns a giant skull found by a museum curator from Ohio State University. This burial is interesting in that it combines several of the burial motifs previously discussed. First of all the skeleton was found inside a log hut buried in the mound. Second, the skeleton's arms and legs were wrapped in half-inch-thick bracelets. Third, the skeleton itself was seven feet tall, with a skull twenty-five inches in circumference.

HUT AND SKELETON FOUND IN BIG MOUND
NEAR CHILLICOTHE

OHIO DAILY GAZETTE, MAY 25, 1897

Clarence Loveberry, curator of the Museum of Ohio State University, has made remarkable discoveries in a large Indian mound. He is excavating just outside the city limits. Several days ago he found a well-preserved log hut in the interior of the mound, and yesterday he found a skeleton of the occupant of the log hut.

The skeleton's wrists were wrapped with copper cerements, indicating it to be that of a distinguished person. The skull was at least half-an-inch in thickness.

SEVEN-FOOTER FOUND IN SALEM, OHIO

HAMMOND TIMES, FRIDAY, JUNE 30, 1939

Discovery of ancient skeletons and priceless relics in an Indian mound in North Benton, northwest of Salem, by two Alliance, Ohio mail carriers, has brought hundreds of visitors to the scene and attracted the attention of expert archaeologists. The two amateur archaeologists Roy Saltsman and Willis Magrath, made the excavation on the farm of John Malmsberry. After examining the mound, Richard G. Morgan, state archaeologist, declared that the work of the two Alliance men was the most important archaeological discovery in this section of the state in recent years. He estimated the age of the findings at more than 2,000 years old.

One skeleton uncovered was that of a man, apparently a chief, estimated to have been seven feet tall, whose skull was 25 inches in circumference.

Other findings included flint arrows, the stones of three sacrificial altars, spear heads, flake knives and beautifully wrought objects of copper.

MASS GIANT BURIAL EVIDENCE OF BLOODY BATTLE

This is one of many accounts that report a giant's jaw was big enough to fit over that of a normal man. In this case the burial field was thought to contain between two and three thousand skeletons.

History of Ashtabula County, 1800

The graves were distinguished by slight depressions in the surface of the earth, deposited in straight rows. The number of these graves has been estimated to be between two and three thousand. Aaron Wright* made a careful examination of these depressions, and found them invariably to contain human bones, blackened with time, which upon exposure to the air quickly crumbled to dust.

Some of these bones were of unusual size, and evidently belonged to a race aligned with giants. Skulls were taken from these mounds of which were of sufficient capacity to admit the skull of a normal man, and jawbones that may be fitted over the face with equal facility. The bones of the upper and lower extremities were of corresponding size.

COPPER-HELMETED GIANTS RULE

There have been a number of intriguing finds in Indiana over the years. The following article describes how an Indiana farmer found eight skeletons, one clad in copper armor, buried together in a circle.

---

*See pages 23–25.

INDIANA'S EIGHT-FOOT GIANTS WORE COPPER ARMOR

OAKLAND TRIBUNE, JANUARY 3, 1926

Another discovery was made of eight skeletons, one clad in copper armor, buried in a perfect circle, made when the Logan Grays, a military group led by A. M. Jones, were conducting military exercises in 1888 on a small island on Eagle Lake near Warsaw, Indiana. Under a flat stone, they discovered a hole that led to the entrance to a secret cave with the skeleton of a 6'9" giant buried next to a stream that led to what was called a sacred pool. It is interesting to note that the dimensions of this secret room are almost identical to one described in Tennessee, i.e. 25 feet long by 15 feet wide by 8 feet deep, branching out at the middle to form two rooms.

INDIANA GIANTS FOUND

BONES OF AN INDIAN GIANT

CINCINNATI COMMERCIAL, OCTOBER 7, 1888

A member of the Logan Grays, the crack military organization of Logansport that held its encampment this year at Eagle Lake, near Warsaw stopped in this city on his way home from camp and told the following story of the discovery by the party of a cavern on an island in Eagle Lake; A.M. Jones rowed to a small island near the southwest corner of the lake and began digging for worms.

He turned over a large, flat stone near a tree, and under it was a small hole, which was an entrance to a cave. Jones called the boys up, and we began an exploration of the cavern, which proved to be twenty-five feet long, fifteen feet wide, and eight feet deep. The walls are of a natural formation of stone, branching out at the middle so as to form two rooms.

In the front room was the skeleton of a man six feet nine inches long. The bones were very large, indicating great strength. Along one side of the cave runs a small stream of water, as pure as crystal. In the front of it forms a small pool. In this were a number of bones. Old settlers in this vicinity of the lake claim that the skeleton is that of Eagleonkie, the giant Indian chief who lived alone on this island and mysteriously disappeared during a severe winter. The island was known after this chief and was once known as Giant Island.

EXCAVATIONS AT ILLINOIS SITES IN 1891

From 1891, we find this news report on skeletons found in the aptly named city of Carthage, Illinois.

PERFECT GIANT SKELETON FOUND

HAWK EYE, BURLINGTON, IOWA, SEPTEMBER 1, 1891

No little excitement has been occasioned by the discovery on a farm near Carthage of several skeletons in a mound that are doubtless those of prehistoric people. In regard to this historic find the *Carthage Republican* newspaper will publish the following.

The Sweney Farm Mounds, located near the south line of the farm quarter, on Section Five, Carthage Township, have been a familiar landmark to the oldest citizens since, and the quarter was entered by Samuels in 1836, or thereabouts.

Last Saturday afternoon the new owner of the Sweney Farm Indian Mounds was plowing on one of his mounds when he hit a series of sandstone blocks. On the removal of several sandstone rocks embedded in the ground, the owner Mr. Felt procured a spade and proceeded to dig out the rocks with some difficulty.

On the removal of these rocks there was revealed an almost perfect skeleton of a man of very large size. The authorities of Carthage College have secured permission to investigate the find to its fullest extent and Rev. Dr. Stephen D. Peet has been notified.

CHICAGO TRIBUNE IN 1892 CONFIRMS RACE OF GIANTS

This definitive report states that the entire country lying between the Illinois and Mississippi Rivers, between Galena and Cairo, is honeycombed with Indian mounds.

HUNDREDS OF BURIALS

CHICAGO TRIBUNE, 1892

Near Carthage, Illinois, about one year ago, a mound was plowed up and the bones, principally the skulls of human beings, were found in sufficient quantities to warrant the conclusion that hundreds of people had been buried there. From measurements taken of some of the skulls and principal bones, it was decided that the persons buried were of a race of giants. Some of the femur bones measured 19¼ inches, and the measurements of the skulls and other bones indicated that these people must have attained an average of seven to eight feet in height.

The entire country lying between the Illinois and Mississippi Rivers, between Galena and Cairo, is honeycombed with Indian mounds and mounds that are believed to be the handiwork of a pre-historic race. Nansook County, especially in localities bordering the Mississippi River, is covered with evidences of Indian burials and their mounds are very numerous. Some interesting discoveries have been made.

Some of the best descriptions of the finds of the mound builders are to be found in county and state historical society reports. This one from 1902 reports the discovery of fields of mounds along Lake Michigan, as well as along related rivers, creeks, and lakes, with the skeletons of giants uncovered measuring between seven and eight feet in height.

The History of Lake County, Illinois, 1902

These mounds were quite numerous along the rivers and in the vicinity of the inland lakes. That they were of great antiquity is evident from the fact that huge trees had come to maturity upon their summits and were awaiting the ax of the pioneer.

Excavations of these piles of earth have revealed the crumbling bones of a mighty race. Samuel Miller, who has resided in this county since 1835, is authority for the statement that one skeleton, which he assisted in unearthing, was a trifle more than eight feet in length, the skull being correspondingly large, while many other skeletons measured at least seven feet. There were extensive burial grounds on the shore of Lake Michigan, mainly south of the Waukegan River, also at various points all through the county. Many of the skeletons found near the lake shore were of an unusually large size.

THE LARGEST NEOLITHIC
BURIAL SITE IN THE WORLD—
THE DICKSON MOUNDS MUSEUM (ILLINOIS)

In 1930, newspapers across the country ran half-page photos of more than fifty skeletons laid out on various dirt platforms in the middle of a large archaeological dig, led by the University of Chicago. It was a truly riveting photo and was used in many year-end features as one of the top stories and photographs of the entire year. Eighty-three years later, in a museum at the site, there is no mention of what was then called "the largest Neolithic burial site ever discovered in the world."

The story of Don Dickson and his mounds could serve as a micro-cosmic primer for many of the stories pertaining to the recovery of ancient bones and the true history of America. In this case, the political correctness fallout that resulted in the Native American Graves Protection and Repatriation Act (NAGPRA) laws once again being misapplied eventually led to a once-thriving tourist destination being shut down and the skeletons it exhibited being buried by a local Indian tribe who have no genetic relation to the skeletons they claim to protect.

To give a little background, Don Dickson, a chiropractor from Lewiston, Illinois, grew up on a farm about ninety miles south of Peoria that was intersected by the Illinois River. In 1927, Dickson was plowing on a hill near the river, and he broke through to a layer of clay and gravel that he immediately recognized as an ancient Indian burial. Dickson then spent the next two years excavating the site, most famously with the help of the University of Chicago in 1929 and 1930.

What they found and how they left it became a national news story. In short, instead of removing 248 skeletons, they exposed them to the air by removing all the dirt surrounding them and leaving them in situ to be photographed and visited like some colossal ancient bone-yard sideshow. In all, it was estimated that the site contained well over three thousand burials, and the University of Chicago was calling it the largest Neolithic burial site in the world.

Fig. 2.6. Don Dickson (courtesy of Illinois State Museum)

In the early 1930s, Dickson constructed a building to house the exposed skeleton field and opened the site to tourists. In the first year he had forty thousand visitors, and the whole venture became a national tourist destination, as people loved being able to see these large skeletons displayed in situ—though in all probability *not* in their original, and far more bizarre, burial positions.

Dickson successfully ran the tourist operation until 1945, when he sold the mounds to the state of Illinois, who made the site part of their state museum system in 1965. The Dickson Mounds averaged about seventy-five thousand visitors a year, who were exposed not only to the skeletons, but also to a history lesson on the mound builders and their extremely ancient history in the area.

All of that came to an acrimonious end beginning in 1990, when Native Americans began to petition and protest that the site be shut down and sealed and that the skeletons should be reburied under NAGPRA, which was then brand new. The NAGPRA laws mandated that all Indian relics and skeletons be returned to their rightful tribal owners. After several years of battle in court revolving around ownership issues pertaining to the lack of genetic associations of the skeletons to the current local tribes, among other controversial subjects, the Indians won out and the mound exhibit was shut down and sealed in 1992. The site remained closed for the next two years, as the tribes involved reburied an undisclosed number of skeletons found at the site, which ultimately is known to have contained more than three thousand burials.

When the "renovated" museum reopened two years later, without the open boneyard exhibit, interest in the site as a tourist attraction immediately disappeared, and although the site remains opened to this day, it generates very little interest from the public in regard to its new, cleaned-up, skeleton-free existence.

SMITHSONIAN INVOLVEMENT IN THE DISAPPEARANCE OF GIANT SKELETONS FOUND IN WISCONSIN INDIAN MOUNDS

It is hard to imagine today, but the historical record is filled with vivid descriptions of how Wisconsin and Minnesota were like the Nazca Lines of burial mounds, so it comes as no surprise that giants have been turning up there for a long time.

This case covers the involvement of the Smithsonian at a Wisconsin site in the 1880s and a collection of ancient skeletons of giants called the Stoddard Collection, so it is of particular interest to our study of that museum's long-standing policy of burying the evidence when it comes to proof of ancient giants ruling America in extreme antiquity.

FIFTY SKELETONS UNEARTHED—REMAINS OF GIANT ABORIGINES DISCOVERED

LA CROSSE TRIBUNE, NOVEMBER 4, 1912

More than fifty skeletons of the ancient mound builders were unearthed Saturday from five mounds in the town of Stoddard, by a party of Normal students and professors, who made a special trip to investigate them. Valuable relics were also recovered that will be on exhibition at the Normal museum.

The country around La Crosse has long been known as the center of Indian activities in centuries long past and as evidences of this fact there are many Indian mounds in this vicinity.

About thirty years ago agents of the Smithsonian Institution in Washington D.C., investigated several mounds in what is now the town of Stoddard. They unearthed much valuable material in the line of skeletons, arrow heads, and spear heads from the first few of a chain of a dozen mounds and at the present time there is in Washington a Stoddard Collection of Indian relics.

Since that time Smithsonian officials have often considered opening more of the mounds but nothing has been done. Spurred on by the generous offer of A. White, who owns the ground on which are located five large mounds, to donate the contents to the Normal School Museum (apparently no help from Smithsonian officials), the Normal authorities recently took the matter up, and several local citizens generously provided a fund for the expenses of an expedition to unearth the contents.

A SIX-FOOT, SIX-INCH SKELETON UNEARTHED

Professors A. H. Sanford and W. H. Thompson of the University of Wisconsin Department of History, and L. P. Deneyer of the Geology Department, together with a company of thirteen students left on Saturday morning with shovels to examine the ancient graves. Professor Austin and some of his students surveyed and made a contour map of the field determining the dimensions of the mounds and the lay of the surrounding country. The expedition was of a scientific character, and the results of the investigations will appear in printed form.

A large mound in the center, probably the grave of an Indian chief, was adjoined by two smaller ones on each side. The latter were investigated first and the efforts of the diggers were rewarded at once by the unearthing of a skeleton about five feet down, which measured six and a half feet in length.

The skull was very large being eight inches in diameter from ear to ear. The teeth were well preserved, but the other bones quickly fell to pieces. The first mound yielded eleven skeletons. The second contained only charcoal and burned bones indicating cremation.

EFFORTS YIELD MANY SKELETONS AND ARTIFACTS

The middle mound, which was the largest, required much effort to excavate. More than twenty skeletons were found besides the bowl of a clay peace pipe, a copper arrow head, copper skinning knife, a sandstone spearhead, and several flint arrow heads. The fourth eminence yielded over twenty five skeletons, pieces of clay pottery, and a bear's tooth. The last mound, after digging about six feet down, brought up a large spear point of quartz with a red coloring design on each side. Adjoining the White farm is property owned by Homer Hart of La Crosse on which are located several more mounds.

GIANT INDIAN BONES: DISCOVERY OF AN EXTRAORDINARY SKELETON NEAR FOND DU LAC

FOND DU LAC BANNER, JUNE 6, 1899

An Indian skeleton was dug up on the farm of Matt and Joseph Leon, one mile south of St. Cloud on Saturday. There is nothing strange in finding an Indian skeleton, but this one was a giant in size, his frame measuring seven feet. He must have been a man of note among his people, for he was buried in a large mound, sixteen handsome arrows surrounding his body. The skull was brought to this city and is on exhibition in one of the Main Street windows.

THE WINONA, MINNESOTA, TEN-FOOT GIANT

THE HISTORY OF WINONA COUNTY, 1883

Indian mounds and relics are found in various parts of this township. Not long since, while some men were digging in Mineral Bluff, some one hundred and fifty feet above the river, a skeleton of unusual size was unearthed. On measuring, the skeleton was found to be ten feet in length, with other parts in proper proportion. In the skull was found a copper hatchet and a dart or arrow-head nine inches long. Another skeleton, nine feet long, was found in the village of Dresbach, while some men were digging a road or trench. These skeletons were of an unusual size to those generally taken from Indian mounds. Their size, form, and structure would lead those well versed in paleontology to believe they belonged to a race prior to the Indian. In many mounds have also been found copper hatchets, chisels, and various kinds of tomahawks and other weapons of war; also these antique races seemed to have had some process for hardening copper unknown to any modern process.

Where they came from, when they lived, and from whence they have gone, is only conjecture and speculation. That they were mighty races, skilled in the mode of warfare, understanding the mechanical arts, for all these we have conclusive evidence. But of their final end we know nothing.

DOCUMENTED DOUBLE DENTITIONS FROM IOWA

Throughout the Indian lore of giants are also stories of skulls being found with double rows of teeth, called double dentitions. (See also "Double Dentitions" on page 37.) While there is often controversy regarding these claims, here is a modest and convincing story.

DOUBLE-TOOTHED GIANT

JOURNAL TRIBUNE, WILLIAMSBURG, IOWA, APRIL 27, 1900

The discovery in Hardin County a short time ago by Joseph Booda and Elliot Charles Gaines of innumerable mound builders' relics, and the subsequent finding, by other parties, of the remains of a man of the prehistoric period, have greatly interested scientists in other parts of the country, the chief among these being Curator Charles Aldrich, of the state Horticultural Society.

Assuring himself of the truthfulness of the various newspaper reports, Mr. Aldrich has arranged to be in Eldora next month and begin a careful and systematic exploration of some of the mounds in the vicinity, the legal permission having been obtained.

In a large show window in Eldora for several days has been exhibited the skeleton of the man, which was found in a mound on the banks of the Iowa River, near Eagle City, six miles north. It has caused much interest and wonderment. Although well preserved, it is estimated that the skeleton is many centuries old. The skull is very large and thick, fully a quarter of an inch. A set of almost round double teeth are remarkably well preserved. They are yellow with age, are perfect in shape, and appear to have been double, both above and below. The femurs are very long showing a giant in stature.

Dr. N. C. Morse, a prominent physician who examined the skeleton, pronounced it that of a person who had evidently been trained for athletics, as the extremities were so well developed.

THE BOODA COLLECTION

Joseph Booda, who has taken much interest in mound exploration, has a rare collection of implements of the stone age, all found near Eldora.

Among these are pottery axes, arrows, beadwork, pestles, mallets, and, although he has offers for the collection, will not part with it, unless he may be induced by Curator Aldrich to loan the collection to the state, to be placed in the historical building in Des Moines when completed.

GIANTS IN MIDDLE AMERICA

IOWA GIANT: SEVEN FEET, SIX INCHES

OAKLAND TRIBUNE, DECEMBER 20, 1925

Out of a mound in Iowa was dug the skeleton of a giant who, judging from the measurement of his bones, must have stood six inches over seven feet high when he was alive. In another there was a central chamber containing eleven skeletons arranged in a circle with their backs against the walls. In the midst was a huge sea shell which had been converted into a drinking cup.

GIANT IN MISSOURI

OAKLAND TRIBUNE, JANUARY 3, 1926

Within the last few weeks it has been reported from Missouri the discovery of the skeleton of a man who was a trifle more than seven feet, two inches tall. Frank Plumb, a student of archaeology who made the find, reported discovering inside the skull a pear-shaped stone such as the Mayas placed in the mouths of their dead.

The article below, which appeared all over Texas and the nation in 1931, omits all information about the size of the skeletons in an obvious effort to hide the skeletons' actual heights. It is standard practice for all archaeologists to give heights for any skeletons they discover.

INDIAN GRAVES ARE OPENED IN TEXAS

TWENTY-FIVE HUMAN SKELETONS DUG UP AND GIVEN TO MUSEUMS

REVIEW-MINER, JUNE 19, 1931

Waco, Texas: Twenty-five complete human frames, those of Indian Braves and Squaws and their papooses with such of their possessions as have survived burial, have been unearthed near here and today are in the museums of three Texas schools.

The twenty-five bodies were placed in the burial mound, each facing East, more than 100 years ago. They were discovered by Dr. K. D. Aynesworth thirty miles west of here in Coryell County. The mound was explored by The Department of Anthropology and Archaeology of The University of Texas.

The first of the three layers of bodies was only 21 inches below the surface and the second layer was just below the first. The third tier was 36 inches deep. Beside the bodies of the women were the large rock bowls and the round-headed clubs they used to grind corn. Arrows and spearheads of flint were found near the bones of the men. One bone knife, ten inches in length, its back notched, was found by the side of one brave.

THE BONES ARE DIVIDED AND GIVEN OUT

The bones were divided between the State University at Austin; Baylor Women's College at Belton; and Baylor University here.

SMITHSONIAN RUSHES TO NORTH DAKOTA FIND

MINNESOTA EVENING TRIBUNE, SEPTEMBER 18, 1963

(*Associated Press*) Kathryn N.D.: The remains of an Indian woman, judged by some to be at least 1,000 years old, have been unearthed from a burial mound on the Vincent Zacharias farm four miles east of here. The skeleton was found about two feet below the surface. The body had been buried in a sitting position and nearly all the skeletal bones were found intact.

Two men from the Smithsonian Institution visited the farm recently and made an analysis of the skeleton. They estimated the remains were those of an Indian woman about 23 to 25 years of age and that she had been buried about 1,000 years ago.

ANOTHER DAM DESTROYS ANOTHER ANCIENT VILLAGE

STANDARD EXAMINER, AUGUST 7, 1959

Ogden, Utah: Evidences of a group of Utah natives who had no housing problems were uncovered by earthmoving machinery at the Willard Bay Dam this week. A bulldozer scraped off the top of an Indian mound in which artifacts and a human skeleton were found. Bureau of Reclamation men stopped work at the site and notified the University of Utah.

James H. Gunnerson of the archaeology department of the university visited the area Tuesday with Robert Robinson of 665 Polk, a field engineer with the bureau. Mr. Gunnerson said the remains were those of a group of Pueblo-type Indians who inhabited the area from AD 1000 to 1200.

"From signs and artifacts, there had been a village of several dirt houses at the site," the Utah University man said.

THEY WERE FARMERS

The Utah scientists said these people were farmers, who raised corn, squash and beans. They had a certain culture, he said, which was indicated by a piece of broken pottery with a decorative line around its rim.

The skeleton was complete, except for the skull. Mr. Robinson said that the scientists estimated the skeleton was that of an adult about 5 feet 10 inches in height, somewhat taller than average for this race of early Indians.

An employee at the University of Utah yesterday quoted Dr. Gunnerson as saying the archaeology department has no plans for further exploration at the Willard dam site.

THE DEATH VALLEY TEMPLE OF THE GIANTS

This story from the *Nevada News* relates how Dr. F. Bruce Russell, following up on reports that the Smithsonian had hidden evidence of giants found in Death Valley, eventually uncovered a complex of thirty-two caves in a 180-square-mile area around the Nevada–California–Arizona border. Inside the complex of caves, he reported finding the skeletons of eight- and nine-foot giants dressed in animal skins that had been tailored into jackets and pants that resembled "prehistoric Zoot-suits." Russell also reported finding hieroglyphics, extensive weapons, religious artifacts, and cooking utensils, and at the end of a hall leading from the main temple he said there was a room filled with the well-preserved remains of dinosaurs, saber-toothed tigers, imperial elephants, and other extinct beasts paired off in niches as if on display.

ATLANTIS IN THE COLORADO RIVER DESERT

NEVADA NEWS, 1947

Near the Nevada–California–Arizona border area, 32 caves within a 180-square-mile area were discovered to hold the remains of ancient, strangely costumed 8–9 foot giants. They had been laid to rest wearing the skins of unknown animals similar to sheepskins fashioned into jackets with pants described as "prehistoric Zoot-suits." The same burial place had been found 10–15 years earlier by another man who made a deal with the Smithsonian. The evidence of his find was stolen and covered up by Darwinian scientists.

Dr. F. Bruce Russell had come to Death Valley from the east coast for the sake of his health. He had taken up mining in the west and was exploring across the Colorado River into Arizona. What he found he described as the burial place of a tribal hierarchy within the ritual hall of an ancient people. He felt that some unknown catastrophe had driven them into these caves. All of the implements of their civilization were there, including household utensils and stoves. Dr. Russell reported seeing hieroglyphics chiseled on carefully polished granite within what appeared to be a cavern temple. Another cave led to their sacred hall, which contained carvings of ritual devices and markings similar to those of the Masonic Order. A long tunnel from this temple led to a room where, Russell said, "Well-preserved remains of dinosaurs, saber-toothed tigers, imperial elephants, and other extinct beasts were paired off in niches as if on display."

Ten to fifteen years earlier the caves had been seen by another miner who had fallen from the bottom of a mineshaft. In his book, *Death Valley Men*, Bourke Lee related a conversation among residents of Death Valley concerning the local

Paiute Native American legends of an underground city at Wingate Pass. After falling through the ceiling of an unknown tunnel, the miner had followed it 20 miles north of the Panamint Mountains to discover a huge ancient underground city. He saw arching stone vaults with huge stone doors and a polished round table in the center of their council chamber, which had once been lit by ingenious lights, fueled by subterranean gases.

Leaning against the walls were their tall gold spears. He said that the designs on their thick golden armbands resembled the work of the Egyptians. The tunnel ended at an exit overlooking Furnace Creek Ranch in California's Imperial Valley. He could see from there that the valley had once been underwater. The tunnel entrance had been a dock or a quay located halfway up the side of the mountain. A deal was made with the Smithsonian Museum for the find, but the miner was betrayed by his partner. The evidence was stolen and the entrance concealed. In a 1940 mining journal, another find was reported of much worked gold found in an 8 mile long cave near San Bernardino.

University of Arizona professor Vine Deloria, himself a Native American, made a similar accusation against the Smithsonian for covering up the remains found within the burial mounds of the Moundbuilder civilization. Surviving diaries from before the time of Darwin attest to these discoveries. The Moundbuilders were a different civilization than that of the Indians, they said. The mounds contained the remains of hundreds of giants along with the bones of giant mastodons. In Cincinnati, Ohio, the giant bones were found with large shields, swords, and engraved stone tablets. In Kentucky and Tennessee the bones of "powerful men of towering stature" were excavated. One of these 7-foot men was buried with an engraved copper plate beneath his head. A woman was also found. She was wearing a silver girdle with letters written on it. The *Detroit Free Press* reported in 1884 the discovery in Gartersville, Mississippi, of the remains of a giant with waist-length jet-black hair. He was wearing a copper crown. With him in his timber burial vault were his children who wore garments decorated with bone beads. The tomb was covered with large flagstones engraved with inscriptions. In Cayuga Township, Niagara, there is a place called "The Cemetery of the Giants," which was discovered in 1880. Those giants were nine feet tall and appear to have died violent deaths. Their axes were found with them.

Giant bones were also unearthed from a rock fissure on Lake Erie Island. In some of the finds of giant bones, the bones lay in confusion as if left on a battlefield. The Smithsonian does display some artifacts of the Moundbuilders found with the bones of the giants: shell discs and carved stone beads. Many of the bones turned to powdery ash within a short time of being exposed to the air. The Smithsonian has been reluctant to test some less fragile finds. The late Vine Deloria said that it is because they "Might find a really early date for the bones" and that it would be distressing: distressing to their Darwinian time-line.

SMITHSONIAN REMOVES 564 SKELETONS IN KERN COUNTY, CALIFORNIA

FIND ALSO CONTAINS FOUR THOUSAND SPECIMENS OF ANCIENT INDIAN LIFE

BAKERSFIELD CALIFORNIAN, MARCH 28, 1934

More than 4000 artifacts and hundreds of Indian burials have been excavated at the site of the Tulamni Company lease near Taft during the past three and a half months. It was revealed here today with the announcement that the camp of workers, supported by federal funds, will all be dispersed by Friday.

The archaeological projects, which have employed varyingly from 190 to the 26 men retained to make the final surveys, have been directed by Dr. W. T. Strong and W. M. Walker, assistant, from the Bureau of American Ethnology of the Smithsonian Institution with Dr. Edwin F. Walker as archaeologist and W. R. Wedel as assistant archaeologist. In the opinion of the directors, two more months could be spent excavating the Kern Indian Mounds.

The artifacts uncovered, classi-fied, and shipped to the Smithsonian Institution include mortar and pestles, flint points, bone tools, textiles, shells, and soapstone beads and other ornaments, stone vessels, and fragments of basketry.

A total of 564 skeletons were uncovered in the burial mounds, of which 348 were taken from the first mound. Not all the skeletons found were considered good specimens. One of the last to be uncovered had been interred in a round hole with the body flexed grotesquely to make it fit the chosen grave. Three thousand specimens were uncovered in the first mound and 1,000 from the second mound, which was conceded to be much older in time than the first.

DOCUMENTING THE FINDS

A topography map of the mounds and the excavation area has been made by

Pavey L. Stanley of Bakersfield, who headed one of the excavation crews, and it will be filed with the collection at the Smithsonian.

Mr. Walker is returning to Washington D.C. and will study the local collection and write a report on the finds for the Smithsonian Institution that will make clear Kern County's contribution to filling in the larger picture of pre-historic human life on the American continent.

SKELETONS OF EARLY INDIANS ARE UNEXPECTEDLY UNEARTHED

LOS ANGELES HERALD EXAMINER, JANUARY 20, 1930

Students of early California history have turned their attention to the discovery of an early Indian burial ground near Carpinteria, uncovered unexpectedly by a crew of workmen making a cut through a cliff for a road to the beach. Some of the traditional Indian burial customs were revealed as the great steam shovel tore open the graves. The skeletons were found lying face down, foreheads resting on surfaced stones, with arrowheads, cooking utensils, and other articles buried with them. The story of the savages' graves was related in Los Angeles by George A. McDonald, local broker, on whose property the burial ground was uncovered by a drilling crew engaged in running a road to the beach for oil-drilling work.

SCORES OF SKELETONS

For 80 feet from the place where a steam shovel started digging into the edge of the cliff, which drops straight to the ocean's edge, skeletons of Indians were uncovered by the score, according to McDonald. In the majority of the graves the Indians were lying on their faces, their heads toward the west. In one grave a mother and her child were discovered, the mother had one arm half-circling the infant. Close by was the skeleton of a brave. Imbedded in his forehead was an arrow, one which undoubtedly struck him down during battle more than a century ago.

Hundreds of arrowheads, a number of grinding and mixing bowls, and other articles were buried with the bodies. Many of the skulls have been removed from the property with the permission of the owner. When Roscoe Eames, drilling superintendent, encountered the old burial ground he immediately halted excavation and made a preliminary investigation. He asked McDonald for permission to continue, and given the right, resumed building the road to the edge of the cliff and throughout the entire distance turned up many of the skeletons.

HUNDREDS OF SKELETONS, SOME STICKING OUT

When word was received of the discovery at Carpinteria, classes from nearby schools were dismissed to visit the old burial grounds and to study the various finds. According to McDonald the cemetery may stretch many feet out and around the road under construction, and hundreds of skeletons probably would be found if that entire area were excavated.

Parts of skeletons could be seen sticking out over the edge of the newly excavated portion of the road, and these were pulled out of the ground by members of the steam shovel crew and tossed in a heap. Sightseers removed the pieces. McDonald owns the property and for many feet into the ocean fronting the old burial ground. The oil well will be drilled out in the ocean and within a stone's throw of the cemetery.

3

HOW OLD?

Clues from Mastodons and Carbon Dating

One of the most amazing aspects of the findings related to the prehistory of America is their extreme antiquity. The dates of early finds were often estimated based on the ages of trees that had grown up over previously inhabited sites, such as in the following excerpt from *A History of Miami County, Ohio, 1880.* As testing became more sophisticated with carbon dating and other analyses, the dates of the finds kept getting pushed back, from hundreds to thousands of years. Scientists are now getting dates of 14,000 BCE for some of their finds in the Americas.

> There were several mounds, which indicate the existence, in this locality, of a prehistoric race. The largest of these earthworks embraces about two acres in extent, and is some three feet high. Various pieces of workmanship found upon the spot, such as arrow-heads, pieces of pottery, and images carved upon stone, go to prove that these people were not totally unacquainted with the fine arts, and that they possessed more than the ordinary intelligence of the Indian.

Upon this mound a human skeleton was plowed up, which, although badly decayed, was judged, by those who examined it, to have been that of a man at least seven feet in height. An ash tree, more than one hundred years old, growing on one of the mounds, shows that they must have been built at a period of time very remote from the present.

At other sites, careful archaeological study resulted in estimates of a few thousand years before, such as the discoveries of the Iowa Archaeological Survey in association with the WPA mentioned in the following article from 1935 or those of the State University of Iowa, as described in the 1958 article.

IOWA INHABITED FOR AT LEAST TWO THOUSAND YEARS

By Ray E. Colton, archaeologist

IOWA ENTERPRISE, ESTHERVILLE, IOWA, AUGUST 21, 1935

Thousands of years before the arrival of the white pioneers to what is now Emmet County, Iowa, there inhabited in this section of Northern Iowa, a strange race of people whom science has named the "mound builders." Evidence of this race has been found at various points in north central Iowa, especially along the shores of Lake Okoboji, and other bodies of water, such as creeks and rivers. These artifacts, in the shape of arrow heads, pottery, spear heads, axes, and some human skeleton remains give to archaeologists the story of this strange race that is believed to have antedated the white pioneers by at least 2,000 years.

Traces of extinct fortifications, burial, ceremonial, and effigy mounds have been found near Milford and Spirit Lake, in Dickinson County, and a line drawn east and west along Emmet and Kossuth counties. These mounds, and other artificial tumuli could have been erected only by the mound builders, as they are known to have been the only cultured race of ancient times of the North American continent capable of erecting these works of antiquity. Owing to their erection of these mounds, the term "mound builder" has been applied to their race and culture.

EXCAVATION OF PREHISTORIC IOWA VILLAGE

MORNING SUN NEWS HERALD, AUGUST 14, 1958

The first excavation of a pre-historic Indian village in Iowa has revealed pottery and some stone tools which indicate the village was established some 3,000 years ago. Although the artifacts are not the oldest found in Iowa, the discoveries 80 inches below the surface of the ground may be considered a major archaeological find, according to R. J. Ruppe, State University of Iowa assistant professor of sociology and anthropology. Dr. Ruppe is directing a field expedition of 16 SUI students on the Indian village site located east of Wapello near Toolesboro in Louisa County.

The site, on a 200-foot-high bluff overlooking the Iowa River, is near a series of large burial mounds where extensive archaeological exploration was carried out in the 1870s by the Davenport Academy of Science. The prehistoric village site was called to Dr. Ruppe's attention after a roadway was cut through the bluff and large black stains in the clay hill indicated it was the site of a number of storage pits, which the Indians filled with broken pottery, flint chips, charcoal, bones, and other trash.

The 3,000-year-old crumbly pottery called "Marion-thick," is extremely thick and coarse tempered. Excavation will be continued through the summer to determine whether the village site may have been inhabited even earlier than 1000 BC. "We're not sure yet how deep we'll have to go to before we hit a 'sterile' level where there are no further artifacts," Dr. Ruppe said.

He explained that the materials found at the various depths show no single, extensive period of occupation to indicate intermittent occupation from 1000 BC to 1400 BC. The articles found at the 30-inch depth indicate that the Indians who used them belonged to the "early Woodland period," which followed from 500 BC. Other artifacts are dated in the "Hopewell period," which followed from 500 BC to AD 500. Artifacts close to the surface are of the "late Woodland period" of 500 to about AD 1400. A broken pottery vessel about 20 inches in diameter and estimated to be 1,400 years old was found by the students at Lake Odessa, several miles from the village site. They have reconstructed about half of the cord-marker, mud colored vessel. "It is one of the few found with all the broken pieces in one place," Dr. Ruppe said.

Thousands of artifacts have been found since the group of SUI students began digging at the village site. In one pit, 4,268 flint flakes were uncovered. Also found were arrowheads, fragments of smoking pipes, fish scalers, various types of bones, much charcoal and obsidian, and a type of volcanic glass used in making tools. Each item, when discovered as the students shave a quarter of an inch of earth with their trowels, is recorded on maps to show exactly where and at what depth it was found. After being carefully cleaned and labeled, all items are sent to SUI to be analyzed further this fall in the classroom. From this information the students will be able to reconstruct the lay-out of the village and gain an insight into the Indian culture.

After carbon dating was developed, truly mind-boggling results emerged, as the articles quoted below make clear. The results have been reinforced by some startling finds that indicate the coexistence of the giants with mastodons, which became extinct some twelve thousand years ago.

HILLTOP DIG NEAR BUFFALO 11,000 YEARS OLD—AREA'S ANCIENT INHABITANTS PROBED ON PHOENIX HILLTOP

By Steve Carlic, Staff Writer

SYRACUSE HERALD AMERICAN, APRIL 3, 1983

It's just about time to dust off the buckets, break out the pickaxes and take another look at North America's earliest residents. They lived just down the road from the village of Phoenix—11,000 years ago. Last summer anthropologists from the Buffalo Museum of Science spent several weeks digging on a hilltop near Route 264 about four miles north of the village. They plan to return May 16 to June 4, to dig again. Michael Gramly, curator of anthropology at the museum, said residents are invited to join in the dig. By studying the hundreds of arrowheads, stone flakes and stone tools found at the site, Gramly hopes to shed light on the mysterious Paleo-Indian people, believed to be the first inhabitants of North America.

The dig site is located on a knoll that provides a view of the Oswego River valley. Gramly believes the site provided hunters with a view of approaching herds of animals migrating south. He said 1,400 artifacts were discovered last summer at one site. At least five Paleo-Indian campsites have been identified at the Phoenix site; only one was excavated by his team of 10 to 15 volunteers and adult education students from Buffalo. The nature of the artifacts and the relative scarcity of them leads Gramly to believe the hilltop was a temporary hunting camp, a place where prehistoric hunters spent two or three weeks during warm weather. Diggers, supported by the National Geographic Society, spent last year sifting dirt from a 275-square meter plot. "The area has been extensively plowed in the past, but that did not disturb the site too much," Gramly said. The site was excavated thoroughly last year and the team is returning this spring to investigate a second of the five campsites.

"We'll be doing the same thing as last year," Gramly said. "We need two areas excavated thoroughly to compare the two. It's possible that the people returned to the area in a different season, which would be evident in certain differences and we've got similarities of the sites. The Phoenix site has been known by anthropologists for decades, but digs were never undertaken for various reasons." A large number of arrowheads and other artifacts discovered by local farmers encouraged Gramly to conduct the dig.

Artifacts discovered last year were cataloged. Gramly has lectured on his findings and a scholarly paper will be written in November that describes his findings.

ONE OF THE MOST IMPORTANT SITES IN THE COUNTRY

In the mid-1970s, excavators removed over twenty thousand artifacts from a dig in the general area of the Delaware Valley, which dated back to 9000 BCE at the earliest and showed thousands of years of continuous habitation.

PALEO-INDIAN CULTURE IN THE DELAWARE VALLEY

By Joe Rattman

POCONO RECORD REPORTER, AUGUST 30, 1975

Archaeologists digging near here have discovered indications of a Paleo-Indian culture in the Delaware Valley no later than 2,000 years after the last glacier receded northward around 9,000 BC. Dr. Charles W. McNett Jr., an archaeologist at the American University in Washington, said fluted points he found at a site he is excavating, confirm that the site's nomadic inhabitants were the first people to live in the area after it was no longer covered by ice.

"Several of my colleagues have said they think this is the most important Paleo-Indian site in the East, if not in the country," McNett said.

The Paleo-Indian artifacts were discovered under eight to ten feet of soil, sand and silt beneath artifacts of more recent cultures on a fertile flood plain of the Delaware River adjoining the Delaware Water Gap National Recreation Area. The 11,000-year-old find this summer predated finds last summer dated to 8800 BC.

MORE THAN TWENTY THOUSAND ARTIFACTS REMOVED FROM SITE

"More than 20,000 artifacts were found last summer alone at the site," McNett said. The river flooded several times over the centuries, gradually building up the soil and placing layers in between the artifacts that indicated occupations at various different times.

"It is not clear where the Paleo-Indians came from but it is speculated that they migrated from western Pennsylvania where they seemed to be living around 14,000 to 15,000 years ago," McNett said.

Some of the oldest spear heads ever found were discovered in the Pee Dee Basin in the South Carolina counties of Florence, Darlington, Marlboro, and Marion. The oldest of these spear points are of Clovis origin and have been carbon-dated to 10,000 B.C. In addition, these points were found in association with mammoth and mastodon kills. In addition to the spear points, some of the oldest pottery ever discovered comes from South Carolina. It is what is called "fiber-tempered" pottery and it was found in association with polished stone tools, various scrapers, projectile points and lithic material.

THE PEE DEES OF SOUTH CAROLINA
DATE TO 8000 BC

FLORENCE MORNING NEWS, AUGUST 4, 1974

Bob Durrett, a Francis Marion College senior majoring in history, has just completed a comprehensive study on the early Indians of the Pee Dee. In his study, the young archeologist focused on the Archaic Period of the Indian culture of the Pee Dee dating from 8000 to 1500 BC. Being, for the most part nomadic, the Archaic Indians moved along river areas in the Pee

Dee basin in search of food, probably sheltering themselves in rough huts of saplings or hides. Occupational sites from this culture were studied in four South Carolina counties: Florence, Darlington, Marlboro, and Marion.

According to Durrett, the people of the Pee Dee have always been aware of the past existence of the Indians of this region. "Farmers have found the artifacts in their fields," he said. "However, people mistakenly associate these artifacts with the historic Indians of early colonial America. In reality, Indians could have lived in this area of South Carolina as early as 12,000 years ago," he added.

SOUTH CAROLINA CLOVIS SPEAR POINTS KILLED MAMMOTHS AND MASTODONS

Durrett bases this opinion on the fact that, in South Carolina, Clovis spear points have been found like those found in the Southwest, which are associated with the bones of now extinct mammoths and mastodons. Carbon-14 dates taken from the pre-historic kill sites of these huge animals go back to about 10,000 BC. Therefore, according to Durrett, since the spear points from the Southwest and from South Carolina are so similar, it is perhaps reasonable to assume that the age of the Clovis artifacts in this state would be close to those from the Southwest, perhaps earlier.

MAMMOTHS AND MASTODONS IN SOUTH CAROLINA

In addition, archeological findings reveal that mammoths and mastodons existed in South Carolina and remains of these animals were found in Darlington County in the 1840s. It was the ancestors of the Archaic Indians, known as the Paleo-Indians, who exploited the large game. Archaics hunted smaller game and added fish, grain, and vegetables to their diets. In his writing, Durrett tries to relate the artifacts to their culture: it was with the Archaic Indians that the "grinding stone" and polished stone tools appeared. In addition, bone pins have been found that were probably used to prepare clothing from hides. It is thought that certain of the "dart or lance" projectile points were used to kill, then to butcher and dress bone or hide. One such artifact was found in a field across from the FMC campus and many have been found in this area. "Artifacts of the polished stone tool are relatively scarce in this area," said Durrett. "However," he added, "many early pot shards from the late archaic period have been discovered in the Pee Dee, this due to the fact that pottery is well preserved in this climate and soil. The pottery of the late-Archaic Indians was fiber-tempered; that is, plant fibers were added to the clay to make it stronger. One of the most common fibers used was the Palmetto fiber, which easily molded with the clay."

EARLIEST POTTERY DATES IN AMERICA

"The earliest dates," Durrett stated, "that have been found on the fiber-tempered pottery in North America come from South Carolina." Durrett's collection of Pee Dee artifacts includes samples of polished stone tools, various scrapers, projectile points, and lithic material. Durrett has included pictures of many of the artifacts with his paper. In his paper, Durrett also includes a word on the importance of preserving Indian artifacts. He warns readers against "pot-holing" or going to historic and prehistoric sites and indiscriminately digging for artifacts.

"Once these artifacts are removed from the context in which they are found, if no careful techniques and cataloging are undertaken," said Durrett, the value of the material is gone forever as far as gaining information. There is no monetary value to the artifacts. "Their value lies in the insight they give into our historic heritage," he said.

Fig. 3.1. View of the eastern face of the Pee Dee Basin excavation under the drip line (photo by Mark McConaughy)

CARBON DATING PUTS FIND AT UP TO
14,225 BC

INDIANA EVENING GAZETTE, JULY 3, 1976

Recent archaeological digging at a cave near Avella, in Washington County, and carbon-14 testing of cave materials, indicate that the prehistoric Indians of our area date to about 14,225 BC. Don W. Dragoo, Curator, Section of Man, Carnegie Museum of Pittsburgh, states that fluted points of the Indian period, dated approximately from 16,000 to 6,000. Most of them have been surface finds, except for one area along the Conemaugh River near Blairsville, which he believes may have been a campsite of these ancient peoples.

SMITHSONIAN INVOLVEMENT
IN THE 1880S AND 1890S

In an *Associated Press* story from 1997, reporter Anthony Breznikan interviewed archaeologist James M. Adovasio about the ten thousand artifacts he had removed from an area of western New York since 1993 in his capacity as a head archaeologist for the Mercyhurst College Archaeological Institute and the Pennsylvania Historic and Museum Commission.

ASSOCIATED PRESS, JULY 29, 1997

"Humans have lived at this site as early as 12,000 years ago," said Dr. Adovasio about the flatlands near the Allegheny River 90 miles south of Buffalo, New York, "when they followed retreating glaciers north. The first year-round residents were the Hopewell tribe from 100 to 500 CE.

"In the late 1800s, archaeologists from the Smithsonian Institution found Hopewell burial mounds in the area. There were many tribes in Pennsylvania who seemed to be imitating what the Hopewell were doing, but the artifacts from these burial mounds appeared to be real."

MARYLAND OCCUPATION DATES TO 10,000 BCE

SITES BEING DESTROYED AT AN ALARMING RATE

ANNAPOLIS CAPITAL, MAY 13, 1981

There is abundant evidence of man's presence in Maryland for 10,000 years or more. Along the Chesapeake Bay and its tributaries are more than 10,000 significant Indian occupation sites. In Anne Arundel County alone nearly 700 sites have been recorded and given permanent identifying numbers by the Maryland Geological Survey. These sites are being destroyed . . . at an alarming rate. Simple pole barns and houses on piers did much to preserve a site. The early farmer with horse drawn plow did little damage to Indian ruins, even though they are usually so thin so as to be contained entirely within the plow zone. But with the advent of the tractor and earth leveling machines, concerned groups of preservationists watched with a little dismay. However, since this was a necessary part of the farming that gave us the free time for our pursuits, not many objected. But in the early 1960s with the mass movement to the suburbs and especially, the waterfront, the time for real concern became apparent.

MOUND BUILDER SITES HAVE NOT FARED WELL

NEW YORK TRIBUNE, 1874

Indian ruins have not fared so well. From Wayson's Corner to Ft. Meade, nearly every shred of gravel has been removed for road building and other construction uses.

Some of those Indian sites extended a quarter mile and farther from the river edge and all the artifacts that once lay there undisturbed for thousands of years, are now in roads, driveways and concrete. We found an Archaic (2000 BC) Indian ax about 20 years ago that was dumped on a Deale driveway. The gravel was from the Patuxent River. Several Indian artifacts were recovered from St. Helena Island in the Severn River. They were found eroding from a decaying concrete bulkhead that was built in the early 1930s. The gravel in the concrete is of the type and color found along the Davidsonville area of the Patuxent. Near Rose Haven in extreme southern Anne Arundel County, a housing development was planned on an Indian site that has been nominated to the National Register of Historic Places.

DEVELOPER ALLOWS A DIG BEFORE DESTRUCTION

The developer was very generous in allowing the Archeological Society of

Maryland Inc. and its chapters to conduct a test excavation in 1977. About 80 people participated in the dig over a period of 10 days. After finding much cultural material, mostly Middle Woodland, (400 BC–AD 400) we found that the primary site was in no immediate danger since it was in a low area encompassed by the so-called 100-year flood plain. We abandoned the project at this point. It is our hope the site will remain forever undug. The longer a site remains untouched, the longer archeologists of the future will have to observe a ruin without its having been destroyed and just written about.

OBSERVATORIES, ALLIGATOR MOUNDS, AND GRAVES

Some [mounds] have the appearance of military structures, and others look as though they were built as observatories, while others seem to be designed for religious or burial purposes. Some mounds have the form of birds, serpents, alligators, and other animals. The "old fort" at Newark, has a mound in the center several feet high and about fifty feet long, built

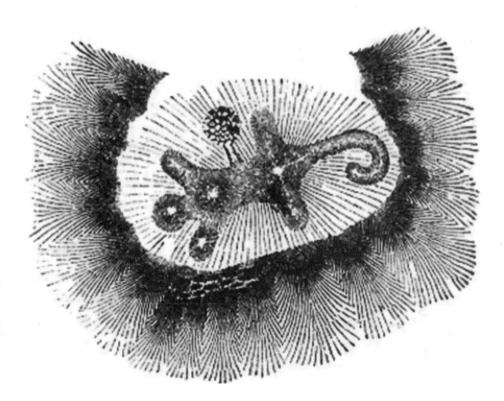

Fig. 3.2. Alligator effigy mound in Ohio, built circa 950 CE

in the shape of an eagle with spread wings.

NOT BARBARIANS

It was certainly no barbaric skill that could have traced out those perfect circles, surveyed those rectangles and octagons, much less controlled the tens of thousands of laborers that must have been necessary to construct these earthen walls and mounds.

But it is all a mystery. One can only wonder that such a mighty people should so completely pass away as to leave no trace of their history but these piles of earth.

SIGNIFICANT FINDS AT THE MEADOWCROFT ROCKSHELTER

The Meadowcroft Rockshelter in western Pennsylvania has recently come into prominence as one of the oldest verified archaeological sites in the United States. Although no skeletons have been recovered from the rock shelter, it must be born in mind that two documented excavations of skeletons in the area predate the rock shelter finds by fifty years. They tell us in no uncertain terms who these people were and what they looked like.

In addition, fossilized bits of bone have been reclaimed from Paleo-Indian, Archaic, and Woodland Indian sites, and radiocarbon dating has revealed continuous use and possible occupation from 17,000 to 14,000 BCE and right up until the present. Digging at the site has gone down 11.5 feet to obtain these results, this being the first site in the Americas that was dug down past the Clovis levels to reveal Solutrean projectile points that predate the Clovis points by thousands of years. Clovis points and other bifacial (two-sided) objects like scrapers have also been recovered, as well as flint from Ohio, jasper from eastern Pennsylvania, and shells from the Atlantic coast, showing that these people engaged in widespread trade in the extremely ancient past.

The Meadowcroft Rockshelter site was first discovered and excavated from 1973 to 1978 by an archaeological team from the University of Pittsburgh led by James M. Adovasio, Ph.D., perhaps the main academic in the forefront of the study of what are called Paleo-Indians, or what should more accurately be referred to as the extremely ancient settlers of the Americas. Not only has Adovasio been at the forefront of the excavations at this site, but he has also been active in the dating and reclamation of the bog mummies in Florida (see chapter 10, page 275). He has published his findings in an excellent book called *The First Americans: In Pursuit of Archaeology's Greatest Mystery*. But despite his expertise in the areas of this study, Adovasio has remained silent on the subject of the previously discovered skeletons, which is odd, as it directly relates to his life's work. Perhaps, like most of the others in the academic field of archaeology, he is simply unaware of the finds or has been brainwashed into believing these old finds were all part of some ongoing hoax. But the only hoaxers are at those at the Smithsonian and the major universities and museums across America who are involved in the ongoing suppression of scientific evidence crucial to understanding the true history of this country.

Fig. 3.3. Meadowcroft Rockshelter in Washington County, Pennsylvania, is a national historic landmark and was first occupied more than 14,000 years ago by pre-Clovis people (photo courtesy of Indiana University of Pennsylvania, Department of Anthropology).

Because of the scientifically confirmed, carbon-14–dated extreme antiquity of the area, as proven by the work of the team at the Meadowcroft Rockshelter, led by Adovasio, the fact that significant skeletons were recovered from this area fifty years ago takes on added significance.

The first skeleton was discovered by William Jacob Holland and his assistant. Holland was the main curator at the Carnegie Museums of Pittsburgh from 1896 to 1922 and was considered the most prestigious anthropologist and archaeologist in the state at that time.

THE CARNEGIE MUSEUM CLAIMS POSSESSION OF AN EIGHT- TO NINE-FOOT GIANT

PHILADELPHIA INQUIRER, NOVEMBER 22, 1920

Dr. W. J. Holland curator of the Carnegie Museum, Pittsburgh and his assistant Dr. Peterson, a few days ago opened up a mound of the ancient race that inhabited this state and secured the skeleton, who, while in the flesh, was from 8–9 feet in height.

The mound was originally about 100 feet long and more than 12 feet high somewhat worn down by time. It is on the J. B. Secrest farm in South Huntington Township. This farm has been in the Secrest name for more than a century. The most interesting feature in the recent excavations were the mummified torso of a human body, which the experts figured was laid to rest at least 400 years ago.

"Portions of the bones dug up and the bones in the leg," Prof. Peterson declares, "are those of a person between eight and nine feet in height." The scientist figures that this skeleton was the framework of a person of the prehistoric race that inhabited this area before the American Indian. The torso and the portions of the big skeleton were shipped to the Carnegie Museum. Dr. Holland and Peterson supervised the explorations of the mound with the greatest of care. The curators believe the man whose skeleton they secured belonged to the mound builder class.

The second very major find from the immediate vicinity of the Meadowcroft Rockshelter was of a cache of forty-nine skeletons that were discovered in Washington County at another mound in the 1930s. The story of this discovery was accompanied by photos of bones,

Fig. 3.4. A fanciful early illustration of our descent from giants.

skulls, and teeth, and one of the accompanying photo captions notes, "Archaeologists are amazed at the excellent condition of the teeth."

THUNDERBIRD IMAGES DATE BACK TEN THOUSAND YEARS

As we pull back the curtain of the true history of the Americas, the first thing that we discover is that many popular, iconographic images that we associate with the American Indians find their roots in the much more ancient culture of the mound builders. A case in point is the classic image of the thunderbird. At a site along the Shenandoah River, estimated to be over one mile long, effigy mounds in a number

Fig. 3.5. Dr. Kenneth Campbell with the reconstruction of a teratorn, the largest bird to fly; it could reach speeds of 150 miles per hour.

of totem styles, including the thunderbird, were uncovered that date back to 10,000 BCE. Giant burials were found in association with these sites, as well as numerous artifacts, including Clovis point arrowheads.

EXTREMELY ANCIENT HISTORY OF VIRGINIA INDIANS

THUNDERBIRD FACTORY SITE MAY BE OLDEST IN NATION

By Ned Burks

STAR STAFF, FEBRUARY 6, 1984

Front Royal: Along the floodplain of the South Fork of the Shenandoah River, about seven miles south of Front Royal, lay the remains of a primitive "factory" that was thriving in the valley long before modern industry came to Warren County.

It is called the Thunderbird site,

and archaeologists who have examined stone artifacts found there say the area was used by a Paleo-Indian culture for the manufacture of hunting and butchering tools almost 12,000 years ago.

The site also contains the oldest evidence yet discovered of a house structure in North America, and evidence gathered there over the past 13 years has allowed archaeologists to construct a working model of one of the oldest known civilizations on this continent.

Amateur archaeologists began to discover Indian artifacts at the site in the 1960s, and their find came to the attention of William Gardner, a professor of anthropology at Catholic University, in 1969. Gardner and his assistants soon discovered that their predecessors had barely scratched the surface of what would become one of the most important archaeological finds in the eastern United States. Gardner is completing a book on the prehistory of the Middle Atlantic Region of North America, in which he is incorporating much of the information he has gathered from the Thunderbird excavation.

He became so fascinated with the area that, with the help of a number of graduate students, he has been excavating and mapping the site ever since.

EXTREMELY ANCIENT DISCOVERY A TOTAL SURPRISE

The "dig" is undisturbed now because of winter weather but excavation will continue next summer.

When Gardner began work on the site with the help of a National Geographic Society grant in 1971, it did not take him long to realize how significant the Thunderbird excavation would be. He thought at first that the artifacts at Thunderbird were strictly from a "surface scatter," similar to so many other sites discovered in the east.

Surface scatters are clusters of stone chips and projectile points that remained in the plow zone of the soil and were frequently disturbed by farmers who settled the valley in modern times, Gardner said. To his surprise, he discovered that the stones at Thunderbird were much older than he had anticipated, and that the site was more than just a temporary stopping point for nomadic Indians who roamed the Shenandoah Valley for food.

"After taking off all the disturbed soil in the plow zone we came down on stains in the ground where posts had been driven," Gardner said. "That was the first evidence, and so far really the only evidence, of a house structure at this time period. It really threw us for a loop." It turned out that Gardner and his crew had stumbled on what had once been a traditional Indian camping ground, first established between 10,000 and 9,000 BC.

Using carbon dating, Gardner discovered that a piece of charcoal found on the site dated to about 8000 BC. He knows the site was probably in use for almost 2,000 years before that, because certain distinctive spear points known as Clovis points also were found near the river. Clovis points discovered in the western United States have been dated as early as 9500 BC, and Gardner's student Bob Verrey has called them "the hallmark of the Paleo-Indian period," the oldest known period of human habitation in North America.

Gardner said that the Indians who occupied the Thunderbird site could confidently be dated to 9500 BC because of stylistic similarities between the spear points found here and elsewhere. "It's like taking a piece of furniture and saying, 'This is Colonial,'" he said.

Gardner also stated that the number of stone chippings found on the site, and the fact that the chippings have been found at varying depths beneath the surface, indicates that the area was used more or less continuously over a period of 2,000 years as a center for making stone hunting and cooking tools.

Further excavation and a painstaking system of mapping, which involves leaving stone chips and projectile points at exactly the level at which they are discovered, allowed Gardner and Verrey to construct a working model of the culture of the earliest known inhabitants of the region. Gardner calls archaeology "history without a written record."

Studying the Paleo-Indian culture in the Shenandoah Valley is compli-cated even more because no human or animal remains have been found at the site. Gardner explained that the well-drained, acidic soils in the Shenandoah Valley have caused all animal and vegetable matter of the period to decay without a trace. Even in the drier soils of the West, no human remains from the period have been found. Consequently, archaeologists are left to make deductions about the early inhabitants of the valley based almost entirely on the evidence of stone artifacts and the patterns in which they are found.

"Though the Indians who once roamed this land in search of deer, elk, and moose remain faceless, certain things can now be said about their lifestyle with some certainty," Gardner said. "The valley would have been attractive to them, with its plentiful supply of game and fresh water. Thunderbird was an ideal place to be in the winter, because the food options were better (than farther north). With the river, you can always break through the ice and get fish and turtle. Sooner or later the animals will come down there too.

"Even more important for the Indians than the abundant game were the outcrops of jasper, an American flint rock that jutted from the cliffs just across the river from the Thunderbird site. Jasper was a stone highly valued by the early Indians because it was especially well suited for making high quality stone tools and weapons. Large piles of stone chippings found at the site indicate that the Indians used the area as a quarry reduction station, whittling rocks down to portable size before making the finished products: knives and spear points for the men who did the hunting, and scraping and cooking tools for the women who prepared the food."

Gardner and Verrey hope to learn more about these early Indians. Excavation at the Thunderbird site will continue for at least four more years, when Gardner's ten-year exca-vation rights to the site expire. The land is owned by Thunderbird Ranch Hunt Club. Together with ongoing research, including the search for more carbon dates that will allow Gardner and Verrey to pin down the oldest date of settlement more pre-cisely, the site is being used to train students. Despite the amount of time spent on the project, a great deal more work remains to be done. By the end of last summer excavation on one household area had been completed, but Gardner estimated there are at least twenty such areas that remain to be unearthed.

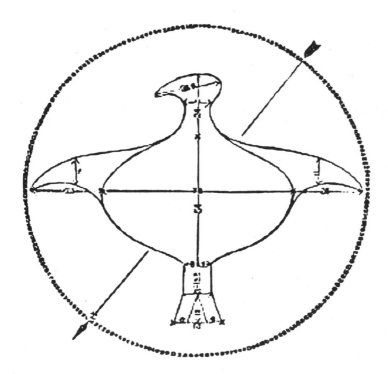

Fig. 3.6. A bird mound, surrounded by a stone circle,
from *The Prehistoric World* by E. A. Allen

**ANCIENT THUNDERBIRD
SITE IS ONE MILE LONG**

*ONLY 2,400 SQUARE FEET
DUG OF ONE-MILE-LONG SITE*

"The Thunderbird site is almost a mile long, and we've dug maybe 2,400 square feet," Gardner said. "We've opened a few small windows in a house of 10,000 windows."

The Thunderbird Museum and Archaeological Park, which houses many of the artifacts discovered at the Thunderbird site and other Indian sites in the Northern Shenandoah Valley, is closed for the winter, but will reopen in mid-March. It is just off U.S. 340, about seven miles south of Front Royal.

THE DISCOVERY OF
THE FAMOUS ELEPHANT PIPE

This detailed account comes from the *Chicago Tribune.* The report is very thorough and covers the excavations of a series of mounds in which were found various burials and a large number of artifacts, the most amazing being the elephant or mastodon pipes illustrated by Davis and Squier in *Ancient Monuments of the Mississippi Valley,* the first book ever published by the Smithsonian.

One of the most impressive earthworks found during this Iowa excavation was the remains of a six-acre octagon with curving sides and a passageway on the western side that led to a freshwater spring.

To give you an idea of the vast extent of some of these sites under investigation, in this report on the Iowa dig, it is reported that a general survey of the area revealed the presence of thousands of mounds that went on for miles and the remains of what is described as a large, ancient city.

GENERAL SURVEY REVEALS
THOUSANDS OF MOUNDS

CHICAGO TRIBUNE, AUGUST 18, 1889

A party of relic hunters, including this writer, arrived one fine morning in early autumn in the region of mounds lying to the north of Toolsboro. Those Mound Builders were a strange race of people. This continent was theirs before the arrival of our modern red man, and their high type of civilization is a cause of wonderment. Their origin, their date, and their disappearance are explained only by theory and conjecture.

Here on this majestic bluff of the Mississippi we are surrounded by huge, unnatural and remarkable elevations of land, undoubtedly the work of human hands, and of so distinctive a character that not even the famed works at Newark or Circleville will excite more archaeological interest.

Just on the outskirts of Toolsboro is the inclined mound known locally as "The Old Fort." Still, it does not appear to have been erected for defensive purposes. To class it as a sacred enclosure would be more in harmony with the theories advanced by scientific men who have made a study of the similar earthworks in the Ohio Valley. As an indication that it was not originally designed as a fortification, we observe that its plan of construction is more ornamental than practical. It was built carefully—not hurriedly—and without regard to strength of position and, further, it is an isolated specimen of an enclosure earthwork. If it was designed as a fortification for practical use in the time of war, there would be other fortifications, or vestiges of war in the immediate neighborhood.

A NORTHEAST LINE OF FORTIFICATION MOUNDS WALLED THE EMPIRE

The line of defense of the Mound Builders extended from New York State diagonally across the country to Wabash, which conclusively proves that the hostilities encountered from the race came from the Northeast, and there was no occasion for a fort in the region.

This enclosure, the only one of importance west of the Mississippi and probably the most unique on the continent stands without counterpart, while the various geometric forms of squares and circles represented by Newark or Circleville are common to other sections of the mound region of the Ohio Valley.

The earthen embankments are now somewhat obliterated, but can still be distinctly traced, the angles and bastions exhibiting the form of an octagon, the sides of which are curved inwards, and enclosing the area of half a dozen acres. A lane or passageway originally extended back from the west side of the enclosure several hundred feet to a spring, which has long ceased to be in existence, though it is remembered by local settlers.

Within the enclosure great quantities of pottery, flint chips, arrow points, polished stone axes and tomahawks, occasional pipes, and copper implements and other articles have been picked up from time to time and found their way into museums and collections.

EIGHT STALWART SENTINEL MOUNDS

Standing upon the margin of this, the highest and most precipitous of the Mississippi river bluffs, are eight stalwart sentinel mounds, drawn up in a line as though zealously guarding through the ages the sacred enclosure just behind. They are conical in shape with a terraced summit; their height is from twenty to thirty feet and their circumference from 60 to 100 feet.

Our first day here was consumed in a general survey of the mound region, which, in addition to the above, includes several thousand burial mounds, some large and some small, extending along the bluffs for miles; and one must naturally conclude that this was the site of a densely populated mound builder's city. Early the following morning, while at work on the mounds, two of the largest were attacked simultaneously. Human remains were first discovered in Mound 1.

When the earth was cleared away exposing the skeleton, it became apparent that the individual had been buried in a sitting posture facing towards the rising sun. The skeleton was that of a man of medium height (very rare); around the neck was a string of shell beads, while scattered about the remains were numerous arrow points and two small stone axes. The cranium was of the short-headed type, the forehead less receding and the crown less dome-shaped than that of the modern Indian. Nothing of consequence was exhumed from Mound 2.

Mound 3, disclosed a perfect skeleton, within a few feet of the apex, which was readily identified as an intrusive burial, and proved to be the remains of a representative American Indian. Intrusive burials are not of uncommon occurrence, as the Indians, feeling an innate reverence for the mounds, frequently appropriate them for their own sepulchers. The practice confused early investigators, but from what is now definitely known of the burial habits of the two races, the question may easily be decided.

The Indian remains were carefully removed and the excavating proceeded. At last the original occupants of the mound were unearthed: two figures in a sitting posture facing eastward. The practice of placing the remains in this position was a common though not universal custom of the mound builders, and is one of the points of evidence on which archaeologists base their opinion regarding them as a race of sun-worshippers.

From this mound were secured relics which would indicate an age somewhat more advanced than shown by Mound 1.

The knives and hatchets were of hammered copper; some being

wrapped in a cloth of coarse texture, though exhibiting skilled workmanship, which only could have been preserved for so many centuries by the chemical action of the copper with which it had lain in contact.

Copper beads and a copper bracelet adorned one of the skeletons. Two finely-carved pipes of catlinite—of curved base variety—one representing a bird with eyes of pearl and the other an animal of questionable description, together with other specimens of less consequence were discovered.

TWO WORLD-FAMOUS MASTODON PIPES ARE FOUND

During the remainder of the week several more mounds were explored and numerous interesting relics of that pre-historic age were added to our collection.

Here it was in the immediate neighborhood that the two elephant pipes—now world famous—were found, furnishing the strongest proof of the antiquity of man on the continent. These pipes, carved from solid stone, representing the form of the elephant or mastodon—*the only one ever known*—were both found in Louisa County, Iowa and both are now to be seen in the museum of the Academy of Sciences at Davenport.

These pipes show beyond a reasonable doubt that the mound builder and the mastodon were contemporaneous. Their genuineness has been

Fig. 3.7. Elephant pipe, from Iowa, illustration from
Ancient Monuments of the Mississippi Valley
by Ephraim Squier and Edwin Davis

called into question, to be sure, but the severe criticism to which they were subjected only proves their value and importance. Their genuineness is attested by scholarly men of the highest character."

On the more traditional front, archaeologists have uncovered evidence of advanced culture and mining activities in Wisconsin dating back to at least 9000 BCE. At sites like Oconto and Osceola, copper artifacts, including spears, arrow points, knives, adzes, gouges, fishhooks, and harpoons have been found in association with textiles, drilled beads, and even bone flutes that can still be played.

OCONTO SETTLED RIGHT AFTER ICE AGE

By John Newhouse

WISCONSIN STATE JOURNAL, DECEMBER 13, 1963

"Dating of the Old Copper Culture, also tells us that the Paleo-Indians, who preceded the Old Copper Culture, arrived shortly after the disappearance of the last glacial age in the state," explained Warren Wittry of the Wisconsin State Historical Society.

The date of the last glacier has been determined as about 11,000 years ago, again by use of the "atomic calendar" (carbon-14 dating) method. The material tested in this instance consisted of wood from a spruce swamp in Manitowoe County that had been flattened by the last glacier. The Paleo-Indians hunted now-extinct bison, elephants, the North American horse, and camels in this country, with those in Wisconsin hunting the bison and probably the mastodons or mammoths of that day. "We have found their tools: a distinctive type of arrow, without the fluting of later Indians and a small flint incising tool with a sharp point. What we hope to find are these tools in association with bones of bisons and mastodons from that period," said Wittry.

"ROYAL" BURIALS AT OCONTO

"Burials at Oconto were in pits just large enough to receive the bodies of the dead, which were put in a variety of positions. Some were flexed, with knees under chins. Some were extended, face up or face down. Some of the pits contained bones and several of these had copper instruments of spatula form but with sharp edges. The supposition is that they were used to dismember the dead before cremation," Wittry observed.

Some pits contained burials in the flesh, as shown by the related pattern

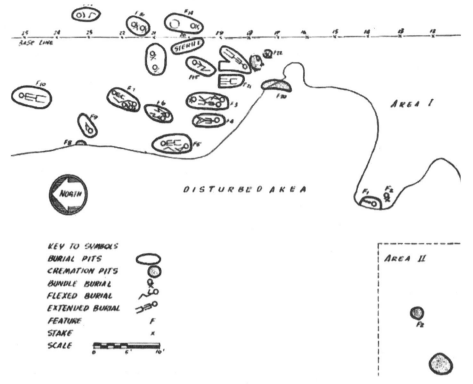

Fig. 3.8. Diagram of the Oconto County, Wisconsin, archaeological dig site

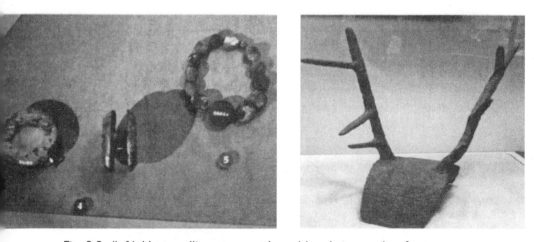

Fig. 3.9. (left) Hopewellian ear spools and bead ring made of copper
(courtesy of the Field Museum); (right) Hopewellian copper headdress
(courtesy of the Field Museum).

of the bones, with bundle burials on top.

"Apparently the Indians waited until a member of the group died in the spring, to dig the grave, then put in the bundles of bones of those who had died during the winter," explained Wittry.

The burials in Oconto were about 2½ feet below the surface. One pit contained the body of a woman and a child about 2 years old. At the base of the child's neck was a whistle made from the tibia of a deer. Markings and placement was distinctive.

"One of the big thrills for an anthropologist came later when I discovered that this was only the fourth such whistle to be discovered," said Wittry. "Two of the other known whistles were found in Kentucky, and one of them was found in the same manner: placed at the base of the neck of a small child."

OCONTO SETTLEMENT REMAINS DATED AT 5,600 YEARS

The date at which at least one group of Indians of the Old Copper Culture lived in Wisconsin has been established as 5,600 years ago, with a leeway of only several hundred years one way or the other as a safety margin. Called one of the most important findings in state anthropology in recent years, the dates were arrived at through the newly-discovered radioactive carbon-14—sometimes called the "atomic calendar"—method of computing age of once living materials.

FORTY-FIVE SKELETONS EXHUMED FROM TWENTY-ONE BURIAL PITS

THIRTEEN-YEAR-OLD BOY MAKES DISCOVERY

The burial ground was discovered in June, 1952, by Donald Baldwin, a 13-year-old boy digging in the wall of an abandoned gravel pit near Oconto. The Oconto County Historical Society immediately acquired the land and kept it under guard, preserving it from vandals and souvenir hunters.

The site, when excavated, yielded bones of 45 individuals in 21 burial pits with the bones in fair to good condition.

"Luckily the burials were in sand over gravel," noted Wittry. "So the drainage was good and the conditions for preservation excellent."

OLD COPPER CULTURE SITE AT POTOSI

The Oconto burial ground of the Old Copper Culture is the second found in the state. In 1945, erosion on the banks of the Mississippi River near Potosi revealed the burial ground of about 500 individuals.

The bones were in a trench, some 20 feet wide and 70 feet long, under a cover of black sand about five feet deep.

8,500-YEAR-OLD CAMPSITE
FOUND NEAR GREEN BAY

ASSOCIATED PRESS, GREEN BAY, WISCONSIN, JULY 3, 1959

An Indian camp site which may have belonged to the earliest Indians yet known in northeastern Wisconsin has been uncovered in the town of Scott, Brown County, not far from the east shore of Green Bay. The site, which is being excavated, was found by Ron Mason, curator for exhibits at the Neville Public Museum, and his wife, Carol. Both are anthropologists. Mason says everything points to the Scottsbluff Indians, who roamed the Plains States from 6,500 to 8,500 years ago.

Mason compared the Scottsbluff period of 6,500 to 8,500 years ago, to the Old Copper Culture site at Oconto. So far, the Old Copper Culture Indians have been the earliest known Indians in northwestern Wisconsin. Two carbon readings have been made at the Oconto site. They fixed the age of fragments at between 5,500 and 7,500 years.

SMITHSONIAN REMOVES TONS OF ARTIFACTS AND
SKELETONS FROM ALABAMA CAVE

ANCIENT ALABAMA CAVE NOW OPEN TO TOURISTS

ALTOONA MIRROR, MARCH 13, 1986

Russell Cave, Alabama, is open to visitors and study of the 9,000-year-old home of the Stone Agers has moved into the laboratory. The cave on a wooded mountainside near Bridgeport is man's oldest known habitation in the southeast. From at least 7000 BCE to as late as 1650 CE, generations of primitive huntsmen found ready-made shelter there, a mild climate, clear fresh water, and a forest full of game.

The Smithsonian Institution and the National Geographic Society explored and excavated the cave several years ago. It is now a national monument.

FIVE TONS OF ARTIFACTS

From a deep working trench, Carl F. Miller of the Smithsonian excavated five tons of artifacts: stone projectiles, arrowheads, fish hooks, bone awls and needles, shell ornaments, human skeletons, animal bones, and the ashes of ancient campfires. Much of this material has been catalogued and studied by the Smithsonian. In a separate project, the National Parks Service has enlisted the aid of several universities to classify animal bones from the new trench.

NEW MEXICO TRADE TIES WITH CALIFORNIA

By Hal Borland

GALVESTON DAILY NEWS, OCTOBER 26, 1930

Last year a joint expedition of the University of Minnesota and the Archaeological Institute's School of American Research excavated a large area in the Mimbres Valley–Cameron Creek section of southwestern New Mexico. There they discovered skeletons, pottery, jewelry, weapons, food, and other relics of a race whose history is believed to extend more than 2,000 years.

Not the least interesting among the finds were shell bracelets and beads identified with the Gulf of California and indicating commercial connections with the West and the South.

This year further exploration of the ruins was carried on by an expedition from Beloit College. Professor Paul Nesbit placed the first period of the Mimbres people at 2,500 B.C., placing them as one of the earliest known American civilizations. These investigations uncovered more evidence of commerce, including a beautifully cast copper bell said to be symbolic of the Central American culture.

GRUESOME RITES OR A HORRIBLE MASSACRE

Other ancient relics were found in the Lowry Ruins of southwestern Colorado last summer by the Field Museum Archaeological Expedition to the Southwest, led by Dr. Paul Martin.

A year and a half ago Dr. Martin announced the discovery of a hitherto unknown savage culture in ruins in that area, more modern, however, than those explored earlier this year. There he found a grim ceremonial room literally heaped with skeletons—and other evidence of gruesome rites—or of a horrible massacre.

COLORADO KIVA PRESERVES 3,000-YEAR-OLD PAINTINGS

This year Dr. Martin worked on two kivas, or ceremonial rooms, one built on top of still older ruins. Remains of these houses and pottery of cultured design representing a highly-advanced Indian tribe were discovered.

"Then," says Dr. Martin, "we penetrated to the lower kiva, where we found that paintings on its walls had been preserved more perfectly than paintings on the room above." The lower kiva was estimated by Dr. Martin to date back about 3,000 years.

GYPSUM CAVE FINDS DATE
FROM 30,000 TO 20,000 BC

MORE DAM DESTRUCTION OF ARCHAEOLOGICAL SITES

BY HAL BORLAND

GALVESTON DAILY NEWS, OCTOBER 26, 1930

The most startling find of the year, however, was that of Dr. Mark Harrington in an expedition to Gypsum Cave, near Las Vegas, Nevada, for the Southwest Museum in Los Angeles. Working in an area that will be submerged by water impounded by the projected Hoover Dam, the party first came on darts from an atlatl, a weapon that preceded the bow and arrow. With these darts they found the skull of a giant ground sloth, which was known to be of great antiquity. Then the excavators set about searching for evidence that man had visited the cave before the sloth.

Eventually they found a patch of real charcoal, presumably from a campfire, under a layer of unbroken strata of the Pleistocene Era, in the top most of which was found remains of the Basket Makers. Other discoveries included numerous bones of the ground sloth, the tiny skeleton of a prehistoric horse, and scores of broken darts and points of obsidian and flint, parts of weapons used by primitive men of that time. At the bottom lay the remains of the campfire.

This seeming link between man and sloth is regarded by many scientists as the most important proof of man's antiquity in America yet brought to light. The sloth is known to have become an extinct mammal 20,000 years ago. This pushes the probable time for America's earliest man back thousands of years further than any reliable previous estimates. It places man in America, in fact, in glacial times.

LEE CANYON, ARIZONA, DINOSAUR PICTOGRAPHS

These finds in Gypsum Cave were forecast a few years ago by the discovery of a series of remarkable pictographs in Lee Canyon in Arizona. Samuel Hubbard, who discovered them said:

"The pictographs included one of an elephant attacking a man, the first elephant drawing by prehistoric man ever found in the United States, as far as this writer knows. Another was of a group of animals, undoubtedly of the ibex, a two-horned antelope still found alive in the mountains of Asia, whose bones have been discovered in European caves but trace of which has never before appeared in the New World. The third, and most valuable, is a pictograph of an animal quite evidently intended to represent a dinosaur.

"The elephant in America dates back at least 30,000 years. The dinosaur belongs to an even earlier tropical era going back millions of years before that. Yet, there in Lee Canyon are pictures of both the elephant and the dinosaur, chipped in the rock by prehistoric man."

EVIDENCE OF CLIMATE CHANGE

There must have been great climatic changes in this thirsty land since these thousands of people lived here. Today there is not an ounce of water to be found anywhere—just a great burned up, heaved up, dried up waste.

Such a great population must have had water and such a population could not have subsisted entirely on game, for certainly rainfall could not have supplied them with sufficient water, nor these mountains with enough game. It is my guess that far back in the past ages a great river flowed at the bottom of these cliffs, that rainfall was plenty, that the inhabitants were farmers, and that what appears to be a fort or reservoir on top of the cliffs was a storehouse for the community's grain.

In the ruins of southern Colorado I am told a great calamity befell the people and that the skeletons lie unburied, and the general confusion denoted a sudden end, but on the Puye ruins, there is absolutely no indication of where these thousands of people went, or how or why they went.

PERSONNEL SET UP MUSEUM OF INDIAN ARTIFACTS FOUND ON ISLAND OF POINT MUGU

PRESS COURIER, JANUARY 18, 1963

Oxnard, California: Sailors and scientists at San Nicolas Island have dedicated their spare time to digging up samples of civilizations long past to break the monotony of the space age. Now on display at the Point Mugu administration building is a collection of primitive artifacts used by Indians who inhabited this land some 4,000 years ago.

The collection is a gift to Capt. J. G. Smith, commanding officer of the Naval Air Station at Point Mugu, donated by two archeology-minded sailors who recently were transferred from the island. Captain Smith, also an amateur archeologist, is credited with the discovery of an Indian fresh water system on the island last April.

San Nicolas Island has long been known as one of the prime archeological sites of the eight Channel Islands that skirt the California coasts. Since first excavations and studies were began in 1875, San Nicolas has yielded hundreds of artifacts from ancient Indian burial sites.

These discoveries have helped

give archeologists a new insight into the ancient history of California. Most extensive studies of the island have been carried on during the past ten years by members of UCLA's Department of Anthropology and Sociology and by other Southern California institutions. Last year, however, sailors who live and work at this small space-age island facility started a new excavation for artifacts during off hours from their regular duty watches in support of satellite and missile firings from nearby Point Mugu, Vandenberg Air Force Base and the Naval Missile Facility, Point Arguello.

Early in 1962, two navy men were assigned to a group of archeologists from UCLA to assist in excavations on the island. James O. Casper, aviation boatswain 3rd class, and Kenneth H. Brittonn, commissary man 2nd class, soon found themselves not only assisting, but genuinely interested in digging for artifacts.

San Nicolas Island is a windswept, almost barren plateau measuring nine miles in length and averaging three miles in width. It is the most remote of the Channel Islands and is located 78 miles west of Los Angeles and 55 miles southwest of the Point Mugu Naval Air Station. Navy and civilian personnel stationed on San Nicolas are virtually isolated from the mainland. Spare-time drags unless used to the best possible advantage.

Consequently, the two sailors found themselves grubbing through sites even after the archeologists had gone. In time, Casper and Brittonn gathered an impressive collection of artifacts from prehistoric burial fields on the island's sandy and dune-covered southern tip. Their collection included a small whistle made of black stone, shell heads, fish hooks fashioned from abalone shell, primitive knives and drills, arrowheads chipped from stone, and a length of rope woven from seaweed. All the artifacts were formed by hand from the only materials the Indians had—those which nature had provided. Radiation dating analysis on similar items indicated that the artifacts range in age from 2,000 to 4,000 years.

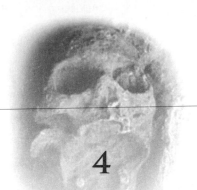

4

COPPER-CROWNED KINGS AND PEARL-BEDECKED QUEENS

It is natural for human beings to link size and power with elevated status. In the legends of giants that have arisen in various parts of the world, giants are often depicted as gods and kings. So it is not surprising that the remains of giants found in America are accompanied by signs of royalty such as copper crowns and other regalia like pearl robes and mica ornaments, as well as being found in ritualistic burial patterns and settings. The kings are also often found buried standing up, surrounded by four megalithic slabs of stone. Sometimes kings and queens are buried in stone sarcophagi, and mummification dating to 8000 BCE has also been scientifically confirmed.

THE SMITHSONIAN
LEADS GEORGIA GIANT SEARCH

The Smithsonian is front and center in this account from 1884 of the discovery of a royal burial.

GIANT CROWNED ROYALTY IS FOUND

ATHENS, GEORGIA, BANNER, MAY 6, 1884

Athens, Georgia: Mr. J. B. Toomer yesterday received a letter from Mr. Hazelton, who is on a visit to Cartersville. The letter contained several beads made of stone, and gave an interesting account of the opening of a large Indian mound near that town by a committee of scientists sent out from the Smithsonian Institution. After removing the dirt for some distance, a layer of large flag stones was found, which had evidently been dressed by hand, and showed that the men who quarried this rock understood their business.

The stones were removed, when in a kind of vault beneath them, the skeleton of a giant, who measured seven feet two inches, was found.

His hair was coarse and jet black and hung to his waist, the brow being ornamented with a copper crown. The skeleton was remarkably well-preserved and taken from the vault intact. Near this skeleton were found the bodies of several small children of various sizes. The remains of the latter were covered with beads, made of bone of some kind. Upon removing these, the bodies were found to be encased in a network made of straw or reed, and beneath this was the covering of an animal of some kind.

In fact, the bodies had been prepared somewhat after the manner of mummies, and will doubtless throw new light on the history of the people who raised the mounds.

Upon the stones that covered the vault were carved inscriptions, which, if deciphered, will probably lift the veil that has enshrouded the history of the race of giants that undoubtedly at one time inhabited the continent.

ALL THE RELICS WERE SHIPPED TO THE SMITHSONIAN

All the relics were carefully packed and sent to the Smithsonian Institution, and are said to be the most interesting collection ever found in America.

The explorers are now at work on a mound in Barlow County, and before their return home will visit various sections of Georgia where antiquities are found. On the Oconee River, in Greene County, just above Powell's Mills, are several mounds, one of them very tall and precipitous.

THE INCREDIBLE PEARLS OF OHIO'S ROYAL GIANTS

Ohio mound builder grave sites are notable for fabulous caches of freshwater pearls found in the burials.

ROYAL MOUND FOUND

OAKLAND TRIBUNE, DECEMBER 10, 1925

Surrounded by bushels of pearls, some of them as large as hickory nuts, skeletons, believed to be from a royal family of the prehistoric mound builders, have been dug out of the largest of the Great Seip group of mounds not far from Chillicothe, Ohio. That ancient mound is 680 feet long, 160 feet wide, and 28 feet high.

Archaeologists have undertaken the task of exploring it by excavation. It is estimated that the skeletons may be anywhere from 1,000 to 2,000 years old. Two of them wore copper helmets, and one of the skulls was provided with a copper nose.

In what is now Ohio, long before Columbus discovered America, pearl fishing was an important industry. The streams of that region were full of pearl bearing mussels, and aboriginal chieftains of the Miami and Scioto Valleys possessed collections of pearls which might well have been envied by European princes and potentates.

MILLIONS OF PEARLS RECOVERED

In one Ohio mound a few years ago were found enough pearls to fill a gallon measure, in size from a millet seed to two-thirds of an inch in diameter. There have been many such finds, one mound yielding two bushels of pearls. From another, 500,000 were obtained. Unfortunately these pearls have no present value. They were buried with the chieftains who owned them, or thrown into altar fires, so that they are either decayed or burned. In some instances they have been found cemented together in masses by water percolating through the soil. An occasional specimen of large size has been salvaged by peeling off the outer coats, a pearl being formed in layers like an onion. Evidence of the great antiquity of the Ohio mounds is afforded by the fact that they contain no buffalo bones. This seems to prove that at the time of their construction the buffalo had not yet extended its range as far east as Ohio.

GIANT KING'S MOUTH STUFFED WITH IMMENSE PEARLS

At another Ohio site immense pearls were stuffed in the skeleton's mouth and a bear's tooth necklace was also adorned with pearls, both indications of royalty. As he was buried together with a woman, she is seen as his queen.

WORLD'S FAIR DIG LEADS TO GIANT MONARCH

GIGANTIC SKELETON, EVIDENTLY OF A
PREHISTORIC MONARCH, EXHUMED IN OHIO

CENTRALIA OHIO ENTERPRISE, NOVEMBER 21, 1891

Chillicothe, Ohio: Warren K. Morehead and Dr. Cresson, who have been prosecuting excavations here for the past two months in the interest of the World's Fair, have just made one of the richest finds of the century in the way of prehistoric remains.

Those gentlemen have confined their excavation to the Hopewell Farm, seven miles from here, upon which are located some twenty-odd Indian mounds. On Saturday, they were at work on a mound 500 feet long, 200 feet wide and 28 feet high.

At the depth of 14 feet, near the center of the mound, they exhumed the massive skeleton of a man encased in copper armor. The head was covered in an oval-shaped copper cap, the jaws had copper mouldings, the arms were dressed in copper, while copper plates covered the chest and stomach and on each side of the head, on protruding sticks were wooden antlers ornamented with copper.

The mouth was stuffed with genuine pearls of immense size, but much decayed. Around the neck was a necklace of bear's teeth set with pearls.

At the side of the male skeleton was also found a female skeleton, the two being supposed to be man and wife. Mr. Morehead and Mr. Cresson believe they have at last found the "King of the Mound Builders."

BODIES WRAPPED IN PRECIOUS GEMS

OAKLAND TRIBUNE, JANUARY 3, 1926

In the United States perhaps the greatest interest was aroused by the discovery near Bainbridge, Ohio, of the remains of four bodies of the ancient mound builders, a race believed by some scientists to have preceded the Indians. . . . In the graves were found fresh-water pearls in such numbers as to convince state archaeologists directing the excavations that the bodies had been wrapped in a covering of precious gems.

When the skeletons were lifted it was found that they had been resting on pearls. Fragments of tortoise shells etched with figures of birds and necklaces made of grizzly-bear claws were found.

INDIANS HAVE NO ORAL TRADITIONS REGARDING THE MOUNDS

Mounds such as the ones uncovered in Ohio are not rarities to the scientist. They were known to the earliest

Fig. 4.1. This couple was buried holding hands, one of the common positions found in American mound burials. Others include man on top and woman on the bottom, as well as woman on top and man on the bottom. This particular image is of skeletons found in central-northern Italy, and the couple was buried holding hands some 1,500 years ago (Soprintendenza per I Beni Archeologici dell'Emilia-Romagna, *Discovery News*).

settlers, but no Indian tradition has ever accounted for them.

Dr. William C. Mills, director of the Ohio State Archaeological and Historical Society, believes that the mound builders once had extensive communities throughout the central portion of North America.

"There is little evidence they were a war-like people. On the contrary, they were a settled, agricultural, hunting and fishing race, given to intensive culture within the limits of their knowledge. They had more than a rudimentary knowledge of mathematics.

"The square, the circle, the octagon, regular polygons, ellipses, exactly measured parallelograms and parallel lines laid out in a large scale were in common use. The bones excavated show that they were a capable people physically. They were fairly broad shouldered and their average height was slightly under six feet."

In 1926, more finds were discovered in Ohio. This time it was toys found with the skeleton of a boy about twelve years old. The discovery of children's toys in the burial mounds is not at all unusual. At other sites small playhouses, toy animals, and game sets have been found. Another recurring theme in the burial mounds is the discovery of houses, temples, vaults, and other structures built inside the mounds. In this instance, the boy had his own cabin, but inside were a number of personal items, including marbles engraved with beautiful designs.

PREHISTORIC ENGRAVED MARBLES

ASSOCIATED PRESS, SEPTEMBER 17, 1926

Chillicothe, Ohio: The skeleton of a twelve-year-old boy, with a number of marbles, prized relics of childhood, was removed from the Bricer Mound of the Seip group, near Bainbridge, eighteen miles west of here, the other day.

This is the second of a group of burials found near the rear of the mound, where last year "the great pearl burial" was unearthed and where this summer five cremated burials, with the usual finds of black, tan, and white wildcat jaws and marine tortoise shell combs were disclosed.

The boy's body had been interred in a cabin-like structure and was covered by a canopy, the mold of which was found. The body had been clothed in a garment of woven fabric. The grave contained many unusual specimens, H. S. Shetrone, curator of the Ohio Museum, said. "We found a number of marbles made from chlorite, a fine, close-grained stone, which takes a very high polish, engraved in beautiful designs. They had been placed there reverently by loving hands.

"We believe playing marbles was an honorable past-time even in the time of the mound builders," Shetrone said.

STONE AND MICA ANIMALS GALORE

Besides the marbles there was found a stone carved in the shape of a turkey vulture; carefully cut down to the feather markings. Another stone was carved like a lizard, with a tail resembling the rattles of a rattlesnake; beads, green chlorite resembling turquoise; many well-cut mica designs, teeth of raccoon, fox, wolf, mountain lion, bear, and other wild animals, which roamed the forest, pierced so that they could be worn as ornaments; woven fabric, obsidian spear points, and a few bits of copper.

Fig. 4.2. Lamantin or sea-cow, illustration from
Ancient Monuments of the Mississippi Valley
by Ephraim Squier and Edwin Davis

CHARLESTON, WEST VIRGINIA—HOME TO GIANTS, ANCIENT KINGS, AND HIGH PRIESTS

In many respects the West Virginia mounds are key to understanding the giants who once ruled America. Not only are the West Virginia mound sites in Charleston, Wheeling, and Moundsville some of the most significant in size and number in the United States, but in 1883, the Smithsonian dispatched a team of archaeologists to conduct an extensive dig of the fifty mounds they found there and issue a detailed report.

The team, led by Col. P. W. Norris and Professor Cyrus Thomas, prepared the detailed report of the work (*Smithsonian Field Report 1883*), which shows quite clearly that they uncovered numerous giants, one of which was decorated with heavy copper bracelets.

As we catalogue the unusual burial practices associated with the mound builders, the sun circle burial arrangement is one of the most dramatic. In this case ten skeletons were found all buried with their feet facing inwards surrounding a central skeleton, presumably that of a King or a high-ranking spiritual or military leader.

In burial mound number 7, a giant seven feet tall was found with his head pointing west. Lying in a circle just above the hips were sixty circular pieces of white perforated shell, each about one inch in diameter and about an eighth of an inch thick. His arm was found to be reaching out towards an oven-shaped vault containing two bushels of corn.

In this burial a covering of flat stones with cup-shaped markings covered the upper layer of the burial. Cup-shaped markings on stones have been found in Europe as well as South America. In this case, further digging revealed a stone slab coffin with a skeleton laid out facing to the east.

Mound 23 was found to be of a hardened pyramidal shape. Digging was difficult, as the mound seemed to be reinforced with a hard cement-like substance. Digs at other mounds across the U.S. have also uncovered similar cement substances, which researchers have likened to a type of Portland cement.

In many of the more elaborate mound burials, actual huts, houses and temples have been uncovered under the mounds. In this case, what had once been a circular or polygonal timbered and conical-roofed vault was found with a number of burials contained inside.

One of the most iconic and unusual of the mound builder burial practices involved the burial of adult couples in romantic embrace, sometimes even kissing. Similar burials have been found recently in Europe [see page 121]. Further down in this burial mound, another couple was found in a sitting posture with their legs interlocked to the knees.

Fig. 4.3. Grave Creek Mound (courtesy of Tim Kiser)

FIFTY MAJOR MOUNDS IN THE CHARLESTON AREA

CHARLESTON DAILY MAIL, SEPTEMBER 23, 1923

Extending along the terrace about five miles over-looking the Kanawha River west of Charleston, above flood level were found about 50 mounds. They range in height from 5 to 35 feet. The principal one is known as the South Charleston Mound, which is 175 feet in diameter at the base and 35 feet high.

In all it is estimated that there are at least 100,000 mounds in the Eastern portion of the United States. These represent the work of millions of people, many nations and tribes, and they were constructed over a long period of time.

FLINT, THE MAJOR INDUSTRY

The leading industry was the quarrying of flint and the manufacture of instruments from this hard quartz-like substance. Many quarries have been discovered where large piles of chipped flint are found. Some copper tools have been found but they are rare. They seem to have been hammered out of bits of the metal that were found in the crevices of the rock.

. . . Beads in great number have been found. They consisted of pearls, shells, copper, bones, and mica. Copper finger rings and bracelets have been unearthed in great numbers.

Many skeletons have been found with their arms covered in bracelets.

ON THE SMITHSONIAN'S DISCOVERY OF THE SEVEN-FOOT, SIX-INCHES-TALL GIANT

The excavation of this mound was made by sinking a shaft from the top, reports the Smithsonian in their 1883 field report. After removing some large stones, a vault was found in which was a decayed skeleton, minus a head. At a depth of six feet another

Fig. 4.4. Carvings of human faces illustration from
Ancient Monuments of the Mississippi Valley
by Ephraim Squier and Edwin Davis

skeleton was found, and three feet deeper, a third one was discovered. The real find was 19 feet from the top. Here a large vault 12 feet square, and 7 or 8 feet high, was discovered. Upright timbers had been placed around the sides to hold up the roof, but they had decayed, and dirt and rocks had fallen into the vault.

In this vault were five skeletons, four of whom had been placed in each corner in an erect position, and the fifth was lying flat on the floor. The four seemed to be standing guard over a chief or important person. This man was a giant, seven feet, six inches tall, and measured nineteen inches between his shoulder sockets. He had been buried in a bark coffin, placed on his back with arms at his side and legs together.

There were six heavy bracelets on each wrist and four others under his head. On the breast was a copper gorget (piece of armor). Three spear heads were found in each hand and others were scattered about the floor of the vault. On the shoulder were three large plates of mica and around the shoulders were many small ornamental shells. While the dirt was being put back a smoking pipe, which had been carved out of gray steatite (soapstone), was found. It was highly polished and similar to others found in mounds in Ohio.

The exploration was made by sinking a shaft 12 feet square at the top and narrowing gradually to six feet square at the bottom, down through the center of the structure to the original surface of the ground and a short distance below it. After removing a slight covering of earth, an irregular mass of large rough, flat sandstones, evidently brought from the bluffs half a mile distant was encountered. Some of these sandstones were a load for two ordinary men.

Other mounds were excavated and records made, writes the Smithsonian in 1883. In one a large skeleton was found surrounded by ten other skeletons. An "altar mound" was excavated. In the center of it were found two skeletons seated, apparently holding, between them and above their heads, a large stone.

SKELETONS OF GIANT MEN ARE DISCOVERED

ONE HILL REVEALS A CENTRAL FRAME OF BONES WITH TEN OTHERS LYING ABOUT IT IN A CIRCLE, FEET POINTED INWARD

Many of these mounds were, however, opened and investigated some 65 years ago by Professors Thomas and Col. Norris of the Smithsonian Institution Washington. Their interesting discoveries including skeletons seven foot six inches tall, underground vaults (ornaments and religious items), and spear heads are preserved in a report in the possession of C. E. Krebs, archaeologist, who by the very nature of his work, is very much interested himself in the mounds of the Kanawha Valley.

The reporter then goes on to reconstruct the story of the mounds as was reported in the now impossible-to-find 1883 Smithsonian report and adds scientific information from the then-recent discoveries made at the mounds in 1923.

THE FOUR SENTINELS

At this point in his downward progress Col. Norris began to encounter the remains of what further excavations showed to be a timber vault about twelve feet square and seven or eight feet high. From the condition in which the remains of the cover were found, he concluded that this must have been roof-shaped and, having become decayed, had been crushed by the weight of the addition made to the mound. Some of the walnut timbers of this vault were twelve inches in diameter.

In this vault were found five skeletons, one lying prostrate on the floor at the depth of 19 feet from the top of the mound and four others, which, from the positions in which they were found were supposed to be standing in the four corners.

The first of these was found standing at the depth of 14 feet, amid a comingled mass of earth and decaying bark and timbers, nearly erect and leaning against the wall and surrounded by the remains of a bark coffin. All the bones except those of the left forearm were too far decayed to be saved; these were preserved by two heavy copper bracelets, which yet surrounded them.

The skeleton found in the middle of the floor of the vault was of unusually large size "measuring seven feet six inches in length and nineteen inches between the shoulder sockets." It had also been enclosed in a wrapping or coffin of bark, the remains of which were still distinctly visible. It lay upon the back, head east, legs together, and arms at the sides. There were six heavy bracelets on each wrist, four others were found under the head, which together with a spear point of black flint, were encased in a mass of mortar-like substance, which evidently had been wrapped in some textile fabric. On the breast was a copper gorget.

In each hand were three spear heads of black flint, and others were about the head, knees, and feet. Near the right hand were hematite celts (ax heads) and on the shoulder were three large and thick plates. About the shoulders, waist, and thighs were numerous minute perforated shells and shell beads.

THE SECOND MOUND IS OPENED

The large mound in South Charleston is conical in form, 173 feet in diameter, and 33 feet high. It is slightly truncated, the top having been leveled off some 97 years ago for the purpose of building a judge's stand in connection with a race course that was laid out around the mound.

A shaft twelve feet square at the top and six feet at the bottom was used to excavate the center shaft in an identical manner to mound one in the report. At a depth of four feet, in a very hard mix of earth and ash, were found two much decayed human skeletons both stretched horizontally on their back, heads *south,* and near their heads several stone implements.

At a depth of 31 feet there was a human skeleton lying prostrate, head *north,* which had evidently been enclosed in a coffin or wrapping of elm bark. In contact with the head was a thin sheet of hammered native copper (a crown?).

By enlarging the base of the shaft to sixteen feet it made the character and content of burial more fully ascertained. This brought to light the fact that the builders, after having first smoothed, leveled, and picked the natural surface, carefully spread upon the floor a layer of bark (chiefly elm), the inner side up, and upon this a layer of fine white ashes, clear of charcoal, to a depth probably of five or six inches, though pressed at the time of exploration to little more than one inch. On this the bodies were properly laid and presumably covered with bark.

The enlargement of the shaft also brought to view ten other skeletons all apparently adults, five on one side and five on the other side of the central skeleton, and like it, extended horizontally, with the feet pointing towards the central one, though not quite touching it. Like the first, they all had been buried in bark coffins or wrappings.

Below the center of the No. 7 Charleston mound, sunk into the original earth, was a vault about eight feet long, three feet wide, and three feet deep. Lying extended on the back, in the bottom of this, amid the rotten fragments of a bark coffin, was a decayed human skeleton, fully seven feet tall, with head *west.* No evidence of fire was to be seen, nor were any stone implements discovered, but lying in a circle just above the hips were sixty circular pieces of white perforated shell, each about one inch in diameter and about an eighth of an inch thick.

The bones of the left arm lay by the side of the body, but those of the right arm, as in one of the mounds heretofore mentioned, were stretched at a right angle to the body, reaching out to a small oven-shaped vault, the mortar or cement roof of which was still unbroken. The capacity of this small circular vault was probably two bushels, and the peculiar appearance of the dark-colored deposits therein, and other indications, led to the belief that it had been filled with corn maize, in the ear.

The absence of weapons would indicate that the individual buried here was not a warrior, though a person of some importance.

One mound, twenty feet in diameter and seven feet high with a beech tree 30 inches in diameter growing on it, was opened by running a trench through it. The material of which it was composed was yellow clay evidently from an extraction in the hillside near it.

Stretched horizontally on the natural surface of the ground, faces up and heads *south*, were seven skeletons: six adult and one child, all charred. They were covered several inches thick with ashes, charcoal, and firebrands, evidently the remains of a very heavy fire that must have been smothered before it was fully burned out. Three coarse lance heads were found among the bones of the adults and around the back of the child three copper beads, of apparently hammered native copper.

Another mound 50 feet diameter and five feet high, standing guard as it were, at the entrance of an enclosure, was opened revealing the following particulars. The top was strewn with fragments of flat rock, most of which were marked by one or more small, artificial, cup-shaped depressions. Below these, to a depth of two or three feet, the hard yellow clay was mixed throughout with similar stones, charcoal, ashes, stone chips and fragments of rude pottery.

Near the center and about three feet from the top of the mound were the decayed remains of a human skeleton, lying on its back in a very rude stone slab coffin. Beneath were other flat stones, and under them charcoal, ashes and baked earth, covering the decayed bones of some three or four skeletons, which lay upon the original surface of the ground. As far as could be ascertained, the skeletons in the mound lay with their heads to the *east*. No relics of any kind worthy of notice were found with them.

Mound 23 of this group shows some peculiarities worthy of notice. It is 312 feet in circumference at the base, and 25 feet high, covered with a second growth of timber. It is unusually sharp and symmetrical. From the top down the material was found to be a light gray and apparently mixed earth, *so hard as to require the vigorous use of a pick to penetrate it.* At a depth of 15 feet, the explorers began to find the casts and fragments of poles or round timbers less than a foot in diameter. These casts and rotten remains of wood and bark increased in abundance from this point until the original surface of the ground was reached.

By enlarging the lower end of the shaft to 14 feet in diameter, it was ascertained that this rotten wood and bark were the remains of what had once been a circular or polygonal timbered and conical-roofed vault. Many of the timbers of the sides and roof had been allowed to extend past the points of support, often 8 or 10 feet, those on the sides beyond the crossing, and thereof the roof downward beyond the wall. On the floor and amid the remains of the timbers, were numerous human bones and two human skeletons, the latter though slightly decayed badly crushed by the weight pressing upon them, but unaccompanied by any ornament of any kind.

A further excavation of about four feet below the floor, or what was supposed to be the floor of this vault, and below the original surface of the ground, brought to light six circular oven-shaped vaults, each about three feet in diameter and the same in depth.

As these six were placed as to form a semi-circle, it was presumed that there are many others under that portion of the mound not reached by the excavation. All were filled with dry, dark dust (presumably cremated remains), or decayed substances, supposed to be the remains of Indian corn in the ear as it was similar to that heretofore mentioned.

In the center of the circle indicated by the position of these minor vaults, and the supposed center of the base of the mound (the shaft not being exactly central), and about two feet below the floor of the main vault, and in a fine mortar or *cement,* were found two cavities resembling in form the bottom of gourd-shaped vessels so frequently met with in the mounds of eastern Missouri and northeastern Arkansas.

Mound 32 of this group seems to furnish a connecting link between the West Virginia and Ohio mounds. . . . It is sharp in outline and has a deep slope, and is flattened at the top; it is 315 feet in circumference at the base and about 25 feet high. It was opened by sinking a shaft 10 feet in diameter from the center of the top of the base. After passing through the top layer of surface soil, some two feet thick, a layer of clay and ashes one foot thick was encountered.

Here, near the center of the shaft, skeletons were lying horizontally, one immediately over the other, the upper or larger one with the face down and the lower one with face up. There were no indications of fire about them. Immediately over the heads were one celt (ax head) and three lance heads. . . .

At the depth of thirteen feet and a little north of the center of the mound, were *two very large skeletons* in a sitting posture, with their extended legs interlocked to the knees. Their arms were extended and the hands slightly elevated, as if together holding up a sandstone mortar which was between their faces.

This stone is somewhat hemispherical, about two feet in diameter across the top, which is hollowed in the shape of a shallow basin or mortar. It had been subjected to the act of fire until bright red. The cavity was filled with white ashes containing small fragments of bone burned to cinders.

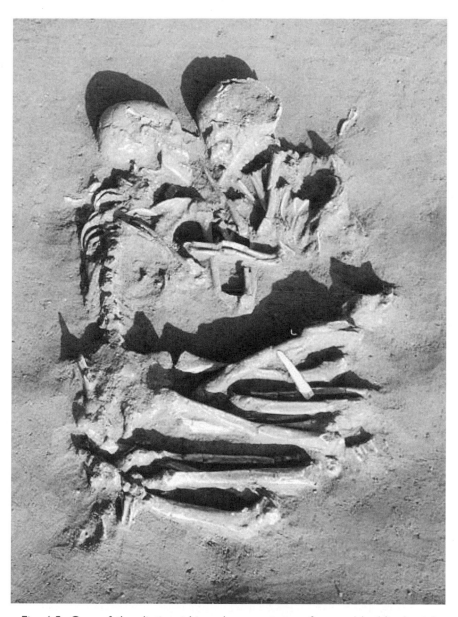

Fig. 4.5. One of the distinguishing characteristics of mound builder burial practices is the paired burial. The interlocked skeletons described by the *Charleston Daily Mail* in 1923 are very similar to these two interlocked Stone Age skeletons—with their "eternal embrace" intact. Discovered near Verona, Italy, the setting of *Romeo and Juliet,* the roughly 5,000-year-old couple has already become an icon of enduring love to many (photo from the Archaeological Society).

Immediately over this, and of a sufficient size to cover it, was a slab of bluish-gray limestone about three inches thick, which had *small cup-shaped excavations* on the underside. This bore no marks of fire. Near the hands of the eastern skeleton were a small hematite celt and a lance head and upon the left wrist of the other two copper bracelets.

At the depths of 25 feet and on the natural surface was found what in an Ohio Mound would be called an "altar." This was not thoroughly traced throughout, but was about *twelve feet long and over eight feet wide.*

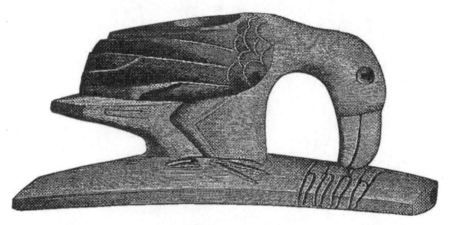

Fig. 4.6. Toucan illustration from
Ancient Monuments of the Mississippi Valley
by Ephraim Squier and Edwin Davis

FIRST-PERSON ACCOUNT OF THE 1883 OPENING OF THE SOUTH CHARLESTON MOUND

By Charles Connor

CHARLESTON DAILY MAIL, APRIL 7, 1952

In looking at the history of the South Charleston Mound, it turns out our best source is A. R. Sines, grandfather of Dr. F. A. Sines, Charleston dentist. Mr. Sines, who died in 1937, had a written account of his part in the mound opening published in the 1920s.

No doubt among the thousands of people who daily pass the large mound at South Charleston, many have often wondered if there is anyone living who can tell what is lying, or once lay, at the bottom of that pile of earth. I am probably the only man now living who stood at the bottom of this mound and assisted with a thorough examination of every foot of its interior from top to bottom in November of 1883.

EMPLOYED BY THE
SMITHSONIAN IN 1883

To help in the excavation by Col. P. W. Norris, an old Indian scout who was then in the employ of the Smithsonian Institution of Washington. Colonel Norris, former superintendent of the Yellowstone National Park, was investigating all mounds of West Virginia, Ohio, and nearby states at that time.

In opening the mound, the men under Col. Norris' supervision first leveled off the top, then dug a round hole ten feet in diameter downward. As they progressed towards the bottom, they dug out a series of shelves around the sides to have a place to throw the dirt.

Four feet from the bottom we made our first discovery. We came upon a large bed of charred wood, something resembling charred bones, and many small pieces which were more intact resembling burnt teeth. This had, beyond a doubt, once been a funeral pyre.

The decayed bones belonged to what once had been a most powerful man. There was but little

left, but the distance from the spot where the heel bone was found to what was left of the skull was 6 feet 8¾ inches.

The shoulder bones were considerably broader than those of men of our present race, although the skull bone was not so large. The teeth were larger than those we have today. The front part of the skull was nearly double the thickness of a human skull today.

A COPPER CROWN AND
A QUEEN

Sines and Colonel Norris found a copper band around the forehead of this buried giant, and similar copper bands around the wrists and ankles. With no copper nearer than Tennessee, they assumed it had been carried here by these mound builders thousands of years ago.

They also found axe-shaped stones grooved in the middle. Sines related that this stone was not familiar to this country and so hard that steel would not make a dent.

"Two miles down near where Sunset Memorial Park is today," Sines related, "they opened a smaller mound and located the bones of what appeared to be the remnants of a woman. There were copper bands on the ankle and wrist bones and larger pieces of copper on each breast."

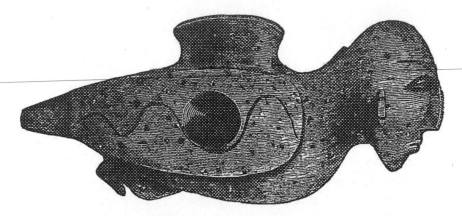

Fig. 4.7. A sacramental pipe in the shape of a human,
illustration from *Ancient Monuments of the Mississippi Valley*
by Ephraim Squier and Edwin Davis

GRAVE CREEK MOUND, WEST VIRGINIA

The best-known mound and the largest in the Ohio Valley region is the Grave Creek Mound at Moundsville. This mound was purchased by the state in 1908. Part of the necessary funds was raised by school children. It is now a public park and is maintained by prisoners of the penitentiary. It is located directly opposite the walls of the state prison.

It was discovered by Joseph Tomlinson in 1772. Two years prior, this pioneer had built his cabin near the site of the now-famous burial ground. Around it he noted a number of smaller mounds. The largest of the group was sixty-nine feet in height and about nine hundred feet in circumference at the base. On it were huge oak trees that indicated that the mound had been built many years before it was discovered by white men.

THE MOUNDSVILLE GIANTS

By Patricia Cantley

RALEIGH REGISTER, JUNE 19, 1963

The largest of the prehistoric remains in this state is the Grave Creek Mound at Moundsville in Marshall County. It looks about 900 feet around at the base and is 69 feet high. When the mound was opened in 1883 by inexperienced workmen, a burial vault was discovered. It contained two compartments: one in the center of the mound on a level with the surrounding land and the other about half way to the top.

In each compartment were found skeletons, two in the lower and one in the upper. Each skeleton was surrounded by ivory beads and other ornaments of various kinds. One skeleton was covered by thin pieces of mica. It was claimed there was also found a stone tablet near the upper compartment, on which were inscribed characters that resembled ancient hieroglyphics.

The second largest mound in the state is in the center of South Charleston. When it was excavated in 1883 by scientists from the Smithsonian Institution, a giant skeleton, about seven feet tall, was found in what appeared to be a vault in the center of the mound.

Around this skeleton were numerous ornaments. Pieces of mica on the shoulders appeared to be epaulets, and a large piece of copper on the chest seemed to be a shield. At each of the four corners of this vault were skeletons.

SALEM PROFESSOR DISCOVERS HUGE SKELETONS IN MOUNDS

DR. SUTTON BELIEVES TRIBE OF GIANTS ONCE INHABITED
CHARLESTON GAZETTE, JUNE 15, 1930

June 14: Excavation of two mounds near Morganville, in Doddridge County, about 11 miles west of here revealed what Prof. Ernest Sutton, head of the history department of Salem College, believes is valuable evidence of a race of giants who inhabited this section of West Virginia more than 1,000 years ago.

Prof. Sutton revealed tonight that he had been excavating the two mounds for the past several months. Skeletons of four mound builders indicating they were from seven to nine feet tall have been uncovered. Professor Sutton believes they were members of a race known in anthropology as Siouan Indians.

The best preserved skeleton was found enclosed in a casting of clay. All the vertebrae and other bones excepting the skull were intact. Careful measurement of this specimen indicated it was a man seven and a half feet tall.

LARGEST MOUND OPENED

The largest mound was excavated in 1883 by A. B. Tomlinson. A tunnel ten feet high and seven feet wide, was driven on the level of the ground toward the center. At a distance of 111 feet, the work men discovered a vault 12 feet long, 8 feet wide, and 7 feet deep. *It had*

Fig. 4.8. This find of a nine-foot skeleton in Indianna was shipped to the Smithsonian, where it immediately went into the "memory hole."

been sunk in the earth before the mound was erected. The vault had been erected by placing upright timbers along each side, and along the ends which supported timbers that formed the ceiling. The top of the vault was then covered with rough stones. With the decay of the timbers, the stones and dirt had fallen into the vault.

When the stones were removed, two skeletons were found. Surrounding one of them were 656 ivory beads and nearby was an ivory ornament about six inches long. There were no ornaments on the other skeleton.

SEVENTEEN HUNDRED IVORY BEADS AND FIVE COPPER BRACELETS MADE FOR A KING

Then an excavation was done from the top of the mound to connect with the tunnel. About the center of the shaft another vault was discovered that contained a single skeleton. This person must have been one of great importance because he was surrounded by many ornaments: 1,700 ivory beads, 500 sea shells, about 150 pieces of obsidian glass and 5 copper bracelets on the wrists.

MORE HEAVILY DEBATED HIEROGLYPHS

In the second vault, about two feet from the skeleton, was found the famous stone that has been the subject of controversy on the part of many antiquarians. Some claim it was a hoax.

On it were certain characters, sort of hieroglyphs, and it was hoped by some that it would prove to be a sort of Rosetta Stone with a message from an ancient race.

Fig. 4.9. The beautiful eight-foot queen in all her glory

ORIGINALLY DUG IN 1838

CHARLESTON DAILY MAIL, 1938

The mound was excavated exactly 100 years ago, the work having been begun on March 19, 1838. The owner and interested neighbor, none of whom were trained antiquarians, did the work. It is possible they over looked many things, that would have thrown light on the life and habits of the mound builders.

THE ANCIENT GIANTS BUILT A STONE WALL EIGHT MILES LONG

Another prehistoric ruin that has been attributed to the mound builders is a stone wall on the hill top above Mount Carbon, about four miles east of Montgomery, overlooking the Kanawha River. It was constructed around the brow of the mountain about three hundred feet from the summit. It is broken in places, but it is at least eight miles long. At intervals there are large piles of stones that indicate that towers or gates were constructed at these points.

ANCIENT HILLTOP TEMPLE

The stones, which were loosely placed together without mortar or cement, are similar to those found at the bottom of the mountain. It was evidently a great task to carry them up the steep hillside. One naturally asks why these walls were constructed: hardly for defense, because there is no evidence of a habitation. No water is to be found on the mountain top. *The walls are built on the highest mountain in the vicinity and they have been for temples of worship.*

THE OHIO CONNECTION

The most important and the most interesting group of mounds erected in West Virginia is found in the vicinity of Charleston. They are distinctive, although they have characteristics similar to the mounds found in Ohio and have been classified with the latter. The ancient people who lived near Charleston were undoubtedly related to those who lived in Ohio.

ANCIENT KING FOUR THOUSAND YEARS OLD FOUND

SAN ANTONIO EXPRESS, NOVEMBER 1, 1936

This summer witnessed the unearthing of a skeleton of a prehistoric Texas man, which has been identified as being from the period of the mound builders. The remains found are estimated to be about 4,000 years old and were located by an expedition from the Department of Anthropology of the University of Texas.

The skeleton was found on the Old Blanco Road, at a point near Klappenbach Hill, just south of New Braunfels.

The burial is evidently that of a chieftain or minor king of the moundbuilder race. Regal artifacts were found near the skeleton to substantiate the theory that this person was of royal birth.

KING CONEHEAD IS DISCOVERED

Throughout my research I ran into reports describing skeletons with "deformed," "elongated," or "flattened" skulls. In almost all the cases where there was more than a cursory description, it turns out that what is being described are what have recently been called "coneheads" (in a humorous reference to a famous *Saturday Night Live* sketch and movie), a condition most clearly seen in the famous statue of Queen Nefertiti.

Traditionally this has been attributed to hydrocephalic deformation or artificial skull-boarding techniques, but as the number of these skulls that have been found and studied increases, it is obvious to researchers that certain skulls are naturally oversized and have increased cranial capacities that are not the result of disease or artificial manipulation.

Fig. 4.10. Egyptian princess Meritaten (daughter of Nefertiti and Akhenaten) with typical elongated skull

EVIDENCE OF CONEHEAD BURIAL

CHARLESTON DAILY MAIL, SEPTEMBER 23, 1923

The removal of a wagonload or so of these stones brought to light a stone vault seven feet long and four feet deep in the bottom of which was found a large and much-decayed human skeleton but wanting the head, which the most careful investigation failed to discover. A single rough spearhead was the only accompanying object found in this vault.

At the depth of six feet, in earth similar to that around the base of the mound, was found a second skeleton also much decayed of an adult of normal size. At nine feet a third skeleton was discovered, in a mass of loose dry earth, surrounded by the remains of a bark coffin. This was in a much better state of preservation than the other two. The skull, which was preserved, was of the compressed or "flat head" type.

In other words, this skeleton exhibited head characteristics similar to those found in South America and Egypt. As digs progressed in other parts of the state, archaeologists in Wheeling, WV found another grouping of giants ranging in height from 6'7" to 7'6" and also displaying unusual skull formations with low foreheads that sloped back gradually.

MOUND BUILDERS HAD
PECULIAR HEADS

Ancient Monuments of the Mississippi Valley

Prof. E. L. Lively and J. L. Williamson of Friendly have made an examination of the giant skeletons found by children playing near the town. The femurs and vertebrae were found to be in a remarkable state of preservation and showed the persons to be of enormous stature. The skeletons ranged in height from 7'6" down to 6'7" inches. The skulls found are of peculiar formation. The forehead is low and slopes back gradually, while *the back part of the head is very prominent, much more so than the skulls of people living today.* The legs are exceedingly long and the bones unusually large. The finding of the skeletons has created a great deal of interest and the general impression is that the bones are the remains of the people who built the mounds, the largest in the country being located at Moundsville in Marshall County.

History of Indiana County, 1880

One child of five or six years had been buried in a stone-lined grave along with two infants. They had possibly been victims of an epidemic. All adults were of medium stature. All but one had head deformities of a lesser or greater degree. The most interesting burials were of a woman under thirty, and a child of eight, to ten years, in the same grave. Around the neck of the woman were several tiny drilled Gulf of Mexico shells, once part of a necklace. The shells are an indication of contact with distant tribes. At the center of her back was found a highly-polished bone tube having worn areas near each end where strings or thongs had probably been placed. This bone, possibly from a swan, could have been a hair ornament.

Around the woman's leg bones were found 1,458 tubular beads cut from birds' long bones. It is surmised that these were fastened to the hem of her skirt. At the foot of the grave was an unusual compound pottery vessel in such good condition that it was easily repaired. It was also found that an intense fire, perhaps of religious significance, had been built directly over the grave.

THE HORNED SKULL OF SAYRE, PENNSYLVANIA

CHARLESTON DAILY MAIL, SEPTEMBER. 20, 1916

Sayre is a borough in Bradford County, Pennsylvania, fifty-nine miles northwest of Scranton. The exact year is not clear, but during the 1880s a large burial mound was discovered in Sayre. It was reported that a group of Americans uncovered several strange human skulls and bones.

The skeletons belonged to anatomically normal men with the exception of bony projections located about two inches above the eyebrows. It appeared that the skulls had horns. *The bones were characterized as giant, as they were representative of people over seven feet tall.* Scientists estimated that the bodies had been buried around 1200 CE. The archeological discovery was made by a reputable group of antiquarians, including Dr. G. P. Donehoo, the Pennsylvania state dignitary of the Presbyterian Church; A. B. Skinner, of the American Investigating Museum; and W. K. Morehead, of Phillips Academy, Andover, Massachusetts.

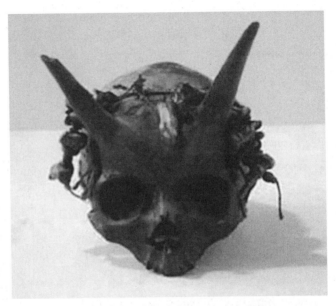

Fig. 4.11. According to historical accounts, the Sayre "Horned Giant" bones were sent to the American Investigating Museum in Philadelphia. The artifacts were later reported missing.

This was not the first time that gigantic horned skulls were unearthed in North America. During the nineteenth century, similar skulls were discovered near Wellsville, New York, and in a mining village close to El Paso, Texas. At one time in history, human horns were used as signs of kingship. Alexander the Great was depicted with horns on some of his coins. In Moses's time, horns were a symbol of authority and power. Apparent pictures of the skulls do exist, but many people claim the discovery to be a hoax. Conversely, many websites suggest that the objects are of extraterrestrial origin.

Fig. 4.12. Evidence of horns. The Vatican Museum possesses Michelangelo's famous statue of Moses.

TWO

Sophisticated Cultures of the Ancient Giants

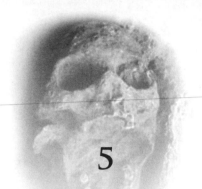

5

PYRAMIDS AND
PICTORIAL MOUNDS

At the turn of the twentieth century there was a national awareness of the mound builders and their extensive earthworks that far exceeded contemporary consciousness on the subject. Since the majority of the country still lived an agrarian lifestyle, awareness of the mounds was reinforced by daily contact with the actual sites themselves. Current estimates put the number of known American mounds at well over one hundred thousand. They ranged in shape from the great pyramids of Illinois to the fantastic pictorial mounds of Wisconsin. It seemed to be common knowledge that giants were found buried in many of these mounds and that these giants were not related to the present-day American Indians living in the region.

THE GREAT PYRAMID MOUNDS
OF ILLINOIS

One of the largest of the mound builder sites in North America is located in southwestern Illinois, near Collinsville. It is commonly called the Cahokia site. The Cahokia mound complex has been compared in scope and grandeur to the Great Pyramid. The site is located at the confluence of the Mississippi, Missouri, and Illinois Rivers, directly across the Mississippi River from present-day St. Louis. During the Middle Ages, Cahokia was a larger city than London, with an estimated population of forty to fifty thousand, yet today it is an abandoned place about which we know almost nothing. Centuries ago, there were more than 120 mounds at the Cahokia site, though the locations of only 106 have been recorded. Many of them have been destroyed or altered because of modern farming and construction, although sixty-eight have been preserved inside of the boundaries of the Cahokia Mounds State Historic Site.

Lawyer and writer H. M. Brackenridge captured the awe of seeing the Cahokia complex in 1811. He crossed the Mississippi at St. Louis and after making his way through the woods along the Cahokia Creek, passed over the plain to the mounds. He referred to them as "resembling enormous haystacks scattered through a meadow."

Journal of a Voyage up the Mississippi River in 1811

By Henri Marie Brackenridge

Pursuing my walk along the bank of the Cahokia, I passed eight other mounds, in the distance of three miles, before I arrived at the largest assemblage. When I reached the foot of the principle mound, I was struck with a degree of astonishment not unlike that which is experienced in contemplating the Egyptian Pyramids. What a stupendous pile of earth! To heap up such a mass must have required years, and labors of thousands. It stands immediately on the banks of the Cahokia, and on the side next to it is covered with lofty trees. Were it not for the regularity and design it manifests, the circumstances of it being on alluvial ground, and the other mounds scattered around it, we would scarcely believe it be the work of human hands.

The site is named after a tribe of Illiniwek Indians, the Cahokia, who lived in the area when the French arrived in the late 1600s. What the actual name of the city may have been in ancient times is unknown. The modern archaeological site is believed to have existed from AD 700 until its decline in 1300. By 1500, it is thought to have been completely abandoned.

As is the case with many of the ancient mound builder sites, a true accounting of the ancient history of the mounds is almost impossible due to the destruction of over half the mounds at the site, coupled with the lack of any modern excavation work that could dig down to the earlier construction at Cahokia, which may be thousands of years earlier than the dates currently assigned by conventional archaeology.

MONKS MOUND

The largest earthwork in the Cahokia complex is a stepped pyramid, which covers about 16 acres. It is often called Monks Mound after Trappist monks who farmed the terraces in the early 1800s. It was apparently rebuilt several times in the distant past. At the summit of the mound are the buried remains of some sort of temple, further adding to the mystery of the site. Monks Mound measures 100 feet tall, with an original base of 1,000 feet. These even measurements in feet have raised the interest of alternative historians, as well as its numerous astronomical alignments that show great similarities to alignments at Stonehenge and Teotihuacan, among numerous significant ancient sites.

MYSTERIOUS MOUND 72

In addition, during the excavation of Mound 72, a ridge-top burial mound south of Monks Mound, archaeologists found the remains of a man in his forties buried on a bed of more than twenty thousand marine-shell disc

Fig. 5.1. Monks Mound, built circa 950–1100 CE and located at the
Cahokia Mounds State Historic Site, near Collinsville, Illinois.
Image courtesy of Skubasteve834.

beads arranged in the shape of a falcon, with the bird's head appearing
beneath and beside the man's head, and its wings and tail beneath his
arms and legs. Archaeologists also recovered more than 250 other skeletons from Mound 72. Scholars believe almost 62 percent of these were
sacrificial victims, based on signs of ritual execution and method of burial.

CIRCULAR WOODEN SUN CALENDARS
CALLED "WOODHENGE"

Some archaeologists believe the last survivors of the mound builders were the Natchez Indians of the Lower Mississippi Valley. These
Indians were known for being devout worshippers of the sun, which
may explain the uses of the mounds at Cahokia and the so-called
"Woodhenge" at the site. These forty-eight wooden posts make up a
410-foot-diameter circle, and by lining up the central observation posts
with specific perimeter posts at sunrise, the exact date of all four equi-
noxes can be determined. Entire books have been written about the
many geological and astral alignments associated with the Cahokia
complex. Although these studies are dismissed by conventional archaeologists as the wishful thinking of wild-eyed amateurs, what cannot be
denied is the amazing similarity between the Woodhenge construction
found at Cahokia and the similarly constructed Woodhenge found next
to Stonehenge in England.

Although these were the finds revealed to the public after the official 1922 excavation, a previous, unofficial dig at the site uncovered
hundreds more skeletons, some giant in nature, which have all disappeared from the historical record.

ONLY FORTY OUT OF 120 MOUNDS
SURVIVE AT CAHOKIA

The wholesale destruction of the Cahokia complex is one of the greatest tragedies in the history of modern archaeology in the United States.
Although the site was recognized as highly important as early as the
seventeenth century, no official efforts were made to preserve and study
the site. As a result, well over half the site was destroyed by farmers and
city planners from St. Louis. Despite national efforts to preserve the
site at the turn of the century, Cahokia was not given National Historic
Landmark status until the 1960s.

EXPERTS SHOW RACISM
BY DISMISSING THE MOUNDS

CHICAGO TRIBUNE, AUGUST 10, 1892

"Racism and prejudice said 'the lazy Indian' couldn't have made the mounds," says archaeologist James Anderson. "That meant excavation of the site—about ten miles east of St. Louis and named Cahokia after a group of Indians that lived in the area in the seventeenth century—was slow in starting, in part, because early 'experts' refused to believe that Indians had built the majestic earthen pyramids that still stand today."

CAHOKIA WAS 6.5 SQUARE
MILES IN AREA

Covering some 6.5 square miles, Cahokia boasted streets, warehouses, man-made lakes, docks, crude but workable astronomical observatories, walled fortifications, and scores of earthen mounds as tall as 10 stories. Flourishing between 900 and 1300 CE, the city dominated the American Bottoms, a fertile 175-square-mile valley near the confluences of the Mississippi, Illinois, and Missouri rivers.

"We know it was a great city," said Anderson, director of the Cahokia Mounds Museum. "But we may be short-changing it. It may have been an empire."

Excavations have revealed that Cahokian commerce reached from the Great Lakes to the Gulf Coast and from the Western plains to the Appalachian Mountains, and controlled such raw materials as copper, mica, sea shells, and flint.

MONKS MOUND TEMPLE

Monks Mound, a flat-topped pyramid named for Trappist monks who lived nearby in the nineteenth century, has a base covering some fourteen acres, rises in four terraces to a height of a hundred feet and is estimated to contain some 22 million cubic feet of earth.

It is thought to have supported a building at least fifty feet high that was the residence of a leader who held both political and religious power in Cahokia.

THREE-MILE-LONG
STOCKADE

While Monks Mound dominated the city center, which was enclosed by a 15-foot-high wooden stockade almost three miles long, other mounds—conical, ridge- and flat-topped—dotted the countryside. The functions of the mounds are not known but there is evidence they were used for burials and as boundary markers.

THREE HUNDRED BURIAL
SACRIFICES, TWENTY
THOUSAND BEADS

"The excavation of one ridge-topped mound revealed some three hundred ceremonial and sacrificial burials, mostly young women in mass graves, and the body of what appears to be a male ruler, about forty-five years old on a blanket of more than twenty thousand seashell beads, and surrounded by the bodies of attendants. The extensive public works and human sacrifices are evidence of a class society in which rulers held sway over life and death and labor," explained Anderson.

Outside the city center were four circular sun calendars of large, evenly-spaced log posts, called "Woodhenges" because of their similarity to Stonehenge in Britain. Probably used to predict the changing of the seasons, they are the most advanced scientific achievement found at Cahokia.

"Of some 120 mounds built at Cahokia—the Indians carried earth in 60-pound basket loads from pits as far as a mile away—only 40 are preserved within a 750-acre state park. The rest are on private lands and have been mostly plowed over by farmers or covered with asphalt in the name of progress," said Anderson, bitterly observing a growing urban sprawl at the foot of the most spectacular of the earthen pyramids, Monks Mound.

ATTEMPTS TO SAVE THE MOUNDS

In 1905, Congress was petitioned to save the mound builder sites from destruction. Although Congress made noises about saving these mound sites from further destruction, funds were not forthcoming. In the case of Cahokia, it took until 1964 for that complex to receive official protection as a National Historic Landmark. Similar tales were told across the nation, since the majority of these sites were on private lands and the government offered no compensation for preservation of the mounds. To compound matters, the mound builders still have no official standing as an indigenous Native American people, as no official descendants of the mound builders have ever been recognized by the courts of the United States.

EARLY BILL CALLS FOR MOUNDS PRESERVATION

GALVESTON DAILY NEWS, AUGUST 20, 1905

A bill now before Congress, having for its objective the preserving and protecting from despoliation, the historic and prehistoric ruins or monuments on the public lands of the United States, especially Colorado and Utah, where the cliff-dweller once dwelt and placing them under the care and custody of the Secretary of the Interior, has served somewhat to revive popular interest in a subject that has been, heretofore, largely dormant except among scientists. While the bill in question applies only to the preservation of monuments on Public Land and particularly to the ruins scattered over the semi-arid regions of Arizona, New Mexico, Utah, and Colorado that have left many evidences of their occupancy of the so-called Pueblo region, it is conceivable that the movement may soon extend and take the form of legislative action looking to similar enclosures with reference to the numerous prehistoric remains of the Mississippi and Ohio valleys.

PRIVATE LANDS, PUBLIC DESTRUCTION

These mound builder sites are located almost invariably on private lands, and though it is true in some few cases the owners have for sentimental reasons maintained the integrity of the mounds and earthworks allotted on their property, in the vast majority of cases the commercial instinct has prevailed, and the original outlines are fast obliterated by time and the abrading wear of the white man's plow. Archaeologists, anthropologists, historians, indeed patriotic Americans of every class, have interest in preserving these relics of bygone days.

Every state in the Union from Wisconsin to the Gulf and from Virginia to Nebraska has more or fewer of the mounds and earthworks, which were built hundreds, perhaps thousands, of years ago. In Mississippi and elsewhere they can be seen from the car windows of railroad trains or from carriages on the highways. These mounds are mostly terraced and truncated pyramids, in shape usually square or rectangular, but sometimes hexagonal or octagonal. They differ greatly in size. One in West Virginia is 70 feet high and 1,000 feet in circumference.

The Cahokia Mound, in Illinois, opposite the northern section of the city of St. Louis, is the largest of them all, rising in terraces from a base of 1,150 feet by 700 feet to a height of 100 feet and covering an area larger than that occupied by the Great Pyramid of Egypt. In Ohio and other states there are mounds approaching these in magnitude, but generally they range from six to thirty feet in height.

The Fort Ancient earthwork on the Little Miami River, in the contour roughly of a Figure 8, and about 22 feet above the surface at its highest, is now enthroned by a public park and watched over by the Ohio Historical Society.

Cahokia was once one of the grandest capitals of this extremely ancient mound-building culture and the artistry of the site alone should have given it supreme protection, but as will be seen in the following shocking exposé of criminal neglect on the part of the Smithsonian and the Parks Division, as early as 1828, these ancient mound sites were already in peril of total destruction.

The following story appeared as a lavishly illustrated Sunday feature in the *Frederick News Post* in Virginia, but this article was also nationally syndicated. Again, the following are the actual headlines and in-depth quotes from this very provocative piece of historical muckraking on behalf of protecting these mound sites from eventual sure destruction.

THE GREAT CAHOKIA MOUND, WHICH SHOULD BE A NATIONAL MONUMENT, IN DANGER OF DESTRUCTION

WORKS OF PREHISTORIC MOUND BUILDERS ARE SCATTERED ACROSS THE UNITED STATES.

BY RENE BACHE

FREDERICK NEWS POST, JANUARY 20, 1928

The largest and most impressive memorial of the prehistoric mound builders is in danger of destruction, and the U.S. Bureau of Ethnology is anxious that it be declared a National monument and thereby preserved.

It is the great Cahokia Mound, across the river from St. Louis, in Illinois. Rising in the midst of a level plain, and rectangular in shape, it is ninety-nine feet high and 998 feet long (100 feet by 1000 feet more likely), an artificial hill that may be seen from the railroad approaching St. Louis from the east.

COMPARED TO THE PYRAMIDS

Students of antiquity regard it as comparable in archaeological interest to the pyramids of Egypt. It is believed to have been, in pre-historic times, the site of a temple, which may have been comparable in size and grandeur to the ancient Sun Temple whose ruins were recently discovered in the far southwest. That structure built of cut stone was 400 feet long. It had only one narrow door and a curious detail that has been preserved is a peephole through which a watcher could inspect persons wishing to enter.

PLEA TO SAVE THE MOUNDS

Here is another of the many public pleas to save the mounds from destruction. In this case from the 1960s, it is a large mound complex located in Whitewater that was scheduled for a suburban subdivision.

RESIDENTS TRY TO SAVE MOUNDS

JANESVILLE GAZETTE, AUGUST 13, 1965

The mounds, covering about 6½ acres of land, range in height from about 1½ to five feet. All have holes or pits on their tops and sides. Formerly situated in lands comprising the Town of Whitewater, the mounds, came under City of Whitewater jurisdiction in 1964 with the annexation of former Tratt Farm property, purchased by Buckingham Developers. Dr. Cummings has urged local acquisition of this land from the Buckingham firm, which presently "owes" the city space in the subdivision equivalent to two lots, having agreed to a planning commission proposal whereby developers of new sub-divisions within the city would allocate a certain amount of space to playground usage. Numerous other groups have sent letters either to Dr. Cummings or City Manager Ronald DeMaad to save the mounds as a historical park site.

CEREMONIAL COPPER-HELMETED AND ARMORED MEN

This report from Cahokia is indicative of the poor quality of the official reports from excavations at the site. As opposed to the detailed descriptions of copper armor found elsewhere in this book (see pages 36, 58), this "official" description merely notes that helmeted and copper-armored men were found, with no description of the finds under discussion.

ON THE CASE OF THE SEVENTY DESTROYED MOUNDS

In this report it is noted that seventy mounds that once surrounded a great mound were destroyed in the construction of the city of St. Louis. With this kind of rampant, wholesale destruction, it is easy to understand why the true history of this site remains obscured to the present day.

HUNDREDS OF MISSING SKELETONS

A true accounting of the number of skeletons found at Cahokia is also shrouded in the same mystery as the destroyed mounds at the site. Officially, there is almost no discussion of the hundreds of skeletons exhumed from this site.

The details and physical descriptions of the finds made during the 1922 dig led by archaeologist Warren K. Morehead of Phillips Academy, in Andover, Massachusetts, are not very detailed and are downright evasive when it comes to the skeletons unearthed during his dig. One might even go so far as to say that Morehead was there to bury evidence, not uncover it.

ANOTHER PYRAMID FOUND

ELISBURG JOURNAL, 1886

W. H. Scoville of Allegheny, and his brother-in-law from Connecticut, while hunting squirrels in the woods towards Irish settlement, found *a pyramidal mound 18 or 20 feet long, walled at the base with stone.* Growing on it were several trees, some of which were six inches through. Mr. Scoville, and son Esca, exhumed two skeletons, one of a dog and one of a tall man, about 8 feet in length. Most of the bones perished away when exposed to the air and handled, but the jaw bone as yet is in Mr. Scoville's possession and is large enough to fit outside his own.

Within the last few months excavations made in the Cahokia Mound have brought to light a number of objects made of sheet copper and representing helmeted and armored men. They were presumably used for some ceremonial purpose and, fashioned very artistically. . . .

The great mound was formerly surrounded by about seventy lesser mounds, some of them forty feet high, which have been destroyed by the plow. . . .

There was a GIGANTIC EARTHWORK of the kind, 319 feet long and 158 feet wide, close to St. Louis, but in the later sixties [i.e., 1860s] the city grew over it and wiped it out.

Digging at the time of the destruction, disclosed inside of it a huge burial chamber seventy feet long, built of logs, which contained HUNDREDS OF SKELETONS. . . .

CAHOKIA ORIGINALLY HAD
OVER 150 MOUNDS

APPLETON POST-CRESCENT, SEPTEMBER 20, 1921

Appleton, Wisconsin: Large earthworks, constructed by the mound builders in the prehistoric past, rise conspicuously in the Illinois lowlands, about ten miles from St. Louis. In several groups, there are about 150 mounds, the largest known as Cahokia Mound, being 1080 feet long, 702 feet wide, and 102 feet high, containing 107,000 cubic yards of earth. The background to these structures built by an unknown race, in the unknown long ago, is a high and sweeping limestone ridge.

Scientists are now opening the smaller mounds in an endeavor to learn of the people who formed them. Of all the prehistoric remnants in North America, the mounds of these groups are the largest, and it is believed, the oldest. As the earthworks seem to have been undisturbed by the Indians, French, Spaniards, and Americans, the scientists hope to dig up skeletons, utensils, and relics that will identify the race that inhabited parts of America before the Redskins.

The exploration of one of the smallest mounds has uncovered what may have been a burial place. Several skeletons have been found in it; next to them red pottery of the mound builders' period. Dr. Warren K. Morehead, of Phillips Academy, Andover, Mass., who is in charge of the research, expects to dig up a complete skeleton.

NO RECORDED SKELETON FINDS FROM
MAIN CAHOKIA MOUND?

Despite the fact that one of the main St. Louis mounds, with more than one hundred human skeletons, was publicly destroyed and desecrated, we are asked to believe that no one has ever made any examination of the nation's largest mound, which has been compared in size to the Great Pyramid. This is despite the fact that every other main mound in the country seems to have been breached at one time or the other in the past.

LITTLE CHANCE OF FURTHER EXPLORATION

EDWARDSVILLE INTELLIGENCER, NOVEMBER 14, 1937

No extensive explorations have been made into the mound at Cahokia. Some years ago members of the Ramey family, former owners, dug a tunnel 90 feet toward the center of the mound. A piece of lead ore was the only article of interest found. Since the entire area has been converted into a state park, there is little probability that any future explorations will be made in any of the mounds.

THE HONEYWELL MOUNDS NEXT LARGEST

The next largest mounds at Honeywell, Ohio, were excavated about thirty years ago. Relics taken from the Cahokia group, at the city limits of East St. Louis, indicated that the Ohio residents traded with those of Illinois. Much interest attaches to the present investigation, as there is a prospect that things of great historic significance will be unearthed. It is proposed to preserve the largest mounds in a state or national park.

CAHOKIA NAMED BY THE FRENCH EXPLORER LA SALLE

Monks Mound with the exception of several smaller ones, is the farthest north of a group of 72 (a very significant number). Years ago the mound was given the name Cahokia Mound. It was named for a tribe of Indians encountered by La Salle, a Frenchman, in his early explorations.

On the southern side of the mound, is a terrace, about 30 feet above the base. The terrace contains an area of over two acres. This is the plateau which may have been used for religious purposes.

Monks Mound is a parallelogram, the longer dimensions extending north and south. The other mounds in the group are of various formations. The bottom of one is circular while another is almost perfectly square. A third along the highway has the longer dimensions extending from east and west.

A HOLLOW METAL BIRD FOUND

OAKLAND TRIBUNE, DECEMBER 20, 1925

Many objects of strange form, of undoubted aboriginal manufacture, have been found in the mounds. For instance, a hollow metal bird with many perforations, and small vessels of odd shapes with numerous holes bored through them. For what purpose could such things be meant? From a mound near Chillicothe came a carving in soft serpentine representing in really exquisite detail a duck riding on a fish. This, however, was a pipe. The pre-Columbian Indians were all of them smokers of tobacco and the mounds yield great numbers of pipes.

In one group of mounds were found hundreds of jaw bones of human beings, bears, and other animals, cut in a most curious way, so as to leave in each case a thin slice of the alveolar structure holding a row of teeth. The work must have been done with a saw so exceedingly thin and sharp that it is a puzzle to know how the Indians could have obtained such a tool. But a more important question is, why should the jaws have been cut that way?

The United States Geological Survey has made a map of the eastern half of the United States showing the entire area sprinkled with red dots, each one standing for an ancient mound or group of mounds. Such mounds are found all over the country, from the Atlantic to the Pacific and from the Canadian border to the Gulf. About 10 percent of them have been more or less excavated, yielding numerous articles of white manufac-ture, such as knives, brass kettles, beads, and so forth. Nearly all of the other objects unearthed are similar to those in use by the Indians today.

Some of the mounds were domiciliary; the old-time Indians lived on top of them because the elevation was an advantage for defense. Thus, a large mound might be a village site. Others were used for purposes of religious ceremonies, yet others were cemeteries. A dead man was buried in a small tumulus, usually in a sitting posture. When another died he was interred in the same place, more earth being added. At every interment the mound grew bigger, and thus in the course of centuries it attained huge size. The usual form of a mound was that of a broad, low-topped cone, which might be eighty or ninety feet high and three hundred feet in diameter at the base. Others were rectangular. Yet others were built like walls, twenty to forty feet wide. The purpose of these last is a mystery; they were not used for burial, and the use to which they were put is likely to remain forever unknown.

MYSTERIOUS EFFIGY MOUNDS FOUND IN MANY PLACES

Although the Cahokia complex stands out because of its size, many other finds of mounds and their contents that are no less fascinating have been made around the United States. Perhaps the most intriguing are the many mounds built in the shape of animals.

SKELETON FOUND IN MOUND NEAR ALTON REVIVES
HOPE OF FACTS ON ANCIENT RACE

MAY HAVE BEEN ABODE OF PEOPLE ANTEDATING THE INDIANS

ALTON EVENING TELEGRAPH, NOVEMBER 10, 1933

Archeological interest in the Alton vicinity is being revived since excavations on the Charles Oerson farm, located on the Newbern road west of the Alton-Jerseyville road have indicated that the several mounds located there are ruins of that race of pre-American Indian dwellers on this continent the mound builders.

ONE-FOOT THICK MIDDEN
OF MUSSEL SHELLS

It was the curiosity of Charles Gerson and Ray Smith that led to the investigation of the dirt formations. Tuesday and Wednesday of this week their curiosity was appeased when a skeleton was unearthed several feet from the surface. Digging deeper more bones and pottery were found. The most interesting, and perhaps the most valuable, of the relics found by two men was a large collection of mussel shells, placed one upon the other to the thickness of a foot. The shells crumbled when exposed to the air, but the fact that they did so may be the factor to determine the antiquity of the mounds as they have been in previous discoveries.

THE DEVIL BIRD PAINTING
OF ALTON BLUFF

Should the mounds prove to be as ancient as the mussel shells indicate there would be a possibility that from the ruins on the Gerson farm aid would be derived to establish the antiquity of the time-honored and be-legended Plasa devil bird painting that for centuries graced the Alton bluffs.

Paleolithic ruins are the most ancient to be found in America and come from the early glacial period. Even at this time the trace of the mongoloid type is found, giving rise to the theory of the immigrations to America over the land bridge that existed between Europe and America and, Alaska and Siberia. Then centuries or perhaps ages later came the mound builders who were neither a Neolithic race nor American Indians.

THE GREAT FRASER
SHELL MIDDEN

Mound Builders were also builders of shell-heaps. The Great Fraser Midden in British Columbia is the greatest known discovery of the shell-heap builders; it is built on the glacial gravel before the post-glacial vegetation had started, and when discovered was covered by a forest from 680 to 700 years old. The shells found crumbled when exposed, but the later mound builders also left mussel shells behind, showing there was a connection between them.

FIVE TYPES OF MOUNDS BUILT

There were five distinct types of mounds built; the effigy or animal-shaped ones, burial and ground work ones combined, burial mounds for that purpose alone, the stockade type, and the pyramidal type, of which the Cahokia mound at East St. Louis is the best known example.

This newly found group of mounds might be of the latter type. But before a label is put on this discovery there is the possibility that it is a burial place of the roving men who succeeded the Mound Builders in this territory. Though no great importance may be placed on the excavation near Alton should it be proved to belong to the American Indian burial ground division, the wealth and beauty of the American Indian relics taken from this vicinity prior to this time will be augmented.

A LINK WITH THE PYRAMIDS

On the other hand, should the discovery be found to correspond with Cahokia and be of the same class, all theories and the romances connected with East St. Louis will be extended to here. Between Cahokia and the early pyramid builders of Central America there is a connecting link. Should the Alton findings be found to be cousins to the Cahokia cluster, it may become a link in the pre-history record of the American continent, a chain of records that stretches from Asia to Alaska, British Columbia, Rio Grande, Guatemala, Yucatan, Florida, and is as near to us as East St. Louis, and has relics ranging from mussel shell heaps to the casa grandes and pueblos of the southwest, down to the more modern calendars and sculptures of the Mayas, and the heavy gold and earth-work of the Itzas, Quiches, and Aztecs. It all depends upon the importance of the slim stratum of mussel shells. To date, mussel shells have not figured as relics found in the graves of the red American Indian, but are a characteristic of the mound builders.

The account that follows describes a particularly stunning serpent mound found in Quincy, Illinois. Inside the mound skeletons were found buried with the skeleton of a snake covering them.

HUGE SERPENT MOUND

HISTORICAL RECORD, QUINCY, ILLINOIS, 1892

A huge serpent mound was recently discovered near Quincy, Illinois, in Adams County. This mound was built by a class of pre-historic people now known as the serpent worshippers. In the mound were found skeletons upon which the bones of a snake reposed.

THE GREAT SERPENT MOUND
OF OHIO ENCHANTS

RALEIGH REGISTER, JUNE 19, 1963

The Great Serpent Mound of Ohio, appeals peculiarly to the imagination. It measures from the upper jaw to the tip of the tail 1254 feet, rising at the head to a height of five feet from the surface and extending in graceful and perfect convolutions, but with receding height to the tail.

The serpent's mouth is open and within the arc of the jaws is a monumental earthwork shaped like an egg, as if about to be swallowed. This striking example of the mound builders' art about which the fancy of the twentieth century weaves traditions of serpent worship in a forgotten civilization is fortunate to be preserved from the ravages of time and vandalism. This is as reported in a feature story about a bill introduced in 1905 to save the mounds from immediate destruction.

As is the case with Michigan's copper mines, the most stunning aspect of Wisconsin's mound building culture is not the plethora of giants unearthed in the area, but the amazing animal effigy mounds that covered the state like a blanket of woodland imagery. It has been estimated that in one county alone in Wisconsin, there were originally over ten thousand effigy mounds. It is no exaggeration to say that Wisconsin was an ancient version of the Nazca plateau in South America, which is famous worldwide for the thousands of animal images cut into the bedrock there. The images that covered Wisconsin were endless and ran the gamut from human forms to snakes, lizards, foxes, rabbits, fish, and mammoths. Unfortunately no official attempt has ever been made to save these mounds from destruction, and at this point in time the vast majority of mounds that once blanketed the state have been destroyed.

In one notable case, it was reported that an eight-foot-tall giant was unearthed near Pelican Lake, while in another report from Westport, giant burials were found in association with ten-pound axes and an eight-foot-high wall, which was fifteen-feet thick and ran along a river embankment for 1,500 feet. It was noted that the wall was made from hard red bricks, some of an immense size. In the woods near the shore, a mound was opened that contained a giant buried with several rolls of textiles and a finely finished grooved stone ax.

EFFIGY MOUNDS
A WOODLAND WONDERLAND

OAKLAND TRIBUNE, DECEMBER 20, 1925

The so-called "effigy mounds" are confined almost wholly to Wisconsin and a small part of Iowa. The entire valley of Prairie du Chien Township is dotted with these mounds, shaped to represent bears, deer, rabbits, antlered elks, and other animals. They form veritable droves, all headed, like the river, to the southwest. The existence of these mounds in such numbers and of so great a magnitude proves that there must formerly have been in that region a large population permanently resident and settled.

They doubtless depended for a livelihood chiefly on farming, as did the eastern tribes until the whites disturbed them. It is worth mentioning that some of their mounds, representing birds, have a spread of 250 feet from wing tip to wing tip, and a remarkable feature of most of them is the imitative curving and rounding of the bodies of the sculptured animals. There are hundreds of these effigy mounds overlooking the Mississippi River, located on bluffs, and hundreds more across the river in Iowa. They are thought to represent the heraldic "totems" of various clans. Thus the Bear clan built mounds in the shape of a bear, the Lizard clan in the form of a lizard, the Snake clan in the likeness of a serpent, and so on.

STRANGE, ANCIENT, SUPERIOR ARROWHEADS FOUND

Around the mound sites in various parts of La Crosse County, archaeologists and parties of Boy Scouts have found many arrow heads of strange design. These points range from the battle or war points to slender points, evidently used for the purpose of shooting small game. Some of the points, which had been found in the area of West Salem, are of obsidian while others found south of La Crosse near the junction of highways 35 and 14, are of flint. While some are of Indian manufacture, others have been identified as being of mound builder construction, and a study of the symmetry and design of both works immediately shows the superiority of the mound builders in manufacturing these artifacts. Scrapers, axes, and pottery have also been found, together with occasional skeleton remains. Beaded ware and middens (refuse from food stuffs) have also been found in La Crosse County.

GIANT SKELETON FOUND

MASSIVE HUMAN BONES AND INDIAN RELICS UNEARTHED NEAR PELICAN LAKE

NEW NORTH WISCONSIN, JULY 23, 1908

That human beings of enormous size inhabited this section of this country ages ago was proven last Sunday, when the massive skeleton of an Indian was unearthed near Pelican Lake. The interesting discovery was made by George Patton and L. H. Eaton, two Chicago tourists, who are spending the summer there.

For several days the men noticed a mound on their travels through the woods, and, at last led by curiosity, decided to excavate it. Procuring spades they fell to work and after digging down to a depth of about four feet were surprised to find the bones of a large human foot protruding through the earth.

Digging further, they gradually uncovered the perfect form of a giant. The skeleton was nearly 8 feet in height and the arms extended several inches below the hips. Buried with the bones were numerous stone weapons and trinkets. Among these were a curious stone hatchet, a copper knife, several strange copper rings, and a necklace made of the tusks of some prehistoric animal.

The skeleton is no doubt that of an Indian who was one of a tribe of giants who roamed this part of the state over one thousand years ago.

RAILROAD WORKERS UNEARTH GIANT

AN INDIAN MOUND OPENED

EAU CLAIRE DAILY FREE PRESS, OCTOBER 7, 1873

A few days ago the men engaged in building the road bed of the Green Bay and Winona railroad, struck an Indian mound near Arcadia. It had been in view for some days, and no little speculation was indulged in as to what the excavation would develop from this cemetery of the red man.

The discovery exceeded all anticipations. The skeleton of an Indian was found of such dimensions as to indicate that the frame must have been that of a giant. The jaw bone easily enclosed the face of the largest laborer to be found on the work. The thigh bones were more like those of a horse than a man, hair heavy and remarkably well-preserved.

Pieces of blanket in which the body had been wrapped were taken out in a tolerable state of preservation. A number of Mexican coins were also found.

The unusual size of the skeleton has excited considerable interest, and the curiosities will be carefully preserved for exhibition.

PERFECT MAN-SHAPED MOUND

SHEBOYGAN PRESS, NOVEMBER 10, 1913

WAUPACA HAS AN ALMOST PERFECT MAN-SHAPED MOUND

Destruction of this was threatened by the street car companies, but the various women's clubs rallied to the rescue with a fund which has ensured the preservation of the prehistoric relic.

ONE WISCONSIN COUNTY HAS OVER 500 ANIMAL EFFIGY MOUNDS

On Doty Island, near Menasha, several mounds have been found of well-defined animal shapes, while in Crawford County are 500 of these tumuli, 100 of which are located in Prairie du Chien and Wauzeka.

The recent discovery in Portage County, by W. A. Titus of the Wisconsin Archaeology Society, of a number of Indian mounds, which have yielded a number of interesting relics, has called to the minds of the members of the state society a large number of tumuli in effigy shape that have been placed on official record in late years. It is of interest to note that, as of now, all known effigy mounds are within the boundaries of Wisconsin.

734 MOUNDS NEAR DEVIL'S LAKE

In seven townships lying about Devil's Lake there are 734 mounds. Best known of these is a bird with outstretched wings, extending 150 feet, tail forked, and wings bent near the tip. The bird seems to be flying toward the lake, the shore of which is but a few rods distant. The head, breast, and body are several feet in height.

WISCONSIN EFFIGY MOUND CAPITAL OF THE WORLD

According to Dr. Cummings, "at one time, probably 20,000 mounds existed in the north-central, Midwest area" and of all effigies constructed, about 95 per cent were built in the territorial limits of Wisconsin, making the state the "effigy mounds capital of the world." Cummings estimated the mounds in Whitewater were built between AD 200 and 1200 and were different from Aztalan mounds in that the local mounds are burial mounds, lacking deposits of artifacts of any significance.

THE BIG FIND IN WISCONSIN

Here is an inventory of the largest effigy and shaped mounds found in Wisconsin. They are in the shapes of a mink, panther, turtle, several massive birds, and several geometric figures.

The earthwork mounds resemble various shapes of varying sizes: mink, 348 long; panther, 120 feet long; bird, body, 57 feet wide, and wings, 69 feet long; conical, 32 feet wide; oval, 32 by 90 feet; conical, 38 feet wide; bird, body, 60 feet wide, 94 feet long; turtle, 143 feet wide, 100 feet long; tapering, 145 feet long; oval, 37 by 60 feet; and tapering, 195 feet long.

In the area around the Dells in Kilbourn, Wisconsin, the discovery of a two-hundred-foot-long giant lizard mound was reported. At an adjacent mound complex consisting of eight to twelve conical mounds as tall as twelve feet, another effigy mound in the shape of a deer was noted.

Mounds Depict Deer and Lizards

One of the mounds at the Dells, near Kilbourn, represents a giant lizard, 200 feet long, the head pointing to the west.

A few miles from the city is a curious group. It occupies a plot of ground five rods wide and 18 rods long. Near the southwest corner is the figure of a deer. To the north is a lizard, several rods long; while around its head are a series of eight or ten conical mounds, some 12 feet in height.

NO TRADITION FOR THE MOUNDS AMONG THE SIOUX

It is evident that the handiwork of the builders of these mounds dates far back into the history of the west, as the Sioux Indians have known the soil for 300 years, and they have no traditions concerning mound building within that range of time.

MOST NORTHWESTERN SITE OF
THE MOUND BUILDERS

The Ross Lake mound group in Wisconsin was the most northwestern site in the continental United States at the time it was investigated and reported in 1935, but since then numerous other mounds have been found farther north in the western United States and Canada.

SUPERIOR QUALITY OF
WORKMANSHIP

The researchers at the Ross Lake site noted that extremely ancient pottery of superior workmanship was found in association with the later and much cruder pottery of the modern American Indian tribes in the area. The earliest form of cord-design pottery can be traced to the Jomon culture in Japan and has been dated as early as 14,000 to 10,000 BCE. The Caucasian origin of the Jomon people is still under debate, but cord-design pottery has been discovered in Wales as well as in the United States, and the swirling design patterns on early Jomon jars resemble the spirals found in later Celtic designs.

EVIDENCE FOR THE
WISCONSIN MAMMOTH

Not only have mammoth and mastodon remains been found in Wisconsin, but bones, tusks, and teeth have been found in association with mound builder burials. In Minnesota, an effigy mound in the shape of an elephant or mastodon has also been reported.

THIRTY-ONE MOUNDS OPENED AT
ROSS LAKE IN 1931

By Cecil L. Munson

WISCONSIN TRIBUNE, FEBRUARY 2, 1935

During excavations recently conducted by Philleo Nash at the site of the Indian Mounds at Ross Lake, three miles south of Nekoosha, many illuminating evidences of fact concerning early Indian life in this area were discovered.

An excellent group of mounds, built by the ancient forebears of the teepee-builders, may be seen in a fine state of preservation on the shores of Ross Lake, three miles south of the city of Nekoosha and about one mile back from the eastern bank of the Wisconsin River. Mr. Nash was majoring in social anthropology at the University of Wisconsin when, in the summer of 1931, he spent four weeks excavating some of these mounds as work preliminary to writing a university thesis in which he hoped to classify the group in its proper anthropological category.

AS A BOY, NASH SAW ANIMAL MOUNDS IN THE WOODS

As a boy he had seen and wondered about these same Ross Lake Mounds, and he knew that, while most mounds found in groups in southeastern Wisconsin rise above the general contour of the earth to a height of little more than 2 feet as an average, their shape and distribution is of historical import.

The mounds at Ross Lake, classified by Mr. Nash as effigy mounds because of the presence of one mound outlined in the shape of an animal, possibly a beaver, were of special interest to him as a student of early Indian mound building because of the presence in the neighborhood of this effigy, of a number of more or less circular and conical mounds averaging 25 inches high by 18 feet in diameter. In the part of the mound area at Ross Lake, still untouched by the plow, or by the spades of marauders, he found 28 such round-topped mounds and three others of various types.

Furthermore, the effigy mound proved to be of special interest to Mr. Nash when he found that it had not been entered and that, as an original deposit of earth over 95 feet long and 33 feet thick through from the haunch-part to the tail, it was as fine an example of the effigy-type mound as could be found in Wisconsin.

ALREADY PARTIALLY DESTROYED

Mr. Nash ascertained that the 31 mounds extant in the group today are but part of the original work of the mound builders on this site.

Crops under cultivation for the last 70 years have doubtless made erosions through the southern part of the original group, obliterating a large number of mounds.

The 31 extant mounds are protected against erosion by a good stand of small timber that has overgrown the mound site, preventing the heavy rains from doing damage to their contours. Being in this dense corner of wooded land, the mounds are hardly visible to the untrained eye. Stretching but a few inches over 2 feet above the sod line of the lake shore at most points, these hummocks of earth have become covered with a dense growth of grass, and that has contributed to hiding the mound builder's work from random relic hunters.

Another characteristic of the group at Ross Lake was made by Mr. Nash on the basis of the external appearance of the mound number 23, called the pointed lineal. This mound, the largest at Ross Lake, over 495 feet long and with an ovoid head, has the characteristics of many other smaller mounds in Wisconsin, but in size it is matched by only one other mound in the United States, the Great Serpent Mound in Ohio.

In a map that he made of the Ross Lake shoreline showing the shape of the 31 mounds, Mr. Nash shows that the most outstanding mound of the group is the long needle-like mound numbered 23, having a bulbous head end fully 25 feet in diameter, and a body that tapers off gradually into the surrounding sod floor to a length of 495 feet.

Using the most approved methods and exercising every care, Mr. Nash found during his excavation of 16,000 cubic feet of earth, that the material used in constructing the mounds was in some cases a kind of red-black sand of a type similar to the subsoil strata of earth found in this vicinity, indicating that the builders had in some cases gone to a considerable depth to find mound material that suited their work.

The most consistently general characteristic of the Ross Lake Mound Group, according to Mr. Nash, is the presence of colored sand in saucer-like pits in almost all of the entrances. Often he found this sand surrounding some bone deposit, although no human bone was unearthed in any of the mounds at the Ross Lake mounds.

It became known through the Nash investigation that the Ross Lake Mound Group locates the point of farthest northwest dispersion of the culture type of the mound-building predecessors of the teepee-building Indians.

Mr. Nash also discovered fragments of a type of native pottery that offered interesting possibilities for exhaustive study. It is well known that the ordinary clay pottery-work done by the teepee-dwellers at the time of the white man's coming was always crude and rarely if ever serviceable.

In the Ross Lake Mounds, however, Mr. Nash discovered a type of pottery far superior to the usual run of later Indian clay products.

To begin with it is evident that upon examining the fragments, that the mound builders were careful in the mixing and molding of their materials. Probably using wooden paddles, wound about with wood or grass, the pottery makers produced strange "cord-imprint" designs on their baked-clay products.

This cord-imprint effect is found only in rare cases in Indian pottery work. On one broken piece of pottery, these strange cord imprints were found to be present both on the inside and outside surfaces, revealing a great amount of skill and patience in the men who made the pottery. Mr. Nash's discovery of cord-imprint pottery at the Ross Lake Mounds sets off the mound builders of that locality as craftsmen far superior to the pottery-making mound builders of the southeastern Wisconsin group.

After the discoveries so far mentioned, Mr. Nash made a study of the mound builders from another angle. He began by making classifications of the mound builders' habits on the basis of the shapes of the various mounds and the relation of those shapes to the shapes of similar mounds found in other areas.

By this method the mound marked number 3 and classified as an effigy mound, was found to be related in general type of contour and surface appearance of burial pits within the mound, to other groups of mounds of the effigy type in the Shawno, Oconto, and Kraniz Creek areas of Wisconsin.

As the evidence, which has been found in the gravel deposits of La Crosse county, shows in the form of teeth, portions of ivory tusks, etc., large herds of hairy mammoths, which we will call scientifically "Elphius Americanum Wisconsinatis," roamed what is today La Crosse county. These giant mammals were about nine to ten feet in height and possessed enormous curved tusks, which were very formidable weapons of offense or defense, whatever the case might have been. Teeth are usually well-preserved, and from studies made on teeth, which have been found in different parts of Wisconsin, including La Crosse county, it appears that moss and lichen composed the diet of these long-vanished brutes. Dental trouble was no doubt unknown among the hairy mammoths and their teeth are in a most excellent state of preservation.

MAMMOTH-SHAPED MOUND IN MINNESOTA

Here is a report of mammoth-shaped mounds being found along the Mississippi River in Wabasha, Minnesota.

MAMMOTH IMAGE DEBATED

By Cecil L. Munson

WISCONSIN TRIBUNE, FEBRUARY 2, 1935

While several pictoglyphs evidently left by the mound builders have been found farther up the Mississippi river in the Wabasha, Minnesota area, showing images of the mammoths, yet, it can hardly be assumed on this basis, that the mammoths were still here when man came. This of course is open to debate.

Erroneously "dubbed" as Indian mounds, several artificial earth tumuli in the form of burial, effigy, fortification, and ceremonial mounds, are to be found in La Crosse county. These mounds appear in the topographical plane in such areas as La Crosse, Onalaska, and West Salem, and only the trained eye of the archaeologist is able to distinguish these mounds from ordinary uplifts of earth and rock.

PANTHERS AND ALTARS

Here is an account of the rare opening of one of Wisconsin's main altar mound complexes, which has earthworks of animal-shaped mounds surrounding it.

WISCONSIN PANTHER MOUND OPENED

WEEKLY WISCONSIN, DECEMBER 26, 1891

Some 30 miles west of Milwaukee, on the banks of the Fox River, are interesting earth works. The high bluffs on the banks of the river offer excellent views of the surrounding country for miles around. At the site of an ancient village, a long neck of land extends into a marsh containing vast quantities of wild rice. Along this high neck of land are found many observation and sacrificial mounds, also a few effigy mounds.

One of the most prominent and imposing of the effigy mounds represents a panther. Near the head of this mound a number of quite remarkable depressions were discovered, having evidently been used for the purpose of storing away whatever valuables the inhabitants of this village may have possessed in case of any threatened danger.

On the summit of one of the high hills overlooking this ancient valley is an altar mound surrounded by groups of effigies. One of its peculiarities is that it is composed of two large burial mounds connected by an oblong mound. Two massive burial mounds by the lowlands nearby, upon being excavated, yielded up large quantities of bones and numerous fragments of rudely ornamented pottery.

INDIAN LEGENDS OF GIANTS

The skeleton was nearly eight feet in height, and the arms extended several inches below the hips. The skeleton is no doubt that of an Indian who was one of a tribe of giants who roamed this part of the state over one thousand years ago.

The Chippewa Indians of our present day tell many legends regarding the prowess and strength of the members of their tribe moons back. One tale was of a giant warrior, who was over ten arrow lengths high and had sufficient strength to uplift tall trees by the roots and hurl huge boulders through the air.

MOUND USED FOR GAME DRIVES

A number of long narrow mounds are placed in such a position as to enclose a large area of land, and this enclosure, it would seem, was used as a game drive. The game was driven from the plateau, down between the lines of the two long mounds, and into this enclosure, where it became an easy prey for the hunter.

The mounds at that distant date were quite high, and the opening between them may have been palisaded. Thus the inhabitants of this village were amply supplied with food from the forest, the prairie, and the river.

THUNDERBIRD EFFIGY MOUND VISITED

Near the city of Waukeesha, another village has been identified by the late Dr. Lapham, and this place was next visited.

It is situated on the high bluffs overlooking a giant swamp. The swamp is even in the present day almost completely over grown with wild rice. It is worthy of note that a tribe of Indians is encamped upon the site of this ancient village at the present time, thus showing the desirability of the location.

The place is guarded by observation and effigy mounds. At the southern extremity of the line of artwork, is an interesting effigy mound of imposing appearance, evidently intended to represent a bird with the wings spread in the act of flying. The head is directed to the south. The wings are long and narrow, and measure 112 feet each way from the body to the extremities. The body and neck are small and the length of the tail is 72 feet. [For other significant instances of the number 72, see the sections about the Monks Mound, on page 138, and Mound 72, on page 139.] It is quite a large and well-formed effigy, and is different from the other bird mounds in having an angle in the wings.

FOXES AND SQUIRRELS DOT THE LANDSCAPE

On the high bluffs many beautiful effigies were discovered, a large majority of them being in the shape of squirrels. The squirrels, some of them large of size, were in every conceivable attitude. One interesting effigy mound represented a fox running, with his head turned around and looking behind him.

The groups on the bottom lands and bluffs adjoining seem to form connecting links. There are three or four lines of effigies on the bluffs, and three or four groups of parallel mounds on the bottom lands. They were arranged in a large circle enclosing an area of some twenty or thirty acres.

THE STRANGE SUGAR-LOAF MOUNDS

In the town of Westport a strange departure from the usual method of building mounds was noticed. The mounds referred to are of the usual conical or "sugar-loaf" form. They are six in number and are situated on the level prairie surrounded by the river and marshes. At the base of each a large perfectly circular pit was excavated and the soil thus obtained was used in the construction of the mound next to it. It was noticeable that great care had been taken to have the base of the mounds of the same size as the circular pits.

Upon excavating one of these mounds the remains of a skeleton that had apparently been cremated was discovered. All the bones, which had not been burned by the fire, had kept their original position standing upright and apparently quite undisturbed in a kind of grayish-colored clay, whereas those portions, which had extended above the clay, had been consumed by the fire, and the surface of the clay was, as far as the fire had extended, covered by a layer of wood ashes, mingled with a layer of small pieces of charred wood and burned bones, together with bones belonging to the spine, ribs, and other parts of the body that had been more or less injured by the fire.

TEN-POUND AXES AND LIMESTONE SLABS

A short distance to the north a very peculiar mound covered with flat lime stones was discovered. The stones had evidently been placed over the mound for the purpose of preventing the wild beasts from penetrating it. Upon excavating this mound it was found to contain a number of charred bones, finely-ornamented pottery, and several implements of stone, very unique and cunning in their design.

Several axes of stone were found, varying in weight from four ounces to ten pounds, with grooves to admit the width for a handle. Also wedges ten inches in length, a double-bitted curved bark peeler, flint flakes for removing dirt, from 5 to 15 inches in length, stone hammers without grooves, perforated ceremonial stones of different sizes, and different types of arrow heads for shooting game in a tree, and those of a keener point for animals of a tougher skin and the small, keen, unextractable ones for war purposes only.

SPECIAL ARROWS FOR SHOOTING FISH

Some of the arrow points were evidently manufactured for the purpose of shooting fish. These points show great ingenuity in their construction and are finely finished. They are barbed, and from a straight base the point inclines at an angle of exactly 45 degrees, which angle would, when the point was shot in the ordinary manner, cause it to deviate the distance required to strike any object under the water.

EIGHT-FEET-HIGH AND FIFTEEN-FEET-THICK WALLS OF THE GIANTS FOUND

About one mile up the river from this place we discovered what appeared to be the remains of an entrenched camp on the west bank of the stream. The northern or upper portion *is at the present time in the best state of preservation. It also lies higher, the ground sloping* both eastward toward the river bank, which forms the fourth side of the camp and toward the south. The north embankment, starting from the river, at a distance of 600 feet, reaches the end of the western embankment, which has a length of 1500 feet and, at its southern extremity, meets another embankment that runs another 700 feet to the river. The enclosure has no wall on the water side, as the river is a sufficient protection.

The bank is steep and rises at once 20 to 30 feet. The observations, or look-out towers, are thirty-six in number. The area of this enclosure is nearly twenty acres. The thickness of the wall is about fifteen feet, and its height varies from three to eight feet but has been plowed down in many places. A large number of mounds are found without the walls, and residents of the neighborhood say that many within have been plowed down.

HARD RED BRICKS USED IN GIANT WALL

One curious feature is that the walls are made of a kind of brick. After building and shaping the walls of clay, they were then burned into brick by means of wood piled up on each side of the structures.

These bricks are of a red color and are quite hard and of irregular forms. The soil is still full of brick fragments, many of them of large size. In the middle of one was a stick one inch thick burned to charcoal. In nearly all of them were holes where the sedge from the river bank had been mixed with the clay and the shape of each stalk and blade was plainly visible. It seemed clear that the soil, a kind of loam, had been thrown up into a rampart and that the whole was treated with clay, matted and massed together with bushes and sedge, that all over was heaped a vast quantity of prairie grass, with perhaps huge trees, and the whole set on fire. Yet it would not have been necessary to burn trees for turning clay to brick. That transformation is wrought in Nebraska, where wood is scarce, with prairie grass alone.

GIANT FOUND SEATED IN STONE BURIAL VAULT

In the tangled woods near the shore was discovered a mound, which, though small, gave evidence from its great age for across the center lay a giant of the forest, prostrated by the elements that for ages it had defied.

The work in question was conical in shape and very difficult to excavate. On removing the outer layer, which was composed of black vegetable mold, a layer of stones entirely covering the top was found. Underneath this came a layer of yellowish dirt about six inches in thickness. In this a finely-finished, grooved stone axe was unearthed. About a foot below this axe was a large flat stone, which, upon being removed, disclosed a cavity.

In this cavity was found the skeleton of an adult mound builder, seated on the floor of clay, baked very hard. Around it were ashes and fragments of pottery, many of which exhibited great artistic skill in their various patterns. Several arrow heads, together with a number of small disks ground from fresh water clam shells, and a number of perfectly round polished stones, some of which have small grooves running completely around both ways, thus quartering the spheres were discovered. The grooves are so slight as to be used only by a small cord.

STONE AXES AND TEXTILES THAT FELL TO DUST

One of the large conical mounds on the outside of the fortification was next opened. After digging through a number of strata of sand, loam, and small pebbles a solid and compact layer of hard clay was reached. Underneath this layer was a number of human bones and fragments of pottery, but no ashes, nor anything to show that any fire had been used. Near the center of this bone depository were several rollers of textile fabric, preserved in shape by the moisture of the earth, but in coming in contact with the air, they were wafted away by the slightest breeze.

Several stone axes, a spearhead, and numerous arrowheads of various types were unearthed. The excavation was continued for several feet through a kind of hard, sandy soil, but nothing being of further interest was discovered.

TWO EFFIGY MOUNDS AT THE UNIVERSITY OF WISCONSIN AT MADISON

In the north the earthworks took more frequently the form of animals, the serpent being the favorite design. Ohio and Wisconsin have several important effigy mounds, and these states have already undertaken the care of them.

Two bird-shaped mounds, rising to a height of between two and a half to three feet above the surface, one forty-three feet long from beak to tail, the other sixty-six feet over all, have been preserved on the college campus of the University of Wisconsin at Madison.

A WISCONSIN CEMETERY CONTAINING ANCIENT GIANTS

Nearly one mile inland from this village the remains of an ancient cemetery were found. A number of cone-shaped mounds of earth were scattered promiscuously over an area of several acres. Two of the most promising then in appearance were next opened. Strata of earth, sand, and cinders were removed to a depth of over ten feet before any remains were found.

Underneath the lowest level of cinders a large number of bones were found, and judging from the different jawbones, at least eight bodies must have been interred in the mound. The excavation was continued through alternate layers of clay, sand, and pebbles until a depth of about ten feet was reached when a large number of bones and pottery were brought to light. The pottery was highly ornamented.

Antiquities of the Badger State, 1855

At the village of Merton are a number of circular and oblong elevations and one called "The Cross." This last is certainly entitled to the name from its striking resemblance to the cross as emblematically used and represented by the Roman Church in every part of the world. And yet there can be no doubt that this mound was erected long before the first Jesuits visited this country and presented the emblem of the Christian faith. An excavation has been made in the mound at the intersection of the arms, and bones of a very large size have been found.

HUNDREDS OF MOUNDS,
EMBALMED NINE-FOOT GIANT,
AND DAMS

SYRACUSE DAILY STANDARD, JULY 23, 1897

While men were excavating with a steam shovel near Mora Minnesota, they found an old copper spear with a point measuring 10 inches in length and tapering to a very fine and tempered point. The weapon shows the maker to have been an adept in working copper metal. Archaeologists believe that at some prehistoric time the country surrounding Mora was densely inhabited by a race of people who were much further advanced in civilization than the Indians.

The many mounds around Fish Lake show that a mighty race of people lies slumbering there, whose history is as yet unwritten—from the mounds of earth, which were used as sepultures for their dead, and which demonstrate beyond a doubt that they were a numerous as well as powerful people.

EVIDENCE OF DAMS

Two investigators excavating a mound found a skeleton apparently embalmed in a kind of cement, which seemed to be prepared for embalming the dead. The skeleton appeared to be in a perfect state of preservation and showed by measurement a height of nine feet for the individual, who was built in good proportion. As soon as the air struck it, the bones crumbled and disappeared.

Taking the country northeast from Fish Lake, where there is a group of 97 mounds, one finds a regular system of dams extending clear to Lake Superior, 100 miles, in which one can see that prehistoric man had a regular means of travel by water from their great city around Fish Lake to Lake Superior, and going south by Snake River to the Gulf of Mexico.

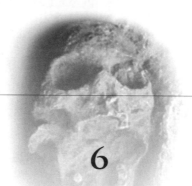

6

CITIES IN CIRCLES AND LINES

In the study of ancient human beings, the presence of cities is regarded as one of the most significant indicators of civilization. This sampling of stories from around the nation makes it clear that ancient America was home to significant urban centers, connected by trade. What is often not understood is that many mound builder centers featured traditional houses that surrounded the ceremonial mounds and that most of the major sites had roads, gates, and walls surrounding them. In addition, evidence of sewage systems and canals has been detected at various sites across the country. In some cases the towns were also manufacturing centers and show signs of high trade and commerce of great sophistication.

THE POVERTY POINT
INDUSTRIAL METROPOLIS

Although the Cahokia mound complex near St. Louis is considered the major mound site on the Mississippi River, the Poverty Point earthworks in Louisiana is the most ancient temple site and trading center on the Mississippi River. As the vast extent of this site has been uncovered, its primacy as the major trading site of ancient America has gradually gained credence with traditional scholars. Poverty Point is constructed entirely of earthworks. The core of the site measures approximately five hundred acres (two square kilometers), although archaeological investigations have shown that the total occupation area extended for more than three miles (five kilometers) along the river terrace. The monumental construction consists of a group of six concentric, crescent-shaped ridge earthworks, divided by five aisles radiating from the center at the riverbank. The site also has several mounds, both on the outside and inside of the ring earthworks. The name Poverty Point came from the plantation that once surrounded the site. The United States nominated Poverty Point for inclusion on the United Nations Educational, Scientific, and Cultural Organization's (UNESCO) World Heritage List in January 2013.

Fig. 6.1. Poverty Point

Most of the artifacts found at Poverty Point are small baked shapes made of loess. They are usually shaped like balls, bicones, or ropes, all of which have been described as Poverty Point objects, or PPOs. Archaeologists have long debated their uses and have concluded that the fired-earth objects were used in cooking. When placed in earth ovens, the objects were shown to hold heat. An alternate way of heating up food before pottery was to stone boil. The soil of the lower Mississippi Valley at Poverty Point does not contain proper pebbles, so the manufacture of artificial stones was necessary.

In recent years, the theory that these anomalous clay balls, fire pits, and other PPOs were used for cooking has come under intense debate, and more recent discoveries linking this site to the copper-producing region of the Great Lakes has led some scholars to posit that what was really going on at Poverty Point was actually the refining of copper for trade goods, the theory being that raw copper was brought down from Michigan during the summer months and then refined for manufacture and trade during the winter in the warmer climate of Louisiana.

LOST CITY IN ONTARIO

A report from 1871 notes that a lost city was found on a farm in Dunnville, Ontario, in association with two tons of charcoal and various implements that indicated the site of an ancient forge.

GIANT SKULLS WITH PERFECT TEETH

DAILY TELEGRAPH, TORONTO, ONTARIO, AUGUST 23, 1871

Dunnville, Ontario: There is not the slightest doubt that the remains of a lost city are on this farm. At various times within the past years, the remains of mud houses with their chimneys had been found and there are dozens of pits of a similar kind to that just unearthed, though much smaller, in the place which has been discovered before, though the fact has not been made public hitherto. The remains of a blacksmith's shop, containing two tons of charcoal and various implements, were turned up a few months ago.

The farm, which consists of 150

acres, has been cultivated for nearly a century and was covered with a thick growth of pine, so that it must have been ages ago since the remains were deposited there. The skulls of the skeletons are of an enormous size and all manner of shapes, about half as large again as are now to be seen. The teeth in most of them are still in an almost perfect state of preservation, though they soon fall out when exposed to the air.

It is supposed that there is gold or silver in large quantities to be found in the premises, as mineral rods have invariably, when tested, pointed to a certain spot and a few yards from where the last batch of skeletons was found directly under the apple tree. Some large shells, supposed to have been used for holding water, which were also found in the pit, were almost petrified. There is no doubt that if there is a scheme of exploration carried on thoroughly, the result would be highly interesting. A good deal of excitement exists in the neighborhood, and many visitors call at the farm daily.

The skulls and bones of the giants are fast disappearing, being taken away by curiosity hunters. It is the intention of Mr. Fredinburg to cover the pit up very soon. The pit is ghastly in the extreme. The farm is skirted on the north by the Grand River. The pit is close to the banks, but marks are there to show where the gold or silver treasure is supposed to be under. From the appearance of the skulls, it would seem that their possessors died a violent death, as many of them were broken and dented.

The axes are shaped like tomahawks, small, but keen, instruments. The beads are all of stone and of all sizes and shapes. The pipes are not unlike in shape the cutty pipe, and several of them are engraved with dogs' heads. They have not lost their virtue for smoking. Some people profess to believe that the locality of the Fredinburg farm was formerly an Indian burial place, but the enormous stature of the skeletons and the fact that pine trees of centuries growth covered the spot go far to disprove this idea.

OHIO ESTIMATED TO HAVE TEN THOUSAND MOUNDS

NEW YORK TRIBUNE, 1874

The first settlers of the Ohio and Mississippi Valleys found various forms of earthworks in the solitudes of the wilderness overgrown with dense forests. It is said that Ohio alone has 10,000 of these in the form of mounds of various sizes, and 1,500 enclosures are scattered through the state.

They are found in Illinois, Wisconsin,

and other Western States, and in the Gulf States, varying in size. Some are small hillocks two or three feet high, while others assume almost pyramidal magnitude, like the mound in Cahokia, Ill., which has a base of more than five acres in area and a height of ninety feet.

One of the most elaborate of all these works is located in Newark, Ohio. It is labyrinthine in structure, containing some fifteen miles of embankment, and after years of investigation archaeologists can do no more than surmise as to what its uses were.

Clearly it cannot have been built for architectural purposes, for the enclosures of which it principally consists have the ditches on the inside of the embankment, while the outside presents no visible obstacle to an invading army.

100-FOOT GATEWAY

One of the largest of the enclosures is known as "Old Fort" and stands one and a half miles southwest of the city of Newark. It consists of a circular embankment more than a mile in circumference, entirely unbroken except on the side toward the city, where a mammoth gateway of a hundred feet [in width] was constructed by the builders. On each side of this passage, the ends of the embankment projected a little from the center of the enclosure, and rose to a height of twenty-five feet, while the general height is about eighteen. Upon this

embankment and within the ditch on the inside, the trees are as large as those upon the undisturbed portion of the ground around and within the fort. The citizen still lives in Newark who cut an oak tree upon this bank sixty years ago which measured 650 rings of annual growth.

PARALLEL MOUNDS LEAD TO OCTAGONAL CENTRAL SQUARE

From this mammoth gateway, two parallel lines of earth, a few rods apart, lead to a rectangular enclosure over half a mile to the Northeast, which has an area of about twenty acres; beyond which, nearer the city, are still other works, traces of which are obliterated.

From this network near the city, two sets of parallel walls run west more than two miles, move to another enclosure in the form of an octagon, containing about fifty acres, to the southwest of which, and almost adjoining it, is another circle about equal in size to "the Old Fort." Both of these are situated on a range of hills.

25-FOOT STONE WATCHTOWER

The ploughshare has performed its work of demolition to some extent upon the walls upon some of these latter enclosures with the exception of one point on the circular embankment. This consists of earth and stone somewhat irregularly built to a height of twenty-five feet, and, as it lies in the extreme southwest of the whole system of works, it is thought by some that this was the watchtower or signal station on the west.

ONE THOUSAND YEARS OF FOREST GROWTH COVER THE SITE

When, by whom, and for what purpose these mammoth works were built, are puzzles which have always baffled the skill of archaeologists. It is evident they were built long ages ago, for, where the timber has not been removed by civilized man, as in the case of the "Old Fort," dense forests covered the works, which must have required one thousand years to grow where they now stand. It is not altogether unreasonable to suppose that generation after generation of forests has grown and decayed on this soil since it was built by the dusky savages into the form we now find it.

THE WHEATFIELD MOUND OF PENNSYLVANIA, FIRST DESCRIBED IN 1806

An ancient mound in West Wheatfield Township, a short distance north of Robinson, Pennsylvania, was known to the earliest settlers as Fort Hill. Earlier digs at the Fort Hill site uncovered textiles of a finely woven nature that did not match those of the local Indians, as well as a number of carved and hollowed stone instruments whose use was unknown at the time they were dug up. The earliest published description is from 1806.

Wheatfield Town History, 1806

In Wheatfield Township there is a remarkable mound from which several antiques have been dug, consisting of a sort of stone serpent, five inches in diameter; part of the entablature of a column, both rudely carved, in form of diamond and leaves; an earthen urn with ashes, and many others of which we have no account. It was thought that it was the ruins of an ancient Indian Temple.

Arm's history states that the mound described was on the inside of "Fort Hill" and that there were found at an early date pottery fragments of much finer texture than that made by the historic Indians; also stones both large and small, of peculiar shapes, carved and hollowed.

Fig. 6.2. Temple mounds enclosed in a circle,
illustration from *Ancient Monuments of the Mississippi Valley*
by Ephraim Squier and Edwin Davis

CIRCULAR VILLAGES
AMID THE TREES

Before the encroachment of modern civilization, the area of western Pennsylvania leading all the way into Indiana was described as a vast sea of trees and high grass that was teaming with wild life and ample plants and herbs for a wide variety of uses. The following description of a circle mound population of two hundred people was first recounted in a court in 1731.

An official report from Jonas Davenport and James LeTort to the Pennsylvania Provisional Council stated that there were three villages along Conemaugh Creek, composed of approximately forty-five families, with a population of around two hundred people. Typical of these kinds of villages, all three were contained within their own earthen rings. Jonas Davenport and James LeTort, two of the very earliest Europeans to trade with the Indians in Western Pennsylvania, reported in an affidavit before the Pennsylvania Provisional Council, October 29, 1731, that "on Conemaugh Creek there were three Shawanese towns" having 45 families and 200 men. Their Chief was Okowala (also Okowelah or Ocowellos) who was suspected of being a "favourer of ye French interest."

In its original wilderness condition at the beginning of historic times, Western Pennsylvania was covered by a vast sea of trees. Many travelers wrote of the view from one another of the mountain ridges as a sea of treetops or the waves of the sea. Here and there were small natural areas of shrubs and high grass. The area west of Indiana, according to the earliest pioneers, was one of these and so was a portion of the southeastern area of Indiana County known as "The Wheatfields."

In the northeastern part of the county were huge white pines, 200 feet or more high along with many hemlocks. In some places the shade of the tall trees was so dense that sunlight seldom ever penetrated. One could walk fairly easily through such mighty forests, but the oppressive silence and the sunless gloom caused many travelers to dread them, and they wrote of them as "Shades of Death."

The three ancient towns are thought to have been Conemaugh Old Town (now Johnstown), Black Legs Town, and Keekenepaulin's Town south of the Conemaugh near Loyalhanna Creek.

Davenport and LeTort also mentioned that the Delawares along the Conemaugh numbered 20 families, and 60 men; their Chiefs being Captain Hill, or "Alaymacapy" and "Kykenhammo." Also named as living in the area was "Sypous, a Dingoe." There seems to have been an Indian town north of New Florence. The Robert Hinkson tract of 301 acres was described as "the old town . . . situate on the north side of Conemaugh opposite Squirrel Hill (the name of the Indian town at New Florence). The Joseph Culbertson Warrantee Survey (B 23-22) indicates an 'Old Indian Town' north of the Conemaugh."

Fig. 6.3. A carving of an otter. Illustration from
Ancient Monuments of the Mississippi Valley
by Ephraim Squier and Edwin Davis

In shape the village was roughly circular consisting of two parallel stockades, the outer one 450 feet in diameter and the inner 430 feet. This fact was ascertained by the finding of rows of "post molds," each mold easily identifiable because of the darker soil in it as contrasted with the lighter surrounding subsoil. There was a plaza area in the center of the village. Refuse pits filled with debris were here and there.

The Indian huts were arranged in a rough circle just within the stockade, and, as shown by the post molds, were from 18 to 20 feet in diameter, having a very narrow entrance less than two feet wide. Inside was a fire pit. Attached to or very near each hut, was a bark-covered, pear-shaped food storage pit. It is believed that tender young saplings were placed in each post hole, arched toward the center, tied at the top, and the whole covered by bark. The staple food seems to have been maize, probably grown in small plots outside the village. Other common foods were fish and mussels, and the meat of animals, particularly deer and elk.

The streams were then clean and sparkling, and fish were abundant. In the smaller creeks were speckled trout; in the larger ones yellow and black bass, white perch, buffalo fish, and mullets. In the rivers were pike, sturgeon, and salmon. Some specimens were as much as four feet long and 35 pounds. Other animals have been noted in connection with the archaeological excavations at the site of the late Prehistoric Indian village near Blairsville.

Other animals known to have been here were gray and black squirrels. The number of panthers is thought to have been rather few. Even more scarced were the wood buffalos, larger than their Western kin (nearly a ton in weight), having no hump and being more nearly black in color, with shorter hair and large hind quarters. The extensive and lucrative fur trade caused the beaver to disappear from the local area.

THE GIANTS CLEARED THE FOREST

The claims of the local Indians of Pennsylvania that they did not clear the wide swaths of forest in the area echo the claims of other Indian tribes across the United States, who also claim no part in the construction of the ancient earthworks found in their tribal domains. The local Indians' claim that giants were responsible for the clearing of forestland and construction of huge earthworks is echoed throughout the United States by widely separated, unrelated Indian tribes.

EXTRA GIANTS: FOUND ON THE NEW YORK–
PENNSYLVANIA STATE LINE

PHILADELPHIA TIMES, JUNE 27, 1885

"Why this man was ten or twelve feet high. Thunder and lightning!" exclaimed Mr. Porter in astonishment. The first speaker, who has won local distinction as a scientist, reiterated his assertion. J. H. Porter has a farm near Northeast, not many miles from where the Lake Shore Railroad crosses the New York state boundary line. Early this week some workmen in Mr. Porter's employ came upon the entrance to a cave and on entering it found heaps of human bones within. Many skeletons were complete and specimens of the find were brought out and exhibited to the naturalists and archaeologists of the neighborhood. They informed the wondering bystanders that the remains were unmistakably those of giants. The entire village of Northeast was aroused by the discovery and today hundreds of people from this city took advantage of their holiday to visit the scene. . . . So far about 150 giant skeletons of powerful proportions have been exhumed and indications point to a second cave eastward, which may probably contain as many more. Scientists who have exhumed skeletons and made careful measurements of the bones say that they are the remains of a race of gigantic creatures, compared with which our tallest men would appear pygmies.

History of Crawford County Pennsylvania, 1850

When first visited by the whites, in the valley of French Creek were old meadows, destitute of trees and covered by long wild grass and herbage resembling the prairies. By whom these lands were originally cleared will probably forever remain a matter of uncertainty. The Indians alleged that the work had not been done by them. A tradition among them attributed it to a larger and more powerful race of inhabitants who had pre-occupied the country.

NUMEROUS MOUNDS AND INDIAN RELICS TO BE FOUND ALONG THE CHEAT RIVER ABOUT HORSE SHOE BEND IN TUCKER COUNTY

By Hugh Maxwell

RALEIGH HERALD, OCTOBER 4, 1906

The center of the prehistoric Indian settlement, which evidently contained a large population, was on a prime piece of bottom land on the Cheat River, in a bend of the stream enclosing one thousand acres or more. It lies in Tucker County, two miles above the village of St. George, and has always been known as Horse Shoe Bend. The tract contained two towns, the sites of which may still be distinguished by the rank vegetation, which flourishes in a soil made fertile by the accumulation of bones and other camp life.

The town sites are about a mile apart. The last inhabitant left them as much as 250 years ago, and perhaps much longer ago, if the evidence handed from the first settlers is reliable, and there is no occasion to doubt it.

The lower town site lies opposite Sycamore Island, on the southwest bank of the Cheat River, a third of a mile below the mouth of Horse Shoe Run, and about an equal distance from the grave which I opened last Wednesday, mentioned in a former article. The town site is on the farm of Joshua Parsons.

The river is rapidly encroaching on its banks at that place, and has been doing so for more than 100 years. It has washed away the greater part of the land that the village stood on and will wash it all away in the next few years. The soil at that place is 14 feet deep.

A STOREHOUSE OF INDIAN RELICS

This region along the Cheat River, above and below the Horse Shoe, is a storehouse of Indian archaeology. *It is covered with sites of camps and towns with graves and mounds.* Many relics have been picked up in the past, but few were saved. If all had been preserved *they would tell a tale of the dim past that would astound the people of today.*

TWO ACRES OF RECTANGULAR STONES

The site of the principal village on the Cheat River, near this place, had a particular nature nearly unknown elsewhere in this region.

When Captain James Parsons in 1769 made his homestead on the river bottom, which is enclosed in the great bend of Cheat River, and is called the Horse Shoe, he found a plot of ground, rudely quadrilateral in shape, and covering about two acres, so stony as to be unfit for cultivation. He therefore

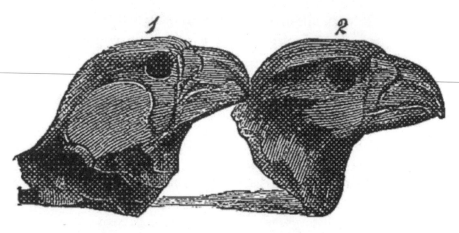

Fig. 6.4. A carving of an eagle. Illustration from
Ancient Monuments of the Mississippi Valley
by Ephraim Squier and Edwin Davis

left it un-cleared until all of his other hundreds of acres had been redeemed from the forest.

PARALLEL ROWS OF STONES FOUND

When the land became valuable, he cut off the trees and began hauling away the stone. He then discovered that all of the stones were on the surface of the ground, while a deep soil lay beneath. What surprised him more was to find that the stones had been laid in parallel rows, and so regularly that he was convinced that it was the work of men.

The stones were worn river rocks, carried no doubt, from the stream which flowed immediately by the spot. The village had been long deserted, even in 1769, when first seen by white men. That was proved by the fact that large trees had grown up through the stone pavement, pushing the rocks aside with their trunks. There were sycamore trees six feet in diameter, and walnuts and oaks nearly as large. Their ages could not have been less than 300 and may have been 500 years. It is not probable that the trees would grow there while the Indians occupied the place. It is, therefore, not unreasonable to presume that we have here the remains of a town antedating the discovery of America by Columbus.

GIANT TOWN

The first recorded settlement on that river bottom [Cheat River] was made in 1769, and there was built the fort in which the settlers found shelter during the Denmore War of 1774. The old settlers called the place where the Indian village stood "The Giant Town." This was not because the town was larger, but from the fact that the skeleton of a very large man was unearthed at that place about 180 years ago. The fact is as well authenticated as any event can be that depends to some extent on tradition.

In the year 1774, or about that time, James Parsons was walking along the river bank at that place (the Cheat River) and discovered the bones protruding from a bank where a recent flood had washed away the soil. He pulled out the thigh bones of a man, and adjusting the bones to his own leg for comparison he found that the bone was seven inches longer than his own. He was six feet tall.

He pulled out other bones until he had the greater part of a skeleton from the knees upward. . . . The lower jaw bone fitted over the outside of his face. He made a partial reconstruction of the skeleton and was sure the man when alive was eight feet tall.

TRADITIONS OF GIANTS

Traditions of giants should be accepted with about the same caution as we accept the measurements of Goliath, who was said to be 11 feet tall. There is no special reason to dispute the truth of Captain James Parsons' statement concerning the bones. He was a man well known in his day, and was reliable. He was frequently spoken of in the frontier histories.

PLEA TO SAVE THE MOUNDS

On the occasion of my present visit I was disappointed and disgusted to find that the owner of the land had attacked it with a plow and scraper, and had leveled it (the mound). He wanted the space for agricultural purposes. A few sheaves of oats were worth more to him than a mound dating back to a prehistoric people. Such is the sentiment that one all too often finds.

The past has no value in comparison with a crop of oats or a bushel of corn. Such people would break up the ruins of Baalbek for material to macadamize a road.

The utter want of appreciation of things that cannot be eaten, worn, or sold, was illustrated in the case of a large earthen mound on the second terrace above both of the village sites, and nearly between them. I had expected to ask the permission of the owner of the land to open it; but I heard it had been opened some months ago. When I asked what was found in it, the answer was: "Not a cent; only some trash."

The people who dug it open expected to find money in it, and failing to find that, they saw no earthly value in the "trash" that was turned up by the shovels. Yet who knows what may have been the bits of weapon wampum, or of stone, bone, or copper jewelry, which would have thrown light on the history and habits of the people who lived and died here at a time of which no syllable has been recorded.

In 1893, the Bureau of American Ethnology at the Smithsonian reported finding a very ancient Indian village near Poplar Bluff, Missouri. According to the article below, over one hundred skeletons were recovered, including those of a chief who measured seven feet, eight inches tall.

MISSOURI MOUNDS ARE A GOLDMINE

ASSOCIATED PRESS, OCTOBER 5, 1964

The farm, long known to be an archaeological gold mine, is identified in archaeological circles as "Koehler's Fort." Diggings were made in 1893, by the Bureau of American Ethnology (of the Smithsonian). Findings established that the Koehler farm was the site of a village populated by 500 Indians of the Middle Mississippian culture. These aborigines pre-dated the tribal American Indian.

THEY LIVED IN HOUSES

They lived in daub and wattle houses under a system of organized government. Identified with the mound builders of Cahokia, Illinois, whose culture extends as far southeast as Georgia, their culture was a peak in civilization.

HOW THE PREHISTORIC RESIDENTS OF IOWA LIVED

IOWA CITY PRESS CITIZEN, JANUARY 13, 1939

Professor Charles R. Keyes of Cornell and director of the Iowa Archaeological Survey, in association with the WPA: "The prehistoric residents of the Miles County (Iowa) district, lived in groups of perhaps 35 in houses averaging 30 feet square. Excavation of about 12 houses in the vicinity revealed large holes in the floor, evidently used as storage or refuse pits," Keyes explained, "while smaller cavities remained where posts supporting the roof had originally been situated."

SKELETON AND HOUSE FOUND AMONG THE SOYBEANS

Fields of lush soybeans and mature cotton now grow on the Walter Koehler farm near Naylor, Missouri, where an Indian village was a ceremonial center for primitive tribes nearly one thousand years ago.

EVIDENCE OF AN ANCIENT HOUSE

ASSOCIATED PRESS, OCTOBER 5, 1964

Poplar Bluff: The skeleton of a woman found with a pottery water bottle gives testimony to the archaeological treasure only inches beneath the soil on the Butler County farm. Jim Price, a sophomore student of archaeology at the University of Missouri, made the find September 5th. The skeleton is that of a woman 35 to 40 years old and dates back to AD 800 to AD 1000. The burial pottery is made of clay and ground river mussel from the Little Black and Black Rivers.

Also discovered by Price, who holds the title of director of the archaeological survey of Missouri for the Missouri Archaeological Survey, was evidence of a house 15 by 20 feet. To the trained eye, the charcoal-streaked soil told that the house had been burned. The place where posts once set in a trench was evident and a broken pot lay on what was once the floor of the house, some three feet from the skeleton.

100 SKELETONS DUG UP— AVERAGED FIVE FEET, SIX INCHES; TALLEST SEVEN FEET, EIGHT INCHES

Koehler has also dug up an estimated 100 skeletons in the shallow graves scattered over his fields. He has been interested chiefly in noting the height of the remains, which he says averaged 5 feet 6 inches. One skeleton measured 7 feet 8 inches.

TEMPLE TO THE SUN

These Indians worshipped the sun as evidenced by the large temple mound clearly visible in the Koehler soybean field. The temple mound is 75 feet in diameter and has been 30 feet high in Koehler's memory.

Three other ancillary mounds, located west of the temple mound, contained houses for the priests. Outlying these mounds was the village area, which includes the Koehlers' chicken yard, where the skeleton was discovered. The site for the village was probably selected for its nearness to water and its high ground.

AN UNUSUAL SQUARE MOUND IS DESCRIBED

On the Big Harpeth River at Dog Creek in Tennessee, a major square-bottomed mound has been described in relation to a much larger complex. The mound is forty-seven feet by forty-seven feet at the base, with a height of twenty-five feet. Two other square-bottomed mounds were also noted in the complex, which are from five to ten feet in height. In all, there are thirteen mounds in this complex.

The Natural and Aboriginal History of Tennessee, 1823

By Dr. John Haywood

On the Big Harpeth river, in a bend of the river below the road, which crosses near the mouth of Dog creek, from Nashville to Charlotte, is a square mound, 47 by 47 at the base, twenty-five feet high, and two others in a row with it, of inferior size, from 5 to 10 feet high. At some distance from them and near to the eastern extremity of the bend, are three others in a parallel row, with a space like a public square between the rows.

Near these mounds are other small ones, to the amount of 13 in all. All around the bend except at the place of entrance is a wall on the margin of the river. The mounds are upon the area enclosed by the wall. Within them also and not far from the entrance is a reservoir of water. Its mouth is square, and it is 15 feet over. The water in it is nearly even with the surface.

There are besides the entrance, two gateways; from thence to the river is the distance of 40 yards. The wall is upon the second bank. On the top of the large mound an image was found some years ago, eighteen inches long from the feet to the head. Soapstone was the material of which it was composed. The arms were slipped into the socket and there retained with hooks. They hung downwards when not lifted up. The trees standing upon the mounds were very old. A poplar stood on one of them, 5 or 6 feet through. A large road leads through the entrance, which is at the point where the river turns off to make the bend, and after making it, returns to an opposite point near it.

Into the river at this latter point runs a branch from near the first mentioned point and the branch is wide enough for a road; and from this point to the branches, is a deep gulley, which is filled up as wide as the road, until made level with the adjoining land on the other side. Over this filled-up interval, passes a road from the great mound between the point where is a high bluff, and the branch in a southwardly direction. It is at this time two or three feet deep and six or seven wide. It crosses the river in less than half a mile.

On the north side of the bend and wall is a gateway and also on the south. On parts of this wall, at the distance of about 40 yards apart, are projected banks like redoubts on which persons might have stood.

THE ANCIENT ROADS LINE UP WITH THE GATEWAYS

Attesting to the primacy of this particular mound complex in ancient history is the fact that the two roads discovered leading to the site pass through the two main gates built into one of the walls and then pass into the main square complex. In addition, numerous walls enclose the mound complex and also line parts of the road leading to the complex.

On the east side of the first large mound, is a way to ascend it, wide enough for two men to walk abreast, and sloping to the top. Steps were no doubt once there, though not now visible. From the gateway on the south side of the bend and wall are the traces of two old roads, one leading to the other works within a mile of these, in another end of the creek, and over an intervening bottom of rich land, made by the winding of the river between the two bends and, in fact, forming a middle or intermediate bend on the opposite side; so that there are three bends, the two outer and the middle.

The other road leading to the mouth of Dog creek and traceable for several miles beyond it; the first of these roads passes from the gateway into the public square, between the mounds to the other gateway on the north side.

Higher up the river, and within a mile of the above-described enclosures, and above the road leading by the mouth of Dog creek to

Charlotte, is another bend of the river, so formed as to leave a bend from on the north or opposite side of the river, and between the two bends on the south side. In the other bend on the south, above the road, is a square wall, abutting on the south side above the river, on a high bluff of the river, upon the bank of which a wall is also built, as it is on the three other sides.

On the outside of it is a ditch, five or six feet wide, with large trees on it. In the eastern wall are two gateways. About the center of this enclosure is a mound of the same dimensions as was the large mound in the other enclosure.

On the east, north, and south sides of it is a raised platform, 10 or 12 feet high on the east side, but less as the hill ascends on the north and south. The top is level; from it to the top of the mound itself, is 10 or 12 feet or more. The top of this mound was ascended to from the west, where the height is a lot more than 5 or 6 feet.

The platform is 60 feet over. Two large gateways are in the eastern wall. From the most southwardly of them, a road leads to the river and across it in a northwardly direction, near the mouth of Dog creek. And from the most northwardly gateway, a road leads to the river and across it, in a northwardly direction, or a little east of north. It then passes over the intermediate bend, or bottom, on the east side of the river and into the enclosures first described.

The bottom on which the second enclosures stand, and also the bottom on the opposite side of the river below this, and that on which stand the enclosures first described, is full of pine knots, which are ploughed up daily. There are no piney woods nearer to these bottoms than 5 or 6 miles. These knots are the most abundant in the intermediate bottom, and but few in the first described enclosures. Mr. Spears supposes, that these are the remains of old field pines, grown to full size after the desertion of cultivation, and the total exhaustion of the lands by long continued tillage. That after allowing their full growth, and after the soil had been restored by long rest, the pines fell down and were succeeded by the growth we now see standing up on the bottom; large oaks, poplars, and sugar trees. One large sugar tree stands there with its roots shooting through the upper part of a large decayed pine stump.

SUN-DRIED BRICK USED
IN MISSISSIPPI

NATIONAL SUNDAY NEWS, SUPPLEMENT, 1905

These ancient remains are prob-ably more numerous in the state of Mississippi, though perhaps smaller, than anywhere else. But here, in some cases, sun-dried brick was used in the embankments and there is a mound sixty feet long, 400 feet wide, and forty feet high.

THE CADDO

When the Spanish conquistador Hernando de Soto led an expedi-tion into what is now the southeastern United States in the 1540s, he encountered a Native American group known as the Caddo. Composed of many tribes, the Caddo were organized into three confederacies, the Hasinai, Kadohadacho, and Natchitoches, which were all linked by similar languages.

At the time of de Soto's visit, the Caddo controlled a large terri-tory. It included what is now eastern Oklahoma, western Arkansas, northeastern Texas, and northwestern Louisiana. Archaeologists have thought that the Caddo and related peoples had been living in the region for centuries and that they had their own local variant of Mississippian culture.

Recent excavations have revealed within that region more cultural diversity than scholars had expected. The sites along the Arkansas River, in particular, seem to have their own distinctive characteristics. Scholars still classify the Mississippian sites found in the entire Caddo area, including Spiro Mound, as Caddoan Mississipian.

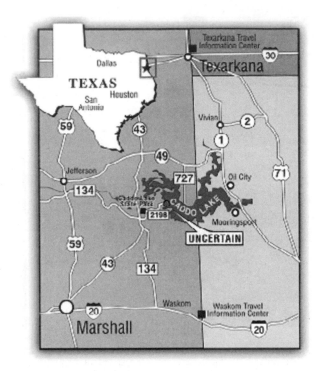

Fig. 6.5. Location of the Caddoan Mississippian culture

CADDO MOUNDS IN ARKANSAS TOURIST ATTRACTION

ARKANSAS TIMES, AUGUST 17, 1975

In 1964, Glen L. Kizzia discovered the site of a Caddo Indian village and burial ground near Murfreesboro: a site that he has given the name Ancient Burial Grounds. The village that Kizzia has unearthed covers about 30 acres in an area where the Little Missouri River once flowed. Located one-and-a-half miles west of Murfreesboro off Arkansas Highway 27, the Indian burials have become popular with tourists who visit the city in search of diamonds at the nearby Crater of Diamonds State Park and in pursuit of outdoor recreation on the cool waters of Lake Greeson.

Early European explorers, who visited the land that was to become Arkansas, reported the Caddo to be an advanced civilization. These Indians were expert in many things, including tanning hides, making pottery, and farming. Kizzia believes that early Caddo pottery is among the finest Indian pottery he has encountered.

An example of a "Temple Mound" is to be found at the Ancient Burial Grounds. The mound has not been excavated, except to show a good cross-section of the various stages that have occurred. The most unusual burial at the site is one, which Kizzia believes to be the largest Caddoan burial on record, probably at least 800 years old. This is a circular burial, measuring two feet deep, by some 15 feet in diameter.

Fig. 6.6. For a thousand years Caddo women made the finest pottery east of the Rockies.

A GIANT RACE: THE INDIAN MOUND CHICKASAWBA

HUMAN SKELETONS EIGHT AND TEN FEET IN HEIGHT—
RELICS OF A FORMER RACE.

EVENING TELEGRAPH, SEPTEMBER 15, 1870

Two miles west of Barfield Point, in Arkansas County, Ark., on the east bank of the lovely stream called Pemiscot river, stands an Indian mound, some twenty-five feet high and about an acre in area at the top. . . . The mound derives its name from Chickasawba, a chief of the Shawnee tribe, who lived, died, and was buried there. This chief was one of the last race of hunters who lived in that beautiful region and who once peopled it quite thickly . . .

Aunt Kitty Williams, who now

resides there, relates that Chickasawba would frequently bring in for sale as much as twenty gallons of pure honey in deerskins bags slung to his back. He was always a friend to the whites, a man of gigantic stature and herculean strength. . . . He was buried at the foot of the mound on which he had lived, by his tribe, most of whom departed for the Nation immediately after performing his funeral rites. . . .

Chickasawba was perfectly honest and the best informed chief of his tribe. . . . A number of years ago, making an excavation into or near the foot of Chickasawba's mound, a portion of a GIGANTIC HUMAN SKELETON was found. The men who were digging, becoming interested, unearthed the entire skeleton and from measurements given us by reliable parties the frame of the man to whom it belonged could not have been less than eight or nine feet in height. Under the skull, which slipped easily over the head of our informant (who, we will here state, is one of our best citizens), was found a peculiarly shaped earthen jar, resembling nothing in the way of Indian pottery, which has before been seen by them. It was exactly the shape of the round-bodied, long necked carafes or water-decanters, a specimen of which may be seen on Gaston's dining table.

The material of which the vase was made was a peculiar kind of clay and the workmanship was very fine. The belly or body of it was orna-mented with figures or hieroglyphs consisting of a correct delineation of human hands, parallel to each other, open, palms outward, and running up and down the vase, the wrists to the base and the fingers toward the neck. . . . Since that time, wherever an excavation has been made in the Chickasawba county in the neighborhood of the mound SIMILAR SKELETONS have been found and under the skull of every one were found similar funeral vases, almost exactly like the one described. There are now in this city several of the vases and portions of the huge skeletons.

One of the editors of the *Appeal* yesterday measured a thigh bone, which is fully three feet long. The thigh and shin bones, together with the bones of the foot, stood up in a proper position in a physician's office in this city, measured five feet in height and show the body to which the leg belonged to have been from nine to ten feet in height. At Beaufort's Landing, near Barfield, in digging a deep ditch, a skeleton was dug up: the leg of which measured between five and six feet in length, and other bones in proportion. In a very few days we hope to be able to lay before our readers accurate measurement and descriptions of the portions of skeletons now in the city and of the artifacts found in the graves. It is not a matter of doubt that these are HUMAN REMAINS, but of a long extinct race.

Fig. 6.7. Illustration of a Haley complicated-incised jar excavated in 1911 by Clarence B. Moore from a grave at the Haley Place, Miller County, Arkansas. (The drawing and watercolor painting was one of the featured color plates in Moore's 1912 report, *Some Aboriginal Sites on Red River*.)

The following article on archaeological finds made in Oklahoma while digging for a new dam opens with an unexpectedly apologetic headline.

DAM DESTROYS EVIDENCE FOR CITY OF 100,000

Ray E. Colton, science writer

DAILY NEWS-RECORD, MIAMI, OKLAHOMA, DECEMBER 4, 1939

While construction of the Grand River Dam in Mayes County will be of vast value to the residents of this area and others, it has already proven a "boon" to archaeological research insofar as finds made in the form of skeleton remains of pre-historic man during excavation work are concerned. During the last week two large burials have been unearthed, one of which contained several dozen decapitated skulls, showing that the early day races of eastern Oklahoma tribes did away with their enemies in a unique manner.

Fig. 6.8. The Great Mortuary: effigy of a man smoking a pipe made of Missouri flint clay (courtesy of Herb Roe).

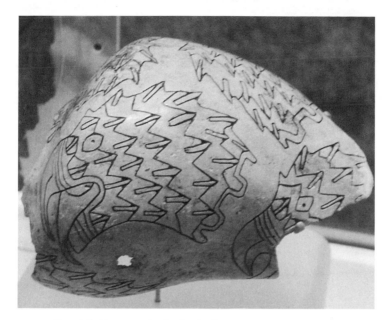

Fig. 6.9. Engraved whelk shell cup with raptor head
(courtesy of Herb Roe)

Fig. 6.10. Craig Mound—also called the Spiro Mound—is the second-largest
mound on the site and the only burial mound. It is located about 1,500 feet
(460 meters) southeast of the plaza (courtesy of Herb Roe).

A cavity created within the mound, about 10 feet (3 m) high and 15 feet (4.6 m) wide, allowed for almost perfect preservation of fragile artifacts made of wood, conch shell, and copper. The conditions in this hollow space were so favorable that objects made of perishable materials such as basketry, woven fabric of vegetal and animal fibers, lace, fur, and feathers were preserved inside it. Such objects have traditionally been created by women in historic tribes. Also found inside were several examples of Mississippian stone statuary made from Missouri flint clay and Mill Creek chert bifaces, all thought to have originally come from the Cahokia site in Illinois.

Fig. 6.11. Copper ear spool (courtesy of Herb Roe)

A DOZEN "ODD" SKULLS;
SEVERAL DOZEN SKELETONS

Centuries before the arrival of white pioneers in what is today the geographical confines of Ottawa, Mayes, and adjoining counties, a strange race, now known to archaeologists as the mound builders, came to establish their governmental seats here.

This was definitely established only a few days ago in the discovery by workmen excavating for the Grand River Dam, near Langley in Mayes County, of two large burials containing several dozen skeletons and a dozen "odd" skulls, ranging from children to adults. An examination of these remains, which appear to be in a fairly excellent state of preservation, by anthropologists from the University of Oklahoma, who are now on the scene, shows that the skeleton remains are unmistakably those of a race of people known as the mound builders.

MOUND BUILDER CAPITAL

The remains of mounds, such as effigy, burial, ceremonial, fortification etc., which have been found throughout northern Mayes and eastern Ottawa counties, and which appear to centralize in this area around Langley, near the Grand River Dam site, give ample proof that this section of eastern Oklahoma evidently was the capital of this vanished race. . . .

SOMETHING TO THINK
ABOUT

Large quantities of arrow-heads, ranging in size from the slender fish-point types, used to hunt small game such as birds, up to the large war-points, ranging up to 10 inches in length have been found during excavation work on the dam. These, together with quantities of pottery and potsherds (potions of pottery) of many designs, which have been found, have given scientists and laymen something to think about as regards the races that inhabited this part of eastern Oklahoma, centuries before the arrival of the white man.

ARCHAEOLOGISTS SHOW
PROOF FOR CITY OF
100,000

Tracing the area as it one-time appeared, and basing theories on the tremendous amount of artifacts found by workmen during digging operations, it is established by anthropologists and archaeologists who are now on the scene, that the "city," if that is what it might have been called, had an area of about 10 square miles, and no doubt supported an estimated population of over 100,000 people.

SEVENTY-FIVE COMPLETE
SKELETONS

The remains of this vanished race consist of about 75 complete skeletons. Two distinct burials were unearthed, one containing dozens of decapitated bodies, while the other contained an equal amount of complete skeletons, which do not appear to have been mutilated.

The skeleton remains do not crumble when exposed to outside air, and appear to have been buried over one thousand years, or more. An estimate of 1,500 years has been given by those who are excavating the remains, part of which will be transferred to the University of Oklahoma at Norman for study and classification.

HEADLESS BURIALS BAFFLE ANTHROPOLOGISTS

This find baffles archaeologists and anthropologists from the University of Oklahoma somewhat, yet it is believed that the mound containing the headless burials is a sacrificial mound, where enemies were buried after their capture during warfare.

The second burial is that of an ordinary burial mound, such as was unearthed near Grove in Delaware County two years ago. Both burials are unmistakably those of mound-builder origin, and are certainly not of Indian origin.

CLIFF DWELLERS

Although the cliff dwellers are generally thought of as a recent tribe, Smithsonian field reports from 1910 on a Puye cliff-dweller excavation describe signs of construction dating back at least five thousand years at some of the kivas that they explored. In a report, Smithsonian correspondent M. J. Brown writes, "It is estimated by the Smithsonian people that 10,000 lived on the face of this one cliff, and that the population of the adjoining cliffs and on the mesas was fully 100,000 people." Brown also comments on the great quantities of Portland cement that were plastered in almost every one of the hundreds of rooms in the settlement.

STAIRWAY TO HEAVEN

Most wonderful of all is the stairway that leads to the top of the cliffs. Here one gets some idea of the ages that these people lived in this spot and the multitude who used this path, for human feet have worn the solid rock to a depth of twelve inches, and when you consider that this outside rock is not of the soft composition of the caves, then you have some conception of the age and the density of the population.

To give a further idea of just how distorted our view of the extent and size of the cliff dweller population is, here is a report from the *Oakland Tribune* of 1926 about the discovery of a six-mile-long city in Nevada.

ARIZONA GIANTS

EL PASO HERALD, APRIL 19, 1915

"The skeleton of a giant fully eight feet tall has been found near Silver City," said H. E. Davis. The thigh bone of this ancient inhabitant of the southwest measures two inches more than the ordinary man and must have been a giant of great strength. The jaw bone is large enough to fit over the jaw of an ordinary man. A peculiarity of the forehead is that it recedes from the eyes like that of an ape. The similarity is still further found in the sharp bones under the eyes. The skeleton was found encased in baked mud, indicating that encasing the corpse in mud and baking it was the mode of embalming. Near the skeleton was found a stone weighing 12 pounds, which, judging from its shape, must have been a club. The wooden handle has rotted away but there are marks on the stone that indicate that it had been bound to a

wooden handle with tongs. It is rather peculiar that less than 30 miles from where this skeleton was found and located on the Gile river are the former houses of a tribe of small cliff dwellers. The existence of these two races so near together forms an interesting topic. "These 'gorilla-like' or 'monkey-like' skulls have been reported in many states several times by Smithsonian personnel. Professor Thomas Wilson, the curator of Prehistoric Anthropology for the Smithsonian, said the following about the find of an eight-foot-one-inch giant skeleton in Miamisburg, Ohio, in 1897. "The authenticity of the skull is beyond doubt. Its antiquity is unquestionably great. To my own personal knowledge several such crania were discovered in the Hopewell group of mounds in Ohio, exhibiting monkey-like traits."

IN NEVADA, A SIX-MILE-LONG STRAIGHT CITY

OAKLAND TRIBUNE, JANUARY 3, 1926

Out in Nevada Governor James Graves Scrugham and archaeologist M. C. Harrington announced the discovery of Pueblo cities that pre-date the birth of Christ. The discoveries gained national attention a year ago when

Harrington first told of the finds.

"The ruins," Harrington said, "run in a continuous line of six miles and are about a half mile wide. The outlines of the houses of stone and adobe and the stone pavement are clearly seen." Everywhere were myriads of pieces of broken pottery. Later Harrington found evidence convincing him that the city had existed 2000 years and was occupied for at least 1000 years. Then followed discoveries of tombs decorated with turquoises and pearl shells cut into small beads.

"These ancient Nevadans," said Mr. Harrington, "probably were the ancestors of our modern Pueblo tribes. . . ."

ANCIENT HIEROGLYPHS FOUND

In New Mexico and Arizona have been found communal dwellings from three to five stories high, in which may have lived as many as 1200 Indians. They are believed to be between 2000 and 5000 years old. Wide interest was aroused among scientists by the reports that certain hieroglyphs found on the walls resemble those of the Chinese.

NO TRADITION OF CLIFF DWELLERS

By M. J. Brown

FIELD REPORT ON THE SMITHSONIAN'S 1910 PUYE CLIFF DWELLER EXCAVATION

"The Pueblos have no traditions, legends, or anything regarding these cliff people."

Smithsonian
representative, 1910

It is estimated by the Smithsonian people that 10,000 people lived on the face of this one cliff, and that the population of the adjoining cliffs and on the mesas was fully 100,000 people.

SMITHSONIAN EXCAVATES 250 SKELETONS OF THE CLIFF DWELLERS

And just beyond this ruin is a burial ground where during the past summer, the Smithsonian people excavated 250 skeletons and all kinds

of trinkets and pottery buried with them. The graveyard is but partially excavated and hundreds of other skeletons yet sleep there. From one of the caves in the cliff, Mr. Hoag showed me some leg bones.

EXPLORING THE KIVA

About in the center of this long cliff is a stone stairway with a kiva at the foot. And I must tell you of the kiva before we go up. The best description of it would be of a well perhaps ten feet across and twenty feet deep.

The roof has long since washed away, and the hole is partially filled up, but the Smithsonian people have excavated it and placed therein a ladder. We descended and there found the only fireplace, or rather the ruins of one, that is to be found in the whole city. The floor is cement, and in front of the fireplace are two rows of holes in the floor, six on a side, and the walls are full of niches, each seeming to conform with similar places on the opposite side.

This kiva is supposed to have been the secret room where the religious and ceremonial rites of these strange people were performed and a room where but few of the cliff dwellers feet ever trod.

THE PORTLAND CEMENT PUZZLE

Where the great quantities of cement came from that plastered almost every room of these hundreds is another for the puzzle department to go to. Nothing has ever been found here of the sticky nature, yet these aborigines must have had a Portland source from somewhere, for it was used in abundance.

In but one room of the hundreds, is there any color. But in one we found the interior painted red, faded through the many generations, but plainly, red, and the picture of some unintelligible man or animal over this door and had first been carved and then painted.

We climbed the cliff, putting our patent leathers in the deep, worn footpath, and our gloved hands in the hand-holds, and gained the top. What a sight!

There in the bright sunshine lay the ruins of a great communal dwelling, one building that once sheltered 1,200 people, a human beehive of the days before history. Ages ago this house fell into ruins, but it has been carefully excavated and cleared away, and the first story and its walls now stand as they did when built.

The great building reminds one of our modern stockyards—an enclosure cut up into little rooms—each room about five by ten feet—and each communicating with the other by a door about three feet high by eighteen inches wide—just one great beehive with no outdoor entrances.

From the quantity of ruins it is pretty thoroughly established that this building was at least three stories high, one great enclosure around a court, and with one main entrance, or street, which is clearly defined. In the center, or court, there are many handsome stone relics, grinding stones, skinning stones, pieces of pottery, and many whose use we can only guess at, but plainly fashioned for some purpose.

CARVING OF A HEART IS FOUND

Over the doors of many of the homes on the cliff's face, are rock pictures—whose meaning I would give much to read—and of some I am sure there are meanings. The sun symbol is prominent, and they were in no doubt sun worshippers, while there are many crude drawings representing men, beasts, and birds. One carving particularly interested me, as representing a heart.

ANCIENT CLIFF DWELLERS HAD DIFFERENT SKULLS THAN THE INDIANS

"There is too great a difference in the heads of the Cliff Dwellers skeletons and the present Indians to allow any connection or relationship," stated Hewitt of the Smithsonian expedition. "The Pueblos have no traditions, legends, or anything regarding these cliff people. Old mountaineers will tell you that a plague exterminated them; others that volcanic fumes stifled them at one stifle; and so on, but as stated, there is absolutely nothing to bear out any change, but that of a slow order of extermination."

NEW MEXICO DISCOVERY: 12-FOOT GIANT FOUND

NEW YORK TIMES, FEBRUARY 11, 1902

Owing to the discovery of the remains of a race of giants in Guadalupe, New Mexico, antiquarians and archaeologists are preparing an expedition further to explore that region. This determination is based on the excitement that exists among the people of a scope of country near Mesa Rica, about 200 miles southeast of Las Vegas, where an old burial ground has been discovered that has yielded skeletons of enormous size. Luciana Quintana, on whose ranch the ancient burial plot is located, discovered two stones that bore curious inscriptions and beneath these were found in shallow excavations the bones of a frame that could not have been less than 12 feet in length. The men who opened the grave say the forearm was 4 feet long and that in a well-preserved jaw the lower teeth ranged from the size of a hickory nut to that of the largest walnut in size. The chest of the being is reported as having a circumference of seven feet. Quintana, who has uncovered many other burial places, expresses the opinion that perhaps thousands of skeletons of a race of giants long extinct, will be found. This supposition is based on the traditions handed down from the early Spanish invasion that have detailed knowledge of the existence of a race of giants that inhabited the plains of what now is Eastern New Mexico. Indian legends and carvings also in the same section indicate the existence of such a race.

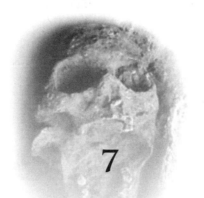

7

A COPPER KINGDOM AND MICA MINES

ISLE ROYALE—THE ROYAL COPPER MOUND CONNECTION

Located in Lake Superior off the northern tip of the Keweenaw Peninsula in northern Michigan, Isle Royale, also known as Royal Island, is one of the most interesting ancient sites in America. Not only is the island literally made out of the highest-grade copper in the entire world, but its name also suggests its royal status in the minds of the ancient giants of the North American copper kingdom. Significantly, a quick look at a modern map of the United States quite clearly shows that the northern border of America was drawn to include this island, showing, again quite clearly, that someone knew of the extreme importance of this innocuous little island.

Because of a freak volcanic event that twisted the copper-bearing bedrock above the water line, thus allowing all the sulfur impurities to burn away in the open air, the copper at Isle Royale is the purest found anywhere in the world. The entire region is scarred by ancient mine pits and trenches up to twenty feet deep. Carbon-dating testing of wood remains found in sockets of copper artifacts indicates that some are at least 5,700 years old, while other open digs around the area have been dated from eight to ten thousand years old.

The most conservative estimates calculate that during a ten-thousand-year period, over five hundred thousand tons of copper were taken from the mines. At the other end of the spectrum, in *Prehistoric Copper Mining in the Lake Superior Region,* published in 1961, Roy Ward Drier and Octave Joseph DuTemple estimated that over 1.5 billion pounds of copper had been mined from the region. Since traditional researchers refuse to analyze European copper for its probable Michigan signature, no one has been able to account for where all this copper went. That it was traded and used extensively across the United States by the mound builders there is no question, but this in no way can account for the magnitude of copper taken out of these unique mines.

Fig. 7.1. Ontonagon boulder of native copper as depicted in Henry Rowe Schoolcraft's 1821 book *Narrative Journal of Travels through the Northwestern Regions of the United States.* Note the relative size of the boulder on the right riverbank versus the men in the canoes. The Ontonagon boulder is actually just three feet, eight inches in its largest dimension and weighs 3,708 pounds. It was initially exhibited in Detroit in 1843 and was eventually acquired by the Smithsonian Institution.

What researchers have determined is a continuous history of mining activity that began in 8000 BCE and then abruptly ended around 1500 BCE, contemporaneous with the volcanic explosion on the Cretan island of Thera (now known as Santorini). Since rock-cut pictures of Cretan trading vessels have been found in the Isle Royale area, this lends credence to the Cretan connection in North America at a very early date. In addition, researchers have also determined that copper mining activity resumed again around 900 CE. This date corresponds perfectly with related evidence of a Viking presence in the area around that same date.

SURFACE EXPLORING COPPER MINERS

In 1863, the Smithsonian published this field report based on Col. Charles Whittlesey's explorations of the copper mines discovered along the Eagle River in the Keweenaw Peninsula. Although the report is mostly observational, it does hint at the magnitude of these mining operations.

ANCIENT COPPER MINING IN THE GREAT LAKES

SMITHSONIAN INSTITUTION, APRIL 1863

Another authority, Colonel Charles Whittlesey, a Civil War veteran and American professional geologist for the government, wrote in 1856 a treatise entitled, "Ancient Mining on the Shores of Lake Superior," based on what he had seen at Eagle River in the Keweenaw copper area. In 1862, Col. Charles Whittlesey drew a map of the position of the ancient copper mine pits for the Smithsonian, and it forms a valuable part of his document on the prehistoric copper miners.

After completing his inspection of the ancient copper mines in the Upper Peninsula on the shores of Lake Superior, Col. Whittlesey reasoned somewhat as follows: an ancient people, of whom history gives no account, extracted copper from the rocks on the Keweenaw Peninsula. They did it in a crude way by means of fire and the use of copper wedges or gads and stone mauls. They had only the simplest mechanical contrivances and penetrated the earth but a short distance. They do not appear to have had any skill with metallurgy or of breaking up large masses of copper. For cutting tools they had chisels and probably axes of pure copper hardened only by beating when cold. They sought chiefly for small masses and lumps of metal and not for large pieces. No sepulture mounds, defenses, domiciles, roads, or canals are known to have been made by them.

No evidence remains for their cultivation of the soil. They made weapons of defense or of the chase such as darts, spears, and daggers of copper. These Old Copper Indians must have been numerous, industrious, and persevering. The amount of work done indicates that they mined the country a long time or the equivalent of 10,000 men over a period of 1,000 years. Col. Charles Whittlesey discovered that the principal prehistoric copper mines in the Keweenaw-Ontonagon area of the Upper Peninsula corresponded to the mining locations of the 1850s. In both the prehistoric and the modern mines three groups of operations appear, one a little below the forks of the Ontonagon River, another at Portage Lake, and the third on the banks of the Eagle River.

These last two sites were located on the Keweenaw Peninsula. It was evident to Whittlesey that centuries ago the old copper miners were only surface explorers, and while the principal mines of the new era followed in the same pattern of location as the ancient, the latter-day miners were able with much better equipment to penetrate the earth to far greater depths.

KNOWLEDGE OF ANNEALING AND EMBOSSING

The ancient North American coppersmiths were the best in the ancient world, as evidenced by the antiquity, quality, and scientific uniqueness of their work. Not only did they know how to anneal, emboss, and engrave copper, but they also produced hardened axes and other instruments whose strength and temper cannot be adequately reproduced to this day. In addition, these ancient coppersmiths produced a unique, ultrapure, high-quality sheet metal superior to that produced in the Mediterranean.

GERMAN BOOK FROM 1857 TALKS OF THE ANCIENT MINERS

In the following newspaper article, reporter Victor F. Lemmor talks about a German book called *Reisen im Nordwesten der Vereinigten*

Staaten (Travels in Northwestern Parts of the United States), with chapters relating to the ancient miners, or "Old People," who legend says were the original miners of the copper in this area. It is interesting to note that the term Old People is a cognate of Anasazi (Ancient Ones), which refers to the original builders of the cliff dwellings in the southwestern United States.

LARGE SKELETONS FOUND IN MINNESOTA

BEMIDJI DAILY PIONEER, OCTOBER 3, 1916

Some large mounds have been found in this territory. In some places a number of pieces of pottery have been unearthed. It will be remembered that when the dam at International Falls was under construction several hundred pieces of tempered copper were unearthed from a depth of 15 feet. The articles consisted of fish hooks, knives, spears, and arrows. The art of tempering copper, which was known by these early mound builders, is now a lost art. An unusually large skeleton was also unearthed and thought to have been a woman. Physicians who have examined the skeleton declare that it represented a type of early prehistoric persons who were seven feet tall or more and who possessed an especially large lower jaw. They drew this conclusion because the skeleton found was that of a person of very large stature. The jaw bone was wide and its construction is said to be a special gift of nature to the early man in order that he could masticate the coarser foods which then made up his subsistence. The skull is very large. The well rounded forehead gives evidence of considerable development of intelligence of the Rainy Lake territory. . . . The skeleton will be sent to the Minnesota Historical Society.

TRACING THE ANCIENT COPPER CULTURE

By Victor F. Lemmor

DAILY GLOBE, NOVEMBER 20, 1969

According to Dr. George I. Quimby, the known world of the Old Copper Indians was the Upper Great Lakes region. Some of these prehistoric people lived as early as 7,000 years ago, and others were still around 3,000 years ago. In addition to being miners, these ancient workmen were the first known fabricators of metal in America. It is believed that the Old Copper Indians must have been rather tall, rugged, and muscular.

Dr. Quimby states that by using as a basis the available archaeological evidence, some of the techniques of the prehistoric copper miners have been reconstructed.

ANCIENT COPPER MINING METHODS REVEALED

Among the discoveries made, which determined these conclusions, are remnants of wooden levers, parts of birch bark buckets, hammer stones, and charcoal from fires found in old mining pits. These prehistoric men dug pits in order to follow the veins of pure copper from surface outcroppings. They broke the copper from the rock formations with the help of water and fire and heavy beach boulders. According to Dr. Quimby, the mining method practiced was to heat the rock surrounding the pure copper with fire and then crack it by sudden dousing with cold water. After that the copper was pounded loose with boulder hammers and then pried away with wooden levers.

The pure copper was fashioned into weapons and tools by cold hammering. To prevent the copper from becoming too brittle, it was alternately heated and chilled. Smelting and casting of copper were unknown.

DATING THE MINES

In addition to these three groups of mines on the Upper Peninsula, the copper on Isle Royale was also known to the aborigines for thousands of years. Professor Roy W. Drier, who is in the department of metallurgical engineering at the Michigan College of Mining and Technology at Houghton, Michigan, informed this writer in November of 1959 that he had found mining that had been done at least 3,000 years ago on Isle Royale.

His evidence points to the possibility of the "Island Miners" being of an earlier race or culture than the "Prehistorics" who mined in the Keweenaw Peninsula. In 1953 Prof. Drier accompanied by Dr. James B. Griffin, director of the Museum of Anthropology, University of Michigan, dug in the old copper pits of Isle Royale to a depth of 70 inches. They unearthed a charred log section, which was dated by carbon methods at the University of Michigan Memorial Phoenix Laboratory as being 3,000 years old plus or minus 350 years. In 1954 Prof. Drier again dug in the same ancient pit and took out another charred log section, which was dated at 3,800 years plus or minus 500 years.

This writer's personal interest in the prehistoric copper miners began just a few years ago at the time he was president of the Historical Society of Michigan. There was called to his attention a German book published in 1857 and written by Johann Georg Kohl, and it is titled *Reisen im Nordwesten der Vereinigten Staaten,* (Travels in Northwestern Parts of the United States). Kohl was a German geographer and researcher who devoted most of his life to scientific investigations.

The chapters relating to the ancient miners or "Old People" as designated by Kohl, were translated from the German into English by Mrs. Helen Longyear Paul, curator of the Marquette County Historical Museum, at Marquette, Michigan. After Mrs. Paul made a detailed study of Johann Kohl's descriptive chapter on the prehistoric copper mines of the Ontonagon country, she and two men from Marquette visited the area referred to in Kohl's book. By following the directions given in Kohl's travels, they, too, discovered the pits and hammer stones that had captivated Kohl over a hundred years before.

FIRST MODERN COPPER MINE IN 1730

The first actual modern mining operations were commenced near the forks of the Ontonagon about 1730 by Sieur de la Ronde, and later in 1761 continued by Alexander Henry, an English traveler and fur trader who became interested in exploiting copper discoveries near Lake Superior.

THE MOST COPPER ARTIFACTS FOUND IN WISCONSIN

While Minnesota and Michigan were nearer these copper sources, it is in Wisconsin that the greatest number of Indian-made articles, that is artifacts of copper, has been found. Indeed, more copper Indian artifacts have been found in Wisconsin than in any other state in the Union. There are on record, at present, over 20,000 specimens of Indian copper manufacture found in Wisconsin and produced from the mines of the Lake Superior region. Copper was found in nuggets of all sizes and in the seams of copper-bearing rock.

It is assumed that the Indians doing the mining took these sheets, a typical size being about three-sixteenths of an inch, and ten inches long by eight inches wide, and the nuggets home to their village artisans who in turn worked them into ornaments and tools.

At Indian sites all along Green Bay there have been found many copper chippings: definite evidence of copper workshops there. At Two Rivers, Sheboygan, Waupaca, and Green Lake especially large amounts of copper chips and other copper pieces have been found as proof of extensive copper manufacture in those parts. The distribution was also extensive.

THE COPPER TRADE WAS SOUTH, EAST, AND WEST

Findings indicate that native copper, as well as the finished artifacts, went in trade east, south, and west. Perhaps in this way Wisconsin Indians secured the ivory-colored flint of Ohio, the obsidian of the Yellowstone, and the beautiful conch shells from the seashores, all of which have been found among the Wisconsin Indian relics. Unmistakably, Wisconsin was the seat of the Indian copper industry, the products of which passed through the avenues of trade to many and distant lands.

With the stone tools that the Indian coppersmith made, he formed the copper artifacts. He found early in his work that hammering on a piece of freshly-mined copper made it crumble, so he experimented until he developed a practical method.

The first step in this method is called annealing and consists of the alternate heating and dipping in water of the copper, which made it tough and manageable. Then by hammering, grinding, cutting, and polishing, he produced the finished object, and by embossing and perforating, he decorated it.

THE MYSTERY OF THE SHEET COPPER AND THE UNIQUE COPPER CONTENT CONTAINED THEREIN

Finding many objects made of sheet copper in Wisconsin brought up controversy as to whether the Indians produced these sheets or got them from Europe in trade. Chemical analysis showed that the Indian coppersmith did not melt or temper copper. The free silver found in the artifacts studied would not be seen if the copper had not been tempered. Analysis shows that the Indian-made sheets, to cite one instance, contained 99.73 percent copper; .34 percent iron and .023 percent silver, while the European trade sheets showed the presence of bismuth, zinc, antimony, nickel, and arsenic and that they were obviously tempered. By annealing and hammering only, the Indian coppersmiths made sheet copper out of chunks and welded pieces upon one another and together.

Copper was used a great deal for decoration, the commonest ornaments being beads. These were made by winding a thin strip of copper around a sort of spindle, the number of times around regulating the size, and by drilling through solid pieces and hammering them into shape. Hammering and polishing made a handsome bead. A chain of copper beads, now famous among finds, was discovered to be over 11 feet long, and to contain over 500 beads, each one-fourth inch in diameter.

Innumerable bangles, rings, pendants, breastplates, bracelets, ear rings, and hair ornaments were made. From the copper breast plate forged as a medal of honor, to the lovely bracelets and hair ornaments goes the story of Indian life and romance, if one cares to read it.

THE SCHUMACHER COPPER COLLECTION, GREEN BAY

Too numerous to mention is the detailed list of other copper artifacts ranging from spears and arrow points, through knives, adzes and gouges, to fish hooks and harpoons. The Schumacher collection of copper artifacts in the Neville Museum in Green Bay offers an exceptional opportunity for study, as do other museum collections in Wisconsin and elsewhere.

For those wishing to read more on the subject, an article "Myths and

Legends about Copper," by Charles E. Brown of the Wisconsin Historical Museum, published in the recent September issue of the *Wisconsin Archaeologist,* will be of much interest.

ALGONQUIAN COPPER WORKINGS THE LARGEST IN THE NATION

"The lands claimed by the Algonquian Menomonies and recognized as theirs by the United States has yielded the greatest number of copper workshops and copper implements of any region in the United States, showing the Indians to have been accomplished artisans, as for centuries they manufactured their copper tools and ornaments," notes W. C. McKern, associate curator of Anthropology at the Milwaukee Public Museum.

EVIDENCE FOR WISCONSIN COPPER MINING 10,000 YEARS AGO

ASSOCIATED PRESS, APRIL 25, 1958

Waukesha, Wisconsin: A power shovel has unearthed a chunk of pure copper, which two Carroll County scientists regard as probable evidence of the primitive "copper culture" 10,000 years ago. John Cooper was operating a power shovel Tuesday when the machine turned up the mass of copper at a subdivision south of here.

Anthropologist Harold Eastman and geologist Benjamin Richason conjectured that the copper chunk, larger than a man's fist, probably was placed in an ancient grave about 100 centuries (10,000) years ago.

SEVEN-THOUSAND-YEAR-OLD FIND AT LEONARD'S POINT

OSHKOSH WISCONSIN DAILY, JUNE 3, 1955

Important new evidence expected to provide scientists with further information concerning the history and culture of ancient Indians in Wisconsin has been uncovered near Leonard's Point on Lake Butte des Morts, it has been revealed by officials of the Oshkosh Museum. The discoveries were made on the Matt Reigh farm, northwest of the city, the same site, which produced an interesting series of prehistoric burials, during excavations carried on by Oshkosh and Madison anthropologists during the summer of 1953. James E. Lundsted, curator of anthropology at the local museum, said Tuesday that three more burials, much older than the 1953 discoveries were found at the Reigh farm site last month.

The remains of the three prehistoric Indians, Lundsted stated, are estimated to date back to a period of between 3,000 to 5,000 BC. The dates of the burials from two years ago have been established at about 500 BC. The new excavations were carried out, beginning May 25 by Lundsted; Stuart H. Mong, director of the Oshkosh Public Museum; and Heinz Meyer, Oshkosh High School history teacher and student of anthropology.

YOUNG BOY
TIPS THEM OFF

Lundsted said the new work came about as the result of a "tip" from Terry Raettig, a boy who lives at Highland Shore, located near the site. The boy called the museum after finding some bones and pottery at the Reigh farm site. The pottery, described as thick and bearing what anthropologists refer to as "cord" markings, dated back to later Indian burials at the Reigh site. "However," Lundsted stated, "the bones of the three prehistoric Indians were in poor condition, it was reported, although the leg bones were well enough preserved to show a heavy and thick conformation, similar to those found during the 1953 excavation. Five copper points were found between the feet of one of the skeletons."

LITERAL RED BONES
DISCOVERED

One of the burials was in a narrow ledge of red material, two to three inches thick. "The red material has not been positively identified," museum officials commented, "but appeared to be sand with a high percentage of iron oxide. The bones had taken on the bright red color and were also heavily impregnated with copper salts."

GRAVE GOODS INCLUDE
ANTLER BEADS

Grave goods—artifacts buried with the prehistoric Indians—included a celt or ax, two crescent-shaped knives, a snail shell bracelet and a number of antler beads. A rolled copper bead was discovered at the site by Penny Foust, a neighborhood girl.

Scientists said the newly-discovered burials near Leonard's Point, were highly important and that they are tentatively believed to be related to what anthropologists know to be the "Old Copper Culture." Other evidence of the "Old Copper Culture" has been found in Wisconsin at Potosi, at Osceola, and, in 1952, at Oconto. Wood charcoal found at the Oconto site was sent to the University of Chicago, where a complicated analysis known as the "carbon 14" test was made. The test indicated the charcoal was about 5,000 years old. The snail beads and crescent-shaped knives found at the Reigh site, a museum official said, are similar to those uncovered at Oconto.

MIDWAY BETWEEN
OCONTO AND OSCEOLA

Mr. Lunsted pointed out that the Reigh site is a logical location for remains of the "old copper culture" being situated about mid-way between Osceola

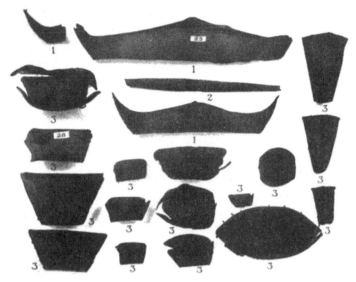

Fig. 7.2. Grave goods from a child's burial on Big Island in Pilley's Tickle,
Notre Dame Bay, Canada (from *The Beothucks or Red Indians*
by J. P. Howley, 1915, plate XXXIV)

Fig. 7.3. Miniature diorama of an archaic copper mine, formerly at the
Milwaukee Public Museum

and the Oconto sites. Further excavations of the archaeologically rich Reigh site will be carried out by Osceola researchers.

FORTY-THREE SKELETONS FOUND

Remains of a total of 43 human beings were uncovered at Osceola by a team of Oshkosh and Madison anthropologists in the summer of 1953. Among the important artifacts discovered at that time were two highly-polished and notched swan bones, a conical copper point, a copper headdress, two axes made of elk antler and a gorget (or neck ornament), made of a conch shell.

The Indians of the "old copper culture" used pure copper in fashioning some of their artifacts but did not have methods for tempering the metal. Instead they worked it by cold pounding and annealing techniques.

THE COPPER HEADDRESS

OSHKOSH DAILY, JANUARY 9, 1954

Another fascinating find was a copper headdress that extended half way around the upper portion of the skull. The headdress consisted of flattened strips of pure copper, which, at one time, were fastened together by a piece of buckskin or fabric. Still another artifact found by the archaeologists was a "gorget," or neck ornament, made of a conch shell. The gorget, which measured about five inches in length, and two inches in width, had three holes on its long axis for suspension purposes. The ornament was shaped like the sole of a sandal.

Among the other unusual artifacts were two swan bones about 7 and 8 inches long, both highly polished and both with a series of notches cut into the sides. The bones may have been used for ceremonial purposes, but their function is not exactly known.

The excavations of last summer also yielded a conical copper point of a somewhat different type than the usual run of such objects.

THE ELK ANTLER AXES

The most interesting specimens found at the site, however, were two axes made of elk antler. The archaeologists' report indicated that the axes found on the Reigh farm were different, so far as is known now, from any previously discovered in the United States.

The 1953 finds at the Reigh farm serve to increase our knowledge of one of the least known periods in Wisconsin archaeology, covering the time period ranging from about 1,000 years before the Christian era, to about 350 AD.

ACCOUNT OF ARROW FOUND IN MASTODON

A newspaper article of 30 years ago noted that such an arrow had been found imbedded in the bones of a mastodon found near the Mississippi River farther north in the state.

A turning point in Wisconsin prehistory came in 1945, when Dr. Robert Ritzenthaler, of the Milwaukee Museum, excavated a site near Potosi. There, the first real evidence of the "Old Copper Culture" was found in situ. The "Old Copper Culture" refers to a cultural group of Indians, antecedent to that of the Early Woodland period, which used copper rather than stone in the manufacture of artifacts.

Dr. R. E. Ritzenthaler, assistant curator of anthropology of the Milwaukee Museum, was sent by his museum to survey the find. The trench in which the bodies were buried, he told the *Wisconsin State Journal,* is about 80 feet long and 15 feet wide. The bodies were laid out on the sand of the reef, in the beginning, and covered with black dirt at a distance of about 5 feet below the present ground level.

"The copper artifacts have been found in the lower level. The copper awls, 5 and 6 inches long, have been sharpened at both ends and were probably used in making clothing. The 'spuds,' tools with sharp edges hafted on handles, were used in scooping out dugout canoes, cleaning skins, and the like," Dr. Ritzenthaler said.

"The instruments were placed in regular patterns," according to Rollo Jamison Beetown, "indicating that the placing of the artifacts was part of a religious ritual. Burials at the upper level were of a bundle burial type, in which the bones, collected during the winter, were buried in a mass ceremony and without placing of copper artifacts."

DAM CONSTRUCTION DESTROYS MORE EVIDENCE

The Potosi burial ground had once been on the banks of the Grant River, but the building of the dam on the Mississippi at Dubuque, raised the waters to include this in the Mississippi and eat away a part of the burial ground.

TWO TYPES OF "COMMON" BURIALS AT OSCEOLA

The dead at the Osceola site were disposed of in two ways: either through bundle burial or partial cremation. (Bundle burials were thought to be of Indians who had died in the winter and whose bodies had been left on platforms in trees until only the bones remained. These were then gathered in a bundle for burial in the spring when the ground thawed.)

ANCIENTS HAD MORE EFFICIENT MINING METHODS

It appears that the ancient miners went on a different principle from what they do at the present time. The greatest depth yet found in these holes is thirty feet—after getting down to a certain depth, they drifted along the vein, making an open cut. These cuts have been filled nearly to a level by the accumulation of soil, and we find trees of the largest growth standing in this gutter, and also timber trees of a very large

Fig. 7.4. This is a modern photo of a ten-ton block of copper being removed from Isle Royale. It is similar in size, but not workmanship, to the smooth-pounded ten-ton block of copper described below.

growth have grown up and died, and decayed many years since; in the same place there are now standing trees of over three hundred years growth. This discovery will lead to a new method of finding veins in this country, and may be of great benefit to some.

TEN-TON CHUNK OF COPPER IS FOUND

Last week they dug down to a new place, and about 12 feet below the surface found a mass of copper that will weigh from eight to ten tons.

This mass of copper was buried in ashes, and it appears they could not handle it, and had no means of cutting it, and probably built fire to melt or separate the rock from it, which might be done by heating, and then dashing on cold water.

CLEAN AS A NEW CENT

This piece of copper is pure, and clean as a new cent, the upper surface has been pounded clear and smooth. It appears that this mass of copper was taken from the bottom of a shaft, the depth of about thirty feet. In sinking this shaft from where the mass now lies, they followed the course of the vein, which pitches considerably; this enabled them to raise it as far as the hole came up with a slant. At the bottom of the shaft they found skids of black oak, from eight to twelve inches in diameter: these sticks were charred through, as if burnt; they found wooden wedges in the same situation. In this shaft they found a miner's gad and a narrow chisel made of copper. I do not know whether these copper tools are tempered or not, but their make displays good workmanship. They have taken out more than a ton of cobblestones, which have been used as mallets. These stones are nearly round, with a score cut around the center, and look as if this score was hatched cut for the purpose of putting a handle around it.

EVIDENCE FOR WIDESPREAD TRADE

OAKLAND TRIBUNE, DECEMBER 20, 1925

There was a well-developed system of trade among those ancient aborigines, and marine shells are often found in the mounds of the Middle West, while articles of native Wisconsin copper occur in those of West Virginia. In Alabama was dug up a skull filled with snail shells, for what purpose can hardly be imagined. A gourd-shaped vessel full of lead ore so pure it was turned into bullets was found in Bellinger County, Missouri. In 1879, the people in the neighborhood of a Mississippi town, where there are mounds exceptionally rich in pottery, discovered that such relics had commercial value. A regular mining fever set in, and men, women and children deserted other tasks to dig for aboriginal bric-a-brac, which was sold to traders and passed on to museums and collectors.

Fig 7.5. A postcard of the Indian Mound Cemetery, Marietta, Ohio

GROUP BURIED WITH COPPER MASKS

In a group of mounds near Chillicothe, Ohio, were found dozens of skeletons wearing copper masks. Presumably the copper came from Wisconsin, where the Indians, long before Columbus landed, obtained the metal by building a fire about a rock containing it and then pouring water on the hot stone, thereby splitting the latter into fragments. The copper thus procured was heated and beaten out into sheets.

"ONE OF THE MOST SUCCESSFUL ARCHAEOLOGICAL EXCAVATIONS EVER MADE IN WISCONSIN"

A number of articles describe the findings of archaeologist Robert J. Hruska at an old copper culture site along the Menominee River.

A WOODEN BURIAL CRYPT

OSHKOSH DAILY, AUGUST 23, 1961

Within 20 inches of the surface, Hruska and his colleagues uncovered a wooden burial crypt, fashioned of oak logs with a roof of sewed birch bark. Because of its proximity to the surface, skeletal material had disappeared, leaving only the enamel of the teeth.

This burial, like others found this summer, gave evidence of red ochre: a substance which appears to have had a religious or ceremonial significance.

THIRTEEN CEREMONIAL BLADES OF UNIQUE DESIGN

Digging down another foot into the pit, the archaeologist found another burial. In association with the skull, all that was left of the skeleton were 13 7-inch ceremonial blades of stone, representing a type never before found with an Old Copper Culture red-ochre burial. So far this summer, Hruska has uncovered four burials with blades, each apparently a set, but differing with each set.

FLEXED BURIALS FOUND

Proceeding another foot down into the pit brought to light the remains of two individuals in "bundle" or flexed burials. One produced a well-preserved skull, which indicates that its owner died right at the site from a severe blow in the face. At each side of the skull, where the ears had been, was a large animal tooth, which Hruska believes may have come from an elk.

EVIDENCE OF CREMATION CEREMONY OR SACRIFICE?

The burial, which was surrounded by upright charred oak logs, consisted of an adult and a child who had been interred in the flesh and beneath them the cremated remains of about five other individuals. "The entire burial," Hruska said, "was impregnated with red ochre, a substance widely used by American Indians for religious or ceremonial purposes."

GIANT FOUND

The other person in this burial was a larger-than-average man. Much of the skeletal material was preserved, due to the chemical properties of a large number of copper beads with which he was buried. At about the 7-foot level, Hruska uncovered another "bundle" burial, this one a cremation.

WRAPPING MATERIAL RECOVERED WITH 44 BLADES

Fortunately, much of the wrapping materials, including strings of beads, some of them braided, were recovered. Around the bones and beads was woven matting which, in turn, was wrapped in the skin of an animal, possibly a beaver. Outer wrapping was a birch bark. Arranged around this burial at the bottom of a pit was found a set of 44 blades, with all the points carefully positioned so as to face north.

200 COPPER BEADS AND 9 BLADES

Around each wrist of the adult were seven strands of copper beads, while a string of some 200 beads was found directly over the skeletal material. Between the two bodies were nine flint blades—spear heads or knives—ranging up to 10 inches in length.

Revealing exceptionally fine workmanship, the blades were manufactured of a type of flint commonly found in Indiana or Illinois, but never before discovered in association with the Old Copper Culture. "The implication that they were imported is clear," commented Hruska.

DISINTEGRATING SKELETONS ARE OF AVERAGE SIZE

Unfortunately human skeletal material had almost entirely disintegrated after 3,000 years in the ground, but enough was left to indicate that physically the Old Copper Culture people were of about average height for their times, and, judging by the thickness of the bones, stocky and robust.

UNUSUAL COPPER AWL FOUND

Among the copper artifacts found with the burials were two large and fine awls, both still showing remnants of wooden handles. One of the awls is fitted at one end with a beaver tooth, probably indicating that the implement performed double duty as a chisel. Other copper grave goods included two toggle-head harpoons: the first of their kind ever.

ONE HUNDRED HUMAN BURIALS UNCOVERED

BY CHARLES HOUSE

APPLETON POST-CRESCENT, SEPTEMBER 18, 1961

One of the most successful archaeological excavations ever made in Wisconsin has come to an end. Archaeologist Robert J. Hruska, the 31-year-old curator of anthropology at the Oshkosh Public Museum, has pronounced the digging as "rewarding beyond my wildest dreams."

The excavations, commenced in July and recently completed, were made at a burial and village site of a copper age culture settlement of Indians known to have lived along the Menominee River near here. Hruska and a crew of volunteer diggers from Menominee succeeded in excavating more than 7,000 cubic feet of ground, from which more than 30 multiple human burials consisting of skeletal remains of about 100 Old Copper Culture age people known to have lived here in prehistoric times were found.

Previous excavations of the Old Copper Culture have shown the Indians to have lived here 3,000 to 5,000 years ago. Of the many human skeletons discovered in the dig only three were of individual burials. Hruska believes that the prehistoric copper people refrained from winter-time burials because of the frozen ground. They retained the bodies of their dead until spring-time thaws and buried all persons who died the previous winter.

RICH MICHIGAN BURIAL FINDS ATTRACT NATIONAL ATTENTION

OSHKOSH DAILY, DECEMBER 16, 1961

Curator Robert J. Hruska: "The dig has attracted national attention in archaeological circles because of the wealth of identifiable new material it produced and the new insights it is yielding into the lives of these rather mysterious early Americans."

The Old Copper Culture—so named because its members fashioned a variety of tools and ornaments of copper—is the most ancient of prehistoric Wisconsin-Michigan Indian cultures. This summer's expedition produced, to say nothing of a vast number of beads, 79 large stone blades, ranging in length up to 10 inches; about 15 copper artifacts, biggest of which is a 12-inch awl, and also including points, knives, axes, and fish hooks; a variety of stone arrow and spear points, scrapers, etc.; and three skulls good enough for exhibit purposes.

TWENTY COPPER CULTURE SKELETONS
UNEARTHED IN MICHIGAN

OSHKOSH DAILY, SEPTEMBER 5, 1962

A total of 20 burials, some of which produced significant artifacts and other grave goods, have been uncovered this summer during the second season of a continuing archaeological dig at Menominee, Michigan. Robert J. Hruska, curator of anthropology at the Oshkosh Public Museum, said that this summer's field work, completed last week, had shed new light on the lives of the rather mysterious prehistoric Indians who comprised what is known as the Old Copper Culture.

SITE IS AT LEAST 3,000 YEARS OLD

This season's excavations, which began in mid-June, have also raised many new questions and pointed the way for further investigations next summer at the ancient burial and village site, located in an unused portion of Menominee's Riverside Cemetery. One of the most interesting aspects of this year's work from the scientific viewpoint was the recovery of a considerable number of pottery shards of a type associated with Early Woodland—a culture marked by cord-wrapped and paddle-impressed pottery, and, probably, a lack of agriculture. It has not yet been definitely established that the Old Copper Culture people had pottery, and this summer's yield of pottery fragments might possibly indicate a temporal overlapping of the final stages of the Old Copper Culture and Early Woodland. The Menominee site is known to be at least 3,000 years old.

MICA AND THE MOUND BUILDERS

Along with the fabled ancient copper mines found in the northern peninsula of Michigan, the mica mines of North Carolina are some of the most significant natural resource sites in North America. The importance of mica to the mound-builder culture cannot be overemphasized. Throughout the United States and Mexico, numerous mound builder burials have revealed a plethora of mica jewelry, ornaments, and decorations, the majority of which can be linked to these mica mines, which archaeologists estimate have been worked since ancient prehistoric times.

EXTREMELY ANCIENT MICA MOUNDS

ACKLEY ENTERPRISE, MAY 23, 1884

At present North Carolina produces two-thirds of all the mica mined in the United States. The center of this industry is at Barkerville, Mitchell County, North Carolina. Senator Clingman, a gentleman of scientific knowledge, had noticed in two geological investigations of the formation of Mitchell County ancient mounds upon which there were large dumps from some ancient mines. He opened several, but found no precious metals, only mica, which he believed worthless. Therefore, the exploration of these mounds was abandoned. A few months later a "cute Yankee" from Connecticut, while prospecting the country for minerals, and coming upon a mound, which Clingman had opened, upon examining the mica, and determining its value, soon afterward obtained a lease upon the property in question and by his energy and practical knowledge of the business soon made a handsome fortune. At the present time there are in this section but two mines that are large producers, the Cloudlook, now 100 feet deep, and the Kay mine, the most valuable property of its kind in the country, which is being worked at a depth of 300 feet and producing two tons monthly. The Clarrisa mine near Barkerville, at one time produced about one-half of the total product of the United States, but after being worked to a depth of 565 feet has been abandoned, as the vein has pinched and the mine is now very wet. A large portion of the product of North Carolina is mined by farmers who eke out a scanty subsistence by prospecting for this valuable mineral.

In this mica belt, which is thirty miles wide and one hundred miles long, the mica is found near the surface and of as good a quality as that found at a considerable depth, which is unquestionably a common experience everywhere, since mica is not as quickly oxidized as other minerals. After the vein is opened a few feet in depth, say 10 or 20 feet, if no pay mica is found the prospect is usually abandoned. These quasi-miners are often satisfied with the finding of a few pockets yielding $100 to $200 return for a season's labor.

THE MOST ANCIENT MICA MINES ARE THE BEST

It is a notable fact that all the best mines of North Carolina are of prehistoric origin. The ancient people working these mines were doubtless contemporaneous with the mound builders of the Ohio Valley, since in Chillicothe, Circleville, and other places have been found in the mounds adjacent sheets of mica covering human remains; also, mica sheets lying upon ancient altars, evidently used for sacrificial purposes, while perforated disks of mica found in graves suggest they were worn as ornaments.

Mica was well known in prehistoric America, traces of its use being widespread. A great shaft near Mount Mitchell, North Carolina, was discovered in 1869, and this not only solved the question as to the origin of the early supply, but gave mica mining in the United States its first impetus. In this region, for many years, mica was largely used as a medium of exchange between farmers and storekeepers.

A DETAILED INVENTORY OF GRAVE GOODS

Mica jewelry and grave goods are common in many mound-builder burials across the country. This not only argues for the high regard the ancients had for mica, but also shows the widespread trade in this material from an extremely ancient date. The sheet mica found in North Carolina is unique, and it should be noted that between the courses of the pyramids at Teotihuacan there are to be found massive sheets of mica. Mica chips are also found in many of the pyramids' walls. Traditional archaeologists say this material came from mines in the Amazon, while the much more likely explanation is that it came from North Carolina.

History of Delaware County, 1879

We were shown some interesting relics consisting of a queen conch shell, some isinglass (mica), and several peculiarly shaped pieces of slate which were found on the farm of Solomon Hill, Concord Township. The mound is situated on the banks of a rocky stream. Two human skeletons were also found in the mound, one about seven feet long, the other an infant. The shell was found at the left cheek of the large skeleton. A piece of slate about one-by-six inches was under the chin. The slate was provided with two smooth holes, apparently for the purpose of tying it to its position. Another peculiarly shaped piece with one hole was on the chest, and another with some isinglass (mica) was on the left hand.

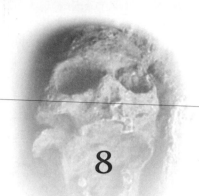

8

TREASURES OF
GIANT BURIAL GROUNDS

The majority of sites that reveal burials of giants also yield evidence of a very sophisticated material culture. The following story gives a reconstruction of the amazing finds made at the extensive complex of mounds in the vicinity of Charleston, West Virginia. These mounds were first breached and studied in 1838 by the state's geological survey team and later by the Smithsonian in 1883. This report is from a front page feature in the state's largest and most respected newspaper at the time, and because it is so precise and detailed and, in many cases, straight from the Smithsonian's own report, I will be quoting from it at length.

THE GIANTS WERE FINE ARTISANS

CHARLESTON DAILY MAIL, SEPTEMBER 23, 1923

Among the most interesting artifacts unearthed were three worked and shaped pieces of cannel coal, a special finely-textured variety of bituminous, which may have come from one of the outcroppings along our local streams.

One was in pendant form, one a disc, and the third of no particular form, probably unfinished. Fragments of seven stone and five clay pipes were found. There were two splendid bone fish hooks and many bone awls and pins. Clay balls about the size of marbles may have been used in chil-

222

dren's games. Miniature "toy" pottery vessels were discovered. Objects of worked antler included a chisel, projectile points, and flakers. There were 341 triangular flint projectile points and 90 flint projectile points of other types. Stone celts, adzes, balls, and a perforated stone disc were brought to light. Other discs of perforated mussel shell were found. A study of the animal and bird bones indicated that the white-tailed deer was very common, also wild turkey, elk and black bear to a lesser extent. Evidence of animals no longer here included elk (28 fragments), bobcat (five fragments), wolf (one) and beaver (eleven).

FOUR HUNDRED SKELETONS UNEARTHED AT ALABAMA MOUND

By Jerome Schweitzer

UNIVERSITY OF ALABAMA, FEBRUARY 27, 1930

EXCAVATIONS OF MUSEUM AT MOUNDVILLE PRODUCE 400 INDIAN SKELETONS—7'6" GIANT AMONG THEM

Some 400 skeletons, the sizes of which vary from unborn infants to male adults and whose ages were estimated at 1,000 to 5,000 years, have been uncovered at the Indian mounds at Moundville by the Alabama Museum of Natural History. From his offices at the University of Alabama, Walter B. Jones, director of the museum, announced that one skeleton measured seven feet six inches in height.

The museum party, headed by Director Jones and Curator William L. Halton and consisting of David de Jarnette, assistant curator, and Carl T. Jones, topographer, is completing its first period of excavations. The party is digging in an area recently purchased by the Museum and which has been designated as Moundville.

In addition to the remains of 400 Indians, the excavation party has taken from the mounds hundreds of valuable artifacts.

AVERAGE HEIGHT OVER SIX FEET

All skeletons unearthed whose bones were strong enough to be preserved have been brought to the Museum. "Most of the large skeletons brought out were found in the vicinity of Mound 'G,'" Dr. Jones said, "the majority averaging over six feet or more in height. All of the graves from which the skeletons were taken were earthen except one, which was a very fine type of stone box burial, which is so prevalent in Tennessee and Kentucky. As a whole the teeth were in very remarkable condition."

Fig. 8.1. Archaeologists have said this stone duck bowl found at Moundville is arguably the most significant prehistoric artifact ever found in the United States (courtesy of Jeffrey Reed).

A MYSTERIOUS STONE DISC UNDER ONE SKULL

One of the most remarkable burials encountered was that of a very prominent member of the tribe, possibly the chief of a tribe that resided around Mound "E." This burial carried a stone disc under the skull, two square pots, and three miscellaneous pots; this pottery is superb ware and beautiful in design.

In addition, the skeleton wore many shell beads at the neck, the wrists and there were seven beads on the right ankle and eleven on the left.

COPPER IS THE ONLY METAL FOUND

The only metal encountered during the excavations was copper, which appeared to be a great favorite with the mound builders.

Red, yellow, and other pigments were met with everywhere, and all discs showed the presence of white to pearl-gray paint, possibly made of lead carbonate, showing that these people carried on elaborate rituals and procedures.

HUNDREDS OF ANCIENT ARTIFACTS FOUND

Director Jones announced that among the group of artifacts, 150 pots of various kinds, four pipes, ten stone discs, one copper pendant, six copper ear plugs, about seventy-five bone awls or piercing instruments, 100 discoidal stones, some made from igneous rocks brought in from other localities, thousands of shell beads ranging from one and one half inches in length to very minute objects. Many of the beads were spool shaped, some discoidal, others irregular.

FOODS WERE PLENTIFUL—REFUSE CAREFULLY BURIED

Their foods consisted of the meats of various animals, fowls, and fresh-water mussel shells. The latter type of food was duplicated in one very fine vessel of earthenware. Numerous bones of deer, bear, turkey, and fish were found with burials in pots and in dumps bordering the burial ground. Incidentally, the dumps, or refuse heaps, appeared to have been buried the same as the human bodies.

Fig. 8.2. Engraved stone palette from Moundville, illustrating a horned rattlesnake, perhaps from the great serpent of the southeastern ceremonial complex (courtesy of Jeffrey Reed)

REMARKABLE SQUARE POT RECOVERED

The most remarkable object met with by the party was a square pot, ornamented by brilliant red and pearl-gray circles. Each circle was fringed by a pearl-gray ring. This is perhaps the finest vessel ever to be taken from Moundville. Several other colored pots were encountered, several of which were very remarkable. In 1904–05, Dr. Clarence Moore, connected with the Philadelphia Academy of Sciences, found only three colored pots, and these were rather rude.

VARIOUS ANIMAL EFFIGIES AT MOUNDVILLE FIND

The art of the mound builders is characterized by various effigies including human heads and sometimes bodies, heads of ducks, owls, alligators, frogs, fish, eagles, serpents, rattle snakes, etc. The rattle snake is often portrayed as having horns and wings, making up what is termed the "flying circle."

The party secured three excellent frog bowls. Although the Indians sometimes exaggerated certain features, there is no question about the great accuracy of their artistic endeavors.

CLAY BRICK FOUND IN MOUND

On Mound "B," 57 feet in height and one of the most remarkable Indian mounds in the world, were found several pots probably placed there during some ceremonial rites, for no human bones were found with them and the pits in which they had been placed were carefully covered with a very nice type of clay brick.

The party was able to spot 33 distinct mounds within the area. Of the 33, the hollow square consists of 16 prominent mounds on the circumference with the largest and finest within the square. It is assumed that the Chief lived on the high mound overlooking the entire area and that tribal ceremonies were carried on upon the great mound just to the south of the Chief's abode. It is further assumed that lesser Chiefs occupied the lesser mounds, while the villagers lived in the areas adjoining the mounds. The northern rim of the hollow square overlooks the Black Warrior River. The entire plain is well above high water level.

In 1871, a Canadian newspaper article reported on a find from Cayuga, New York, in which two hundred skeletons were removed from a collapsed mound. . . . These skeletons were said to be in a perfect state of preservation and that "the men were of gigantic stature, some of them measuring nine feet, very few of them being less than seven feet."

NIAGARA'S ANCIENT CEMETERY
OF GIANTS

DAILY TELEGRAPH, TORONTO, ONTARIO, AUGUST 23, 1871

A REMARKABLE SIGHT: TWO HUNDRED SKELETONS
IN CAYUGA TOWNSHIP

A SINGULAR DISCOVERY BY A TORONTONIAN AND OTHERS—A VAST
GOLGOTHA OPENED TO VIEW—SOME REMAINS OF THE "GIANTS
THAT WERE IN THOSE DAYS" FROM OUR OWN CORRESPONDENTS.

Cayuga, New York: On Wednesday last, Rev. Nathaniel Wardell, Messers Orin Wardell (of Toronto), and Daniel Fredenburg were digging on the farm of the latter gentleman, which is on the banks of the Grand River, in the township of Cayuga.

When they got to five or six feet below the surface, a strange sight met them. Piled in layers, one upon top of the other, were some two hundred skeletons of human beings nearly perfect: around the neck of each one being a string of beads.

There were also deposited in this pit a number of axes and skimmers made of stone. In the jaws of several of the skeletons were large stone pipes, one of which Mr. O. Wardell took with him to Toronto a day or two after this Golgotha was unearthed.

These skeletons are those of men of gigantic stature, some of them measuring nine feet, very few of them being less than seven feet. Some of the thigh bones were found to be at least a foot longer than those at present known, and one of the skulls being examined completely covered the head of an ordinary person.

These skeletons are supposed to belong to those of a race of people anterior to the Indians.

Some three years ago, the bones of a mastodon were found embedded in the earth about six miles from this spot. The pit and its ghastly occupants are now open to the view of any who may wish to make a visit there.

EARLY EASTERN OUTPOST FOR
THE MOUND BUILDERS

The primacy of river routes in relationship to the placement of mound builder sites can be seen everywhere in the United States. In this case the Allegheny River is singled out as a major ingress route into western Pennsylvania and New York State.

RICH BURIALS AT SUGAR RUN ATTRACT SMITHSONIAN

On October 20, 1941, we have this report on the Smithsonian's involvement in excavations at the Sugar Run Indian Mounds in Warren, Pennsylvania, by Dr. Wesley Bliss and Edmund Carpenter, in association with the state historical commission and representatives from the Smithsonian, including Dr. William N. Fenton.

> The central or most important find, was of two rock cists each containing an uncremated skeleton in good preservation. Deposited with one of these, beneath the skull, were fifty-three cache blades; near its feet, quantities of red and yellow ochre, a gorget and a sheet of mica. Near the center of the same burial was *a lump of galena (crystal lead)*. Mica, and cache blades were found, too, with the second skeleton.
>
> The earlier Sugar Run people appear to represent an eastern outpost for the "mound builders" of the Mississippi drainage basin. The Allegheny River suggests itself as the corridor through which these people penetrated into Western Pennsylvania and New York. These people probably flourished until at least 1000 CE.
>
> No intimate connection can be traced between the mound builders of Sugar Run and the "Cornplanter" band or the other Senecas living just across the line in New York State. The former appear to have lived along and disappeared from the upper Allegheny many years before the ancestors of the present Senecas first appeared hereabouts.

MATERIAL TO BE CATALOGUED
AND PLACED IN SMITHSONIAN MUSEUM

As we have seen time and time again in this book, major caches of archaeological material are handed over to the Smithsonian, only later to disappear down the memory hole of traditional research. The article by Fenton continues . . .

"Material recovered from this site will be studied by experts over several months," said Dr. C. E. Schaeffer of the state historical commission in a speech also attended by Dr. William N. Fenton of the Smithsonian, who was there to consult as a Seneca specialist.

When the returns are all in formal reports of the investigations will be published and distributed in professional quarters to make the information available to archaeologists in other areas. Leaflets, illustrated talks, exhibits, and the like, will be prepared for the non-professional.

Finally, the artifacts will be placed in permanent storage or on exhibition at some central repository for the benefit of the serious or casual student of archaeology.

1880 HISTORY OF INDIANA COUNTY
REVEALS INDIAN LORE

A great deal of local Indian lore is recorded in the old *1880 History of Indiana County*. A few colorful Indian names have continued until the present, reminding us of earlier times. The name "Kiskiminetas" is of Indian origin, but there is some difference of opinion as to its meaning. Based on stem words from the Indian language, one meaning is "plenty of walnuts." Rev. John Heckewelder, a Moravian missionary from the time of the Revolutionary War, said it meant "make daylight." John McCullough, captured in Franklin County by Indians in 1756, wrote of being taken to an old-town at "Keesk-kshee-man-nit-teos," meaning "cut spirit" and located at the junction of the Loyalhanna and the Conemaugh. Conemaugh is also a name of Indian origin and means "long fishing place" or "otter creek."

SEVENTEEN BURIALS UNCOVERED

As we begin to catalogue the mound builder burial practices, one of the major burial styles is "flexed" burial, where the knees are drawn up to the chest.

Seventeen burials were uncovered in the excavated portions of the tract; ten children and infants, four adult males, two adult females, and one unidentified adult. "Most had been buried in a flexed position, with knees drawn up to the chest."

THE MISSING GIANTS IN
NORTH CAROLINA

In North Carolina, significant finds were made in the Yadkin Valley of Caldwell County in 1883 that included one group of four skeletons in seated positions and a pair lying on their backs. One of the recumbent skeletons was of a man who was reported to be seven feet tall. At another site in the North Carolina foothills, twenty-six skeletons were found in unusual burial positions associated with other mound builder sites. In yet another location, sixteen skeletons were found in seated, squatting, and prone positions in the center of which was a skeleton standing upright in a large stone cist, which is a burial chamber made of stone or a hollow tree.

The following section is from an October 18, 1962, *Associated Press* article that includes extensive quotes from a report written for the Smithsonian. It was published in the North Carolina–based *Lenoir News* and the *Virginia Bee* and was also syndicated nationally. This article is of great interest as it documents the Smithsonian's involvement in the dig, as well as the institution's confiscation of the evidence for further study.

SIXTEEN NORTH CAROLINA SKELETONS
SHIPPED TO THE SMITHSONIAN

By Nancy Alexander

ASSOCIATED PRESS, OCTOBER 18, 1962

In 1883 the foothill section of North Carolina became the site of intense excavations for Indian relics. Dr. James Mason Spainhour, a Lenoir dentist and Indian authority, discovered several large mounds in the area. Relics, which he and others unearthed, so aroused the interest of officials of the Smithsonian Institution in Washington that a representative, J. P. Rogan, was sent to the area to assist with the excavations.

Rogan wrote a comprehensive report of Caldwell County findings using sketches to illustrate each of five notable mounds discovered. All were located in the Yadkin Valley area now known as Happy Valley. After skeletons were carefully removed and labeled, they were sent to the Smithsonian. Later one of the mounds was carefully reproduced in miniature for public viewing.

It was on the T. F. Nelson farm about a mile and a half southeast of Patterson, that two important discoveries were made. "The first mound was only about 18 inches in height from first appearances," writes Rogan. "Of circular shape it was about 38 feet in diameter. A pit had been dug about three feet deep, with the center area being about six feet in depth.

"Sixteen skeletons were found in various positions, some squatting, some reclining, while others were in small stone sepultures of water-worn rocks," continues Rogan in the official Smithsonian report. "In the center was a skeleton standing upright in a large stone cist. Also found were stones shaped like disks and pitted. There were celts, crude bones and soapstone pipes, black paint made from molded nuts and charcoal."

TWENTY-SIX MORE
NORTH CAROLINA
SKELETONS FOUND

"On the W. D. Jones property two miles east of Patterson, a fourth excavation was made," reports Rogan to the Smithsonian.

In a low circular mound about 32 feet in diameter and three feet in depth, 26 skeletons were discovered. Relics included celts, disks, shell beads, food cups, crescent shaped pieces of copper, pipes, red and black paint, broken pottery, and charcoal.

As a result of the excavations excitement spread throughout the region. People began exploring hillocks and mounds in all vicinities. Other discoveries, which went unrecorded, were made. John P. Perry and John M. Houck, exploring an old Indian camp site near the present Brown Mountain Beach, found many relics.

THE MANY MOUNDS OF TENNESSEE

I have already included excerpts detailing some of the amazing accounts in Dr. John Haywood's wonderful book from 1823, *The Natural and Aboriginal History of Tennessee*. Perhaps the most amazing finds described in the book were the tiny mounds that contained caskets of the three-foot-tall "moon-eyed children," who were pygmies that were said to accompany the giants. The three-foot-tall pygmies were originally said to have come from North Carolina, and legends say they were mischievous and only liked to come out at night. Comparisons with leprechauns immediately come to mind reading this. Cherokee lore recounts that they waged war against these moon-eyed people and drove them from their home in Hiwassee, a village in what is now Murphy, North Carolina, pushing them west into Tennessee.

In addition to numerous giants and pygmies, Haywood discovered grave goods, including bloody axes, a stone trumpet hunting horn, carved mastodon bones, and soapstone statues and pipes. In a cave on the south side of the Cumberland River, a secret room was discovered that was twenty-five feet square and showed signs of engineering, as it contained a large rock-cut well and the skeleton of a blond-haired giant.

Outside of Sparta, a standing stone was discovered that marked the burial of more oversized skeletons. In another burial at the top of a nearby hill, carved ivory beads were found of the "finest and best quality," while in a dig at Ohio Falls, Roman coins depicting Claudius II and Maximinus II were uncovered. It was reported that in 1794, an ancient furnace was discovered and in association with it a bar of iron was found, as well as annealed and hardened copper implements.

The Natural and Aboriginal History of Tennessee, 1823
BY DR. JOHN HAYWOOD

It would be an endless labor to give a particular description of all the mounds in Tennessee. They are numerous upon the rivers,

Fig. 8.3. An illustration of the Tennessee dig led by
Dr. John Haywood, 1823

which empty into the Mississippi, running from the dividing ridge
between that river and Tennessee. They are found upon Duck river,
the Cumberland, upon the Little Tennessee and its waters, and upon
the Big Tennessee, upon Frenchbroad and upon Elk river.

The trees are of more recent growth which are upon the mounds
that are found in the last settlements of the Natchez; for instance,
near the town of Natchez, and on the waters of the Mississippi
within the present limits of Tennessee than those are which grow
upon the mounds in other parts of the country: a circumstance,
which furnishes the presumption, that the ancient builders of the
latter were expelled from the other parts of Tennessee, at a period
corresponding with the ages of the trees which the whites found
growing upon them.

A careful description of a few of these mounds in West and East
Tennessee will put us in possession of the properties belonging to
them generally. In the county of Sumner, at Bledsoe's lick, eight

miles northeast from Gallatin, about 200 yards from the lick, in a circular enclosure, between Bledsoe's lick creek and Bledsoe's spring branch, upon level ground, is a wall 15 or 18 inches in height, with projecting angular elevations of the same height as the wall and within it, are about 16 acres of land.

Fig. 8.4. Engraved shell from a Tennessee mound, from *The Problem of the Ohio Mounds* by Cyrus Thomas, Smithsonian Institute, 1889

In the interior is a raised platform, from 13 to 15 feet above the common surface, about 200 yards from the wall to the south, and about 50 from the northern part of it. This platform is 60 yards length and breadth, and is level on the top. And is to the east of a mound to which it joins, of 7 or 8 feet higher elevation, or 8 feet from the common surface to the summit, about 20 feet square. On the eastern side of the latter mound, is a small cavity, indicating that

steps were once there for the purpose of ascending from the platform to the top of the mound.

In the year 1785, there grew on the top of the mound a black oak
three feet through. There is no water within the circular enclosure
or court. Upon the top of the mound was ploughed up some years
ago, an image made of sandstone. On one cheek was a mark resembling a wrinkle, passing perpendicularly up and down the cheek. On
the other cheek were two similar marks. The breast was that of a
female, and prominent. The face was turned obliquely up, towards
the heavens. The palms of the hands were turned upwards before
the face and at some distance from it, in the same direction that the
face was. The knees were drawn near together, and the feet, with the
toes towards the ground, were separated wide enough to admit of
the body being seated between them.

The attitude seemed to be that of adoration. The head and upper
part of the forehead were covered with a cap or mitre or bonnet
from the lower part of which came horizontally a brim, from the
extremities of which the cap extended upwards conically. The color
of the image was that of a dark infusion of coffee. If the front of the
image was placed to the east, the countenance obliquely elevated,
and the uplifted hands in the same direction would be toward the
meridian sun.

About ten miles from Sparta, in White county, a conical mound
was lately opened, and in the center of it was found a skeleton eight
feet in length. With it was found a stone of the flint kind, very hard,
with two flat sides, having in the center circular hollows exactly
accommodated to the balls of the thumb and forefinger. This stone
was an inch and a half in diameter, the form exactly circular. It was
about one third of an inch thick, and made smooth and flat, for
rolling, like a grindstone, to the form of which, indeed, the whole
stone was assimilated. When placed upon the floor, it would roll for
a considerable time without falling.

The whole surface was smooth and well-polished, and must have been cut and made smooth by some hard metallic instrument. No doubt it was buried with the deceased, because for some reason he had set a great value on it in his lifetime, and had excelled in some accomplishment to which it referred.

The color of the stone was a dingy white, inclining to a darkish yellow. At the side of this skeleton were also found two flat stones, about six inches long, two and a half wide at the lower part, and about one and a half at the upper end, widening in the shape of an ax or hatchet from the upper to the lower end. The thickness of the stone was about one tenth of an inch. An inch below the upper end exactly equidistant from the lateral edges, a small hole is neatly bored through each stone, so that by a string run through, the stone might be suspended off the side or from the neck as an ornament.

One of these stones is the common limestone. The other is semi-transparent, so as to be darkened by the hand placed behind it and resembles in texture those stalactical formations, like white stone, which are made in the bottoms of caves by the dripping of water. When broken, there appears a grain running from one flat side to the other, like the shootings of ice or saltpeter, of a whitish color inclining to yellow. The latter stones are too thin and slender, for any operation upon other substances, and must have been purely ornamental.

The first described stone must have been intended for rolling.

For why take so much pains to make it circular, if to be used in flinging? Or why, if for the latter purpose, so much pain taken to make excavations adapted to the thumb and finger. The conjecture seems to be a probable one that it was used in some game played upon the same principles as that called ninepins; and the little round balls, like marbles, but of a larger size, were so disposed as that the rolling stone should pass through them.

Such globular stone, it is already stated, was found in a mound in Maury County. With this large skeleton were also found eight beads and a human tooth. The beads were circular and of a bulbous form. The largest about one fourth of an inch in diameter, the others smaller. The greater part of them tumescent from the edge to the center, at which a hole was perforated for a string to pass through and to connect them. The inner sides were hard and white, like lime indurated by some chemical process. The outside was a thin coal of black crust.

OKLAHOMA PICTURE WRITING

BY RAY E. COLTON

DAILY NEWS-RECORD, MIAMI, OKLAHOMA, DECEMBER 10, 1939

Yes! The tombs of a long-vanished race of mound builders have been found near Langley, in Mayes County, site of the Grand River dam, and much is expected to be learned from these finds after investigating archaeologists and anthropologists complete their studies of the finds which have been made.

The pottery, consisting of drinking vessels, water bowls, and so forth has been found in the excavated mounds near Langley, and also recently in mounds unearthed near Grove in Delaware County, even to designs such as the Thunder Bird. Arrow heads, which have been found at Langley and also in the Grove "diggings," are of many designs and sizes.

In the slender fishing or hunting point type, made of some material resembling glass, the symmetry and design are perfect, thus reflecting a remarkable degree of ability on the part of the manufacturers. Battle or war points, ranging in size from eight to ten inches, and about two inches in width at their widest point near the center, are of two types of material, namely obsidian "black" and flint "gray." A study in the area of the vicinity of these finds by geologists fails to show any material corresponding to these types of rocks, and on the basis of these finds, it is assumed that the material to make these points was brought from some distant point in either southern Kansas or central Missouri, where some of this material exists. The balance of the war points is perfect and when held in the palm of the hand, remains in a perfect balanced position.

Picture writings which have been found near Grove show in crude design a hunter chasing a buffalo with a spear of this type.

MUCH LARGER THAN PRESENT-DAY HUMANS

Some of the burials, which have been unearthed at the dam site, appear with head to the north, while others appear with head to the south. The meaning of this has not been determined. Some evidences of the

Fig. 8.5. Examples of copper and stone work: pre-Columbian copper artifacts from Oklahoma, Missouri, and Illinois (courtesy of Herb Roe)

practice of masonry are noted in some of the finds, and it is believed that the mound builders had knowledge of this craft. Certain skeleton remains have considerable arrow heads, beaded work, and other artifacts around them. It is theorized that the person possessed some rank of standing within the tribal councils and was thus designated by the artifacts buried with him.

Most of the skeleton remains are much larger than present day humans and the race must have presented a strange sight owing to the extreme heights of its members.

A GIANT RACE

MEMPHIS DAILY APPEAL, AUGUST 15, 1870

THE INDIAN MOUND CHICKASAWBA—HUMAN SKELETONS EIGHT AND TEN FEET IN HEIGHT—RELICS OF A FORMER AGE

Two miles west of Barfield Point, in Arkansas County, Ark., on the east bank of the lovely stream called Pemiscott River, stands an Indian mound, some 25 feet high and about an acre in area at the top.

This mound is called Chickasawba, and from it the high and beautiful country surrounding it, some twelve square miles in area derives its name: Chickasaw. The mound derives its name from Chickasawba, a chief of the Shawnee tribe, who lived, died, and was buried there.

STILL ACTIVE AS TRADING MOUND IN 1820

From 1820 to 1831, Chickasawba and his hunters assembled annually at Barfield Point, then, as now, the principal shipping place of the surrounding country, and bartered off their furs, peltries, buffalo robes, and honey to the white settlers and the trading boats on the river, and receiving in turn powder, shot, lead, blankets, money, etc.

A GIANT EIGHT TO NINE FEET TALL IS FOUND

A number of years ago in making an excursion into or near the foot of Chickasawba's mound, a portion of a gigantic human skeleton was found. The men who were digging, becoming interested, unearthed the entire skeleton, and from measurements given to us by reliable parties the frame of the man to whom it belonged could not have been less than eight or nine feet in height.

Under the skull, which easily slipped over the head of our informant (who, we will here state, is one of our best citizens) was found a peculiarly shaped earthen jar, resembling nothing in the way of Indian pottery, which had before been seen by them.

It was exactly the shape of the round-bodied, long-necked carafes or water-decanters, a specimen of which may be seen on Gaston's table.

EXQUISITE HIEROGLYPHS FOUND ON FINELY-CARVED VASE

The material of which the vase was made was of a peculiar kind of clay, and the workmanship was very fine. The belly or body of it was ornamented with FIGURES OR HIEROGLYPHICS consisting of a correct delineation of human hands, parallel to each other, open, palms outward, and running up and down the vase, the wrists to the base, the fingers towards the neck. On either side of the hands, were tibia or thigh bones, also correctly delineated, running around the base.

MORE SKULLS, MORE VASES UNDER THEIR HEADS

Since that time, whenever an excavation has been made in Chickasawba country in the neighborhood of the mound SIMILAR SKELETONS have been found and under the skull of every one were found similar funeral vases, almost exactly like the one described. There are now in the city several of the vases and portions of the huge skeletons. One of the editors of *The Appeal* yesterday measured a thighbone, which is fully three feet long.

The thigh and shin bones, together with the bones of the foot, stood up in proper position in a physician's office in this city, measure five feet in height, and show the body to which the leg belonged to have been from nine to ten feet in height. At Beaufort's Landing, near Barfield, in digging a deep ditch, a skeleton was dug up, the leg of which measured from five to six feet in length and other bones in proportion.

THREE

Pre-Columbian Foreign Contact

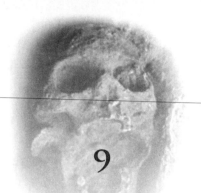

9

HOLY STONES,
A CALENDAR STELE, AND
FOREIGN COINS

As we have seen, there is compelling evidence that America's giants belonged to sophisticated indigenous cultures. Along with that there are strong indications of very ancient cultural exchanges with other parts of the world. In this chapter I review reports related to tablets carved with inscriptions, a calendar stele, and ancient foreign coins.

GEORGE S. MCDOWELL REVEALS HIEROGLYPHIC TABLETS IN THE POSSESSION OF THE CINCINNATI SOCIETY OF NATURAL HISTORY

One of the most extraordinary documents I have run across in my research is a newspaper article published in 1891, which goes into a detailed description and translation of tablets in the possession of a historical society's museum in Cincinnati, textiles matching those in Assyria, evidence of surgery, and so forth. The author was a respected writer, and the article was widely syndicated nationally in 1891.

RARE TREASURES CONTAINED IN THE MUSEUM OF THE CINCINNATI SOCIETY OF NATURAL HISTORY

By George S. McDowell

CINCINNATI ENQUIRER, JULY 15, 1891

FURTHER EXPLORATIONS NOW IN PROGRESS IN OHIO

Continued explorations among the ancient monuments remaining in the Ohio valley maintain the general interest in those people whose existence was before the time of written history, whose relations to the rest of mankind have never been discovered, and who are distinguished simply as mound builders; that is, they are known only as the authors of the most enduring of the monuments that survive them: those great piles of earth, whether raised for sacrifice, sepulture, or war.

The museum of the Cincinnati Society of Natural History is filled with a wealth of these curious peoples, in many cases inexplicable antiquities, and the explorations, which are in progress among the mounds and forts of the Little Miami Valley, under the direction of Dr. Metz, of Madisonville, Ohio, are almost every day bringing to light additions to the remarkable collection, which is equaled only by the one at the Peabody Museum, that was filled and still supplied by the same sources.

A study of these shows that the mound builders were an agricultural people, industrious in the arts of peace as well as the precautions of war, with considerable educational and scientific attainments, and that they had rites and ceremonies of religion and burial as distinctive as any that characterize the people of the present day.

ROWS AND ROWS OF GRINNING SKULLS

Illustrative of the physical characteristics of the people, the Cincinnati Museum has a number of skeletons taken from the mounds around the city and the newly-excavated cemetery near Madisonville, and there are rows upon rows of grinning skulls from which the learned members of the society have drawn many lessons touching on the mental qualifications of these ancient people.

They have determined that the shape and the phrenological points preclude the possibility to their having belonged to any Indians of whom our histories furnish us information.

There is also in the rooms of the society a piece of woven cloth taken from one of the mounds, in this case found lying close to a skeleton that occupied almost the center and bottom of the mound (so that it must have been placed there with the corpse) that in texture is almost identical with cloth found among the ruins of ancient Babylon and Assyria and the farther east.

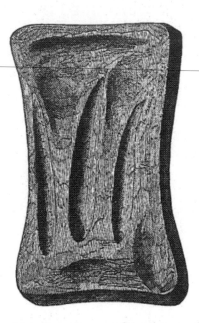

Fig. 9.1. Cincinnati tablet. Sometimes referred to as the great American Rosetta stone, the Cincinnati tablet was discovered in the Old Mound at the corner of Fifth and Mound Streets in Cincinnati in 1841. At first declared a fraud, it was later shown to be authentic. Some have speculated that it is a stylized representation of the Tree of Life. (Illustration from *Ancient Monuments of the Mississippi Valley* by Ephraim Squier and Edwin Davis.)

THE SENSATIONAL CINCINNATI TABLET

Similar to the textile in its ancient connections to advanced civilization, are two other relics in the possession of the Society—one known as the "Conjuring Stone" and the other as the "Tablet of Life" or more commonly the "Cincinnati Tablet" because it was taken from one of the mounds marking the site of the city—the former a mathematical, the other a psychological witness.

The tablet is a remarkable and curious stone. Two others of similar hieroglyphical decoration, but plainly of less advanced philosophical idea, according to the learned men who examined them have been found in Ohio mounds, one near Wilmington and the other near Waverly.

And not only does the Cincinnati Tablet exhibit a more advanced idea, it is also of superior workmanship and preservation. An examination of the drawing of the Cincinnati Tablet will discover upon it several fetal designs that have been interpreted as symbolical of those gestative and procreative mysteries that must have powerfully affected the minds of man in the remotest early ages. The design of the tablet shows that its author had knowledge of the stages of development at various periods of fetal growth, and the tablet, bearing these symbolizations of the existence before life, was no doubt used in connection with the ceremonies of sepulture and possibly by way of comparative conjecture concerning the hidden things of life beyond the grave.

THE MEASURING STONE

Regarding the next in importance to the "Tablet," is the "Measuring Stone." This is a piece of sandstone, about $5/8$ inch thick, a half ellipse in shape, exactly nine inches on the flat side and twelve inches on the curve, the dotted lines in the drawing indicating the completed ellipse, which is an exact model of the mound in which it was found.

Learned mathematical analysis shows this stone to have been the basis for all measurements of the great mounds and earthworks in the Ohio Valley, and that the same numbers 9 and 12 are the key numbers of the measures used in the construction of the architectural works of the Chaldeans, Babylonians, pre-Semites, and Egyptians, while the latter number remains to this day the English standard.

EVIDENCE OF BRAIN SURGERY

The skull taken from an excavation near Cincinnati shows that these people were well-versed in surgery. It is the skull of a man who had once received a terrible blow to the side of the head, which crushed the skull, but after careful treatment recovered from the effects of the blow. Dr. Langdon, an eminent surgeon of Cincinnati, examined the skull and said that the adjustments to the parts of bone and the way in which they had healed show knowledge of practical surgery scarcely excelled at the present day.

FORGES, POLISHING BONES, AND IRON

The relics in the Museum of the Cincinnati Society show also that these people were well-versed in the industrial arts, there being the remains of hammers, knives, mica ornaments, beads, wampum, decorated shells, pottery, and many other things. Among these are some that have puzzled the scientists to determine to what uses they have been applied such as a certain leg bone.

It is a femur almost worn in two by some friction, as though it must have been used for polishing. Thousands of pieces of these bones have been found, having been so worn away that they broke in use.

There is also a kind of needle, made from long fish bones resembling in length the present crocheting needle and the carpet needle in construction. They may have been used in the making of clothing.

~~There are found the remains~~

of forges, and great quantities of furnace slag and cinders and scaling like those that fly from beaten white-hot iron.

HIEROGLYPHICS ALSO FOUND IN MARIETTA

It may be that one of the tablets with "similar hieroglyphical decoration" referred to by McDowell in 1891 is the one described below as part of the findings of an elaborate giant burial in Muskingum County, Ohio.

REMAINS OF NINE-FOOT GIANTS IN OHIO

CINCINNATI ENQUIRER, JULY 14, 1880
(SEE *MARION DAILY STAR,* JULY 14, 1880, FOR ORIGINAL STORY.)

The mound in which these remarkable discoveries were made was about sixty-four feet long and thirty-five feet wide top measurement and gently sloped down to the hill where it was situated. A number of stumps of trees were found on the slope standing in two rows, and on the top of the mound were an oak and a hickory stump, all of which bore marks of great age.

All of the skeletons were found on a level with the hill, and about eight feet from the top of the mound. In one grave there were two skeletons, one male and one female. The female face was looking downward, the male being immediately on top, with the face looking upward. The male skeleton measured nine feet in length, and the female was eight.

The male frame in this case was nine feet, four inches in length and the female was eight feet.

In another grave was found a female skeleton, which was encased in a clay coffin, holding in her arms the skeleton of a child three and a half feet long, by the side of which was an image, which being exposed to the atmosphere, crumbled rapidly.

The remaining seven, were found in single graves and were lying on their sides. The smallest of the seven was nine feet in length and the largest ten. One single circumstance connected with this discovery was the fact that not a single tooth was found in either mouth except in the one encased in the clay coffin.

On the south end of the mound was erected a stone altar, four and a half feet wide and twelve feet long, built on an earthen foundation nearly four feet wide, having in the middle two large flagstones, from which sacrifices were undoubtedly made, for upon them were found charred bones, cinders, and ashes. This was covered by about three feet of earth.

AN ANCIENT TABLET WITH POSSIBLE HIEROGLYPHS

What is now a profound mystery may in time became the key to unlock still further mysteries that were centuries ago commonplace affairs.

I refer to a stone that was found resting against the head of the clay coffin above described. It is irregularly shaped red sandstone, weighing about 18 pounds, being strongly impregnated with oxide of iron, and bearing upon one side TWO LINES OF HIEROGLYPHS.

HOLY STONES IN OHIO AND ILLINOIS?

Other ancient engraved tablets found in Ohio and Illinois deepen the mystery.

IS IT REALLY THE TEN COMMANDMENTS?

OHIO STATE UNIVERSITY WEB ARCHIVE

In November of 1860, David Wyrick of Newark, Ohio, found an inscribed stone in a burial mound about ten miles south of Newark. The stone is inscribed on all sides with a condensed version of the Ten Commandments or Decalogue, in a peculiar form of post-Exilic square Hebrew letters. The robed and bearded figure on the front is identified as Moses in letters fanning over his head.

The inscription is carved into a fine-grained black stone. It has been identified by geologists Ken Bork and Dave Hawkins of Denison University as limestone; a fossil crinoid stem is visible on the surface, and the stone reacts strongly to HCl.

It is definitely not black alabaster or gypsum as previously reported here. According to James L. Murphy of Ohio State University, "Large white crinoid stems are common in the Upper Mercer and Boggs limestone units in Muskingum Co. and elsewhere, and these limestones are often very dark gray to black in color. You could find such rock at the Forks of the Muskingum at Zanesville, though the Upper Mercer limestones do not outcrop much further up the Licking." We therefore need not look any farther than the next county over to find a potential source for the stone, contrary to the previous assertion here that such limestone is not common in Ohio. The inscribed stone was found inside a sandstone box, smooth on the outside and hollowed out within to exactly hold the stone. The Decalogue inscription begins at the non-alphabetic symbol at the top of the front, runs down the left side of the front, around every available space on the back and sides, and then back up the right side of the front to end where it begins, as though it were to be read repetitively.

Fig. 9.2. The Newark "holy stone"
(courtesy of J. Huston McCulloch)

David Deal and James Trimm note that the Decalogue stone fits well into the hand, and that the lettering is somewhat worn precisely where the stone would be in contact with the last three fingers and the palm if held in the left hand. Furthermore, the otherwise puzzling handle at the bottom could be used to secure the stone to the left arm with a strap. They conclude that the Decalogue stone was a Jewish arm phylactery or tefilla (also written t'filla) of the Second Temple period. Although the common Jewish tefilla does not contain the words of the Decalogue, Moshe Shamah reports that the Qumran sect did include the Decalogue.

THE KEYSTONE ALSO FOUND AT NEWARK MOUNDS

Several months earlier, in June of 1860, David Wyrick had found an additional stone, also inscribed in Hebrew letters. This stone is popularly known as the "Keystone" because of its general shape. However, it is too rounded to have actually served as a keystone. It was apparently intended to be held with the knob in the right hand, and turned to read the four sides in succession, perhaps repetitively. It might also have been suspended by the knob for some purpose. Although it is not pointed enough to have been a plumb bob, it could have served as a pendulum.

The material of the Keystone has been identified, probably by geologist Charles Whittlesey, immediately after its discovery as novaculite, a very hard fine-grained siliceous rock used for whetstones. [For more on Whittlesey, see "Ancient Copper Mining in the Great Lakes," on page 203.] The inscriptions on the four sides read:

Fig. 9.3. The Keystone (courtesy of J. Huston McCulloch)

- Qedosh Qedoshim, "Holy of Holies"
- Melek Eretz, "King of the Earth"
- Torath YHWH, "The Law of God"
- Devor YHWH, "The Word of God"

Wyrick found the Keystone within what is now a developed section of Newark, at the bottom of a pit adjacent to the extensive ancient Hopewellian earthworks there (circa 100 BC–AD 500). Although the pit was surely ancient, and the stone was covered with 12–14 inches of earth, it is impossible to say when the stone fell into the pit. It is, therefore, not inconceivable that the Keystone is genuine but somehow modern.

The letters on the Keystone are nearly standard Hebrew rather than the very peculiar alphabet of the Decalogue stone. These letters were already developed at the time of the Dead Sea Scrolls (ca. 200–100 BC), and so are broadly consistent with any time frame from the Hopewellian era to the present. For the past 1000 years or so, Hebrew has most commonly been written with vowel points and consonant points that are missing on both the Decalogue and Keystone. The absence of points is therefore suggestive, but not conclusive, of an earlier date.

Note that in the Keystone inscription, "*Melek Eretz,*" the *aleph* and *mem* have been stretched so as to make the text fit the available space. Such dilation does occasionally appear in Hebrew manuscripts of the first millennium AD. Birnbaum,

The Hebrew Scripts, vol. I, pp. 173–4, notes that "We do not know when dilation originated. It is absent in the manuscripts from Qumran. . . . The earliest specimens in this book are . . . middle of the seventh century [AD]. Thus we might tentatively suggest the second half of the sixth century or the first half of the seventh century as the possible period when dilation first began to be employed." Dilation would not have appeared in the printed sources nineteenth-century Ohioans would primarily have had access to.

The Hebrew letter *shin* is most commonly made with a V-shaped bottom. The less common flat-bottomed form that appears on the first side of the Keystone may provide some clue as to its origin. The exact wording of the four inscriptions may provide additional clues.

Today, both the Decalogue Stone and Keystone, or "Newark Holy Stones," as they are known, are on display in the Johnson-Humrickhouse Museum in Roscoe Village, 300 Whitewoman St., Coshockton, Ohio.

THE WILSON MOUND STONES

One year after Wyrick's death in 1864, two additional Hebrew-inscribed stones were found during the excavation of a mound on the George A. Wilson farm east of Newark. These stones have been lost, but a drawing of the one and a photograph of the other are reproduced in Alrutz.

The two stones from the Wilson farm, known as the "Inscribed Head" and the "Cooper Stone" at first caused considerable excitement. Shortly afterwards, however, a local dentist named John H. Nicol claimed to have carved the stones and to have introduced them into the excavation, with the intention of discrediting the two earlier stones found by Wyrick.

The inscription on the Inscribed Head can be read in Hebrew letters as J–H–NCL. In Hebrew, short vowels are not represented by letters, so this is precisely how one would write J–H–NiCoL.

The Cooper stone is less clear, but appears to have a similar inscription. The inscriptions themselves therefore confirm Nicol's claim to have planted these two stones. Nicol was largely successful in his attempt to discredit the Wyrick stones, and they quickly became a textbook example of a "well-known" hoax. It was only with Alrutz's thorough 1980 article* that interest in them was revived.

Although the Decalogue is of an entirely different character than either of the Wilson Mound stones, it is disturbing that Nicol was standing near Wyrick at the time of its discovery.

THE JOHNSON-BRADNER STONE

Two years later, in 1867, David M. Johnson, a banker who co-founded the Johnson-Humrickhouse Museum, in conjunction with Dr. N. Roe Bradner, M.D., of Pennsylvania, found a fifth stone, in the same mound group south of Newark in which Wyrick had located the Decalogue. The original of this small stone is now lost, but a lithograph, published in France, survives.

The letters on the lid and base of the Johnson-Bradner stone are in the same peculiar alphabet as the Decalogue inscription, and appear to wrap around in the same manner as on the Decalogue's back platform. However, the lithograph is not clear enough for me to attempt a transcription with any confidence. However, Dr. James Trimm, whose Ph.D. is in Semitic Languages, has recently reported that the base and lid contain fragments of the Decalogue text. The independent discovery, in a related context, by reputable citizens, of a third stone bearing the same unique characters as the Decalogue stone, strongly confirms the authenticity and context of the Decalogue Stone, as well as Wyrick's reliability.

---

*The negative of the sketch of the Inscribed Head was somehow flipped over in producing Alrutz so that it appears there in mirror image. The profile should face left, not right. With this correction the Hebrew letters have their proper orientation and may be read right to left.

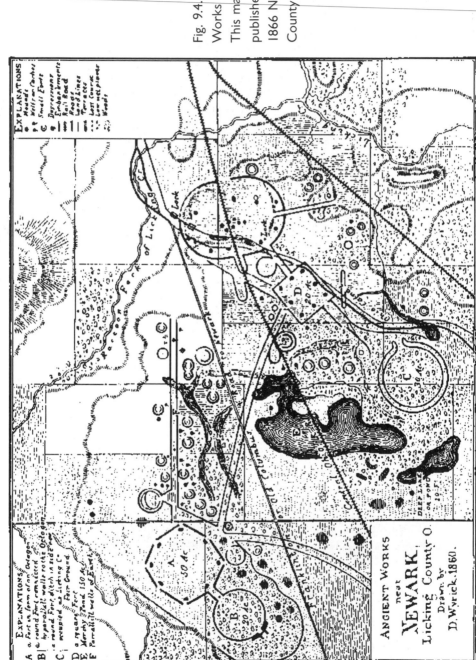

Fig. 9.4. Ancient Works at Newark. This map was published in the 1866 Newark County Atlas.

Fig. 9.5. These skeletons found in a recent excavation in Germany are from the Neolithic Period and are typical of the multiple burials found in many of America's Indian mounds (courtesy of Arthur W. McGrath).

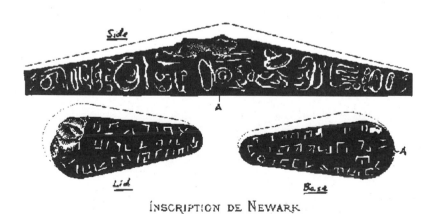

INSCRIPTION DE NEWARK

Fig. 9.6. Lithograph by Nancy J. Royer, *Congres International des Americanistes* (courtesy of J. Huston McCulloch)

Mr. Myron Paine of Martinez, Calif., has cogently noted that the Johnson-Bradner stone, if bound in a strap so as to be held as a frontlet between the eyes, would serve well as a head phylactery, while the Decalogue stone was being used as an arm phylactery per the Deal-Trimm hypothesis noted in the first section above.

THE MYSTERIOUS STONE BOWL

A stone bowl was also found with the Decalogue, by one of the persons accompanying Wyrick. By Wyrick's account, it was of the capacity of a teacup, and of the same material as the box. Wyrick believed both the box and the cup had once been bronzed (Alrutz, pp. 21–2), though this has not been confirmed.

The bowl was long neglected, but was found recently in the storage rooms of the Johnson-Humrickhouse Museum by Dr. Bradley Lepper of the Ohio Historical Society. It is now on display along with the Decalogue stone and Keystone. (Photo courtesy of Jeffrey A. Heck, Najor Productions, njor@tcon.net).

An interview in the Jan/Feb 1998 issue of *Biblical Archaeology Review* ("The Enigma of Qumran," pp. 24ff.) sheds light on the possible significance of the stone bowl. The interviewer, Hershel Shanks, asked how we would know that Qumran, the settlement adjacent to the caves in which the Dead Sea Scrolls were found, was Jewish, if there had been no scrolls. The four archaeologists interviewed gave several reasons: the

Fig. 9.7. The Decalogue stone, the Keystone, and the ritual cleansing bowl (photo by Jeffrey A. Heck)

presence of ritual baths, numerous Hebrew-inscribed potsherds, and its location in Judea, close to Jerusalem. Then Hanan Eshel, senior lecturer in archaeology at Hebrew University and Bar-Ilan University, gave a fourth reason.

ESHEL: We also have a lot of stone vessels.

SHANKS: Why is that significant?

ESHEL: Stone vessels are typical of Jews who kept the purity laws. Stone vessels do not become impure.

SHANKS: Why?

ESHEL: Because that is what the Pharisaic law decided. Stone doesn't have the nature of a vessel, and therefore it is always pure.

SHANKS: Is that because you don't do anything to transform the material out of which it is made, in contrast to, say, a clay pot, whose composition is changed by firing?

ESHEL: Yes. Probably. Stone is natural. You don't have to put it in an oven or anything like that. Purity was very important to the Jews in the Late Second Temple period.

In an article in a subsequent issue of *BAR*, Yitzhak Magen goes on to explain that in the late Second Temple period, the Pharisees ordained that observant Jews should ritually rinse their hands with pure water before eating, and that in order to be pure, the water had to come from a pure vessel. Pottery might be impure, but stone was always pure. The result was a brief "Israeli Stone Age," during which there flourished an industry of making stone teacups to pour the water from and stone jugs to store it in. After the destruction of the Second Temple in AD 70, this practice quickly disappeared.

The stone bowl therefore fits right in with the Decalogue Stone as an appropriate ritual object. It is highly doubtful that Wyrick, Nicol, McCarty, or anyone else in Newark in 1860 would have been aware of this arcane Second Temple era convention.

Perhaps the stone box is another manifestation of the same "Stone Age" imperative: The easy way to make a box to hold an important object (or a prank) is out of wood. Carving it from stone is unnecessarily difficult, and would be justified only if stone were regarded as being significant in itself. According to Wyrick the bowl and box were made of the same sandstone.

Two unusual "eight-square plumb bobs" were also found with the Decalogue. Their location is unknown, though they might also turn up in the Museum's collections.

HUNTERS FIND STONE TABLETS UNDER A TREE

SMITHSONIAN INVOLVED IN ILLINOIS TABLET FIND

A REMARKABLE FIND ON THE PRAIRIES OF ILLINOIS:

QUAINT LETTERING, INDIAN RELICS,

AND THE MOUND BUILDERS

CHICAGO TRIBUNE, AUGUST 10, 1892

A remarkable discovery was recently made on the virgin field a few miles from LaHarpe, in the historic old county of Hancock, in Illinois. Wyman Huston and Daniel Lovitt were chasing a ground squirrel on the farm of Huston, when the dog trailed the squirrel to its hole under an old dead tree stump, which was easily pushed over by one of the men. In grabbing for the squirrel, the old stump was taken out, and under its roots were found two sandstone tablets, about 10 × 11 inches, and from one-fourth to half-an-inch in thickness.

The tablets lay one upon the other, and the sides that faced contained strange inscriptions in Roman-like capital letters that had been cut into the stone with some sharp instrument. The men brought the tablets to LaHarpe, where they were inspected by several antiquarians but none of them could decipher the inscriptions. Mr. Huston allowed the stones to be forwarded to the Smithsonian in Washington D.C., where they are to be held for scientific investigation.

SMITHSONIAN BAFFLED BY INSCRIPTIONS

The authorities of the Smithsonian Institution state that the find is a remarkable one, and that they hope to throw some light upon the meaning of the lettering etched upon the tablets. But, so far, however, they have been unable to do so, or at least they have not announced the result of any discoveries, they may have made in the matter.

THE DAVENPORT STELE

When the Davenport Stele is added to the mix, things get even stranger. The stele was found in an Indian mound in 1877, and according to

Harvard Professor Barry Fell, the stele contains writing in Egyptian, Iberian-Punic, and Libyan. The Smithsonian, of course, says it and others like it are fakes.

SMITHSONIAN INVOLVED IN STRANGE ANCIENT IOWA TABLET "HOAX" WITH *AMERICA B.C.'S* BARRY FELL

By Otto Knauth

DES MOINES REGISTER, FEBRUARY 20, 1977

"Egyptian and Libyan explorers sailed up the Mississippi River 2,500 years ago and left a tablet where Davenport now stands," a Harvard Professor said. "That's absurd," countered a former Iowa state archeologist, who says the Professor is perpetuating a 100-year-old hoax. Harvard's Dr. Barry Fell, a marine biologist by profession and an epigraphist by avocation, said he had deciphered the front and back of a table that was found in an Indian mound in 1877. "The tablet," he stated, "contains writing not only in Egyptian hieroglyphics but also in Iberian-Punic and Libyan."

He likened it in importance to the famed Rosetta Stone, which, because it said the same thing in three languages, enabled scientists to decipher hieroglyphics.

"It is unquestionably genuine," he stated.

"Not so," said University of Iowa archeologist Marshall McKusick.

"The tablet is part of 'one of the most thoroughly documented hoaxes in American archeology.' Members of the old Davenport Academy of Science inscribed the tablets and buried them in a mound on the old Cook farm, knowing the tablets would be found by a member they wanted to ridicule," McKusick says.

But the hoax got out of hand when the Smithsonian Institution got involved and the discovery of the tablets received national publicity. McKusick documented the hoax in a 1970 book, *The Davenport Conspiracy.*

"That all may well be true," Fell said in a recent telephone interview, "and two of the three tablets in the mound probably are fake. But the third, which he refers to as the Davenport Calendar Stele, definitely is not." This stele with the spring equinox scene on is described in Barry Fell's book, *America B.C.,* as "one of the most important ever discovered. It is used in the ceremonial erection of a New Year pillar made of bundles of reeds called 'Djed,'" Fell said.

"Writing in the curving lines above says the same thing in Iberian and Libyan. The Egyptian hieroglyphics along the top explain how to use the stone.

"Two Indian pipes carved in the shape of elephants found in the mound also are genuine," Fell says.

BARRY FELL PUBLISHES CONTROVERSIAL *AMERICA B.C.*

Fell's account of deciphering the tablet and the implications of its message are contained in his book just published, *America B.C.: Ancient Settlers in the New World*. The book deals with a wide variety of finds, particularly in New England, but also ranging as far west as Oklahoma, which Fell contends prove that ancient Egyptians, Libyans, Celts, and other people were able to reach America and settle here well before the birth of Christ. Portions of the book are reprinted in the February issue of *Reader's Digest*. "The Davenport stele," Fell writes, "is the only one on which occurs a trilingual text in the Egyptian, Iberian-Punic, and Libyan languages.

"This stele, long condemned as a meaningless forgery, is in fact one of the most important steles ever discovered," he writes.

"One side of the tablet—since its discovery it has separated by cleavage so that each face is now separate—depicts the celebration of the Djed Festival of Osiris at the time of the Spring equinox (Mar. 21)," Fell says. The other side contains the corresponding fall hunting festival at the time of the autumnal equinox (Sept. 21). The writing runs along the top of the spring tablet. "The Iberian and Libyan texts," Fell says, "both say the same thing—that the stone carries an inscription giving the secret of regulating the calendar." This "secret" is given in the Egyptian text of hieroglyphics.

"This Egyptian text," Fell says, "may be rendered in English as follows":

To a pillar attach a mirror in such a manner that when the sun rises on New Year's Day it will cast a reflection onto the stone called the Watcher. New Year's Day occurs when the sun is in conduction with the zodiacal constellation Aries, in the House of the Ram, the balance of night and day being about to reverse. At this time (the spring equinox) hold the Festival of the New Year and the Religious Rite of the New Year.

"This festival," Fell says, "consists in the ceremonial erection of a special New Year pillar made of bundles of reeds called a "djed." The tablet, shows long lines of worshippers pulling on ropes with the pillar in the center."

HOW DID ANCIENT HIEROGLYPHS GET TO IOWA?

"How did this extraordinary document come to be in a mound burial in Iowa?" Fell asks. "Is it genuine?

"Certainly it is genuine," he says, "for neither the Libyan nor the Iberian scripts had been deciphered at the time Gass [Rev. Jacob Gass] found the stone. The Libyan and Iberian texts are consistent with each other and with the hieroglyphic text.

"As to how it came to be in Iowa, some speculations may be made. The stele appears to be of local American manufacture, perhaps made by a Libyan or an Iberian astronomer who copied as an older model brought from Egypt or more likely from Libya, hence probably brought on a Libyan ship.

"The Priest of Osiris may have issued the stone originally as a means of regulating the calendar in far distant lands. The date is unlikely to be earlier than about 800 B.C., for we do not know of Iberian or Libyan inscriptions earlier than that date," Fell writes.

"The explorers presumably sailed up the Mississippi River and colonized in the Davenport area," he says, and he hazards a guess that they came on ships commanded by a Libyan skipper of the Egyptian navy, during the Twenty-second, or Libyan, Dynasty, a period of overseas exploration. "An Egyptian astronomer-priest probably came with the explorers," he speculates, "and it was he or his successors who engraved the stone.

"The hunting scene tablet is engraved in Micmac script and is the work of an Algonquian Indian of about 2,000 years ago," Fell says. He does not explain the discrepancy in time, but goes on to say that the Algonquian culture shows evidence of contact with early Egyptians. The approximate translation is:

Hunting of beasts and their young, waterfowl and fishes. The herds of the Lord and their young, the beasts of the Lord.

"It is the earliest known example of Micmac script," Fell says. Fell makes no mention in his book of McKusick's account of the Davenport fraud but this is not because he was not aware of it.

AVOIDING OLD DISPUTES

"I just felt it was kinder not to mention it," he said recently. "It was my desire to avoid raking up old disputes. Who cares whether somebody defrauded somebody else a hundred years ago? I attach no importance to those things."

NINETY-FIVE PERCENT OF "FRAUDS" TURN OUT TO BE TRUE

The Smithsonian, which was the first to declare the tablets fraudulent, had no experts in ancient languages. "Only those who thought they were," Fell said.

"And McKusick himself makes no claim to being a linguist," he says. Fell said he has been investigating similar archeological finds that had been labeled frauds, "and we find that 95 per cent of them are genuine.

"There is a tendency on the part of those established in a field of science either to ignore or label as fraud anything that does not fit in with their pre-conceived notion of how things should be," he said.

"It is much easier to cry fraud at something out of the ordinary than to investigate it," he said. "Americans are throwing away 2,000 years of their history that way."

Fell concedes he has never been in Iowa and was not allowed to see the tablet, which is now in possession of the Putnam Museum in Davenport. He says he did his deciphering from photographs, which is the usual way epigraphists do their work. McKusick has taken up the challenge by writing a report to *Science,* the weekly publication of the prestigious American Academy for the Advancement of Science. He said the Davenport frauds were first exposed in *Science* in the 1880s and later reviewed in 1970. McKusick pointed out that the slate for one of the tablets (not Fell's Davenport stele) came from a wall of the Old Slate House, a notorious

early-day house of ill fame. "The third tablet, a piece of limestone with a tablet, is engraved on a piece of slate," said University of Iowa Archeologist Marshall McKusick.

In 1970 McKusick wrote a book about the Davenport Conspiracy that surrounded the finding of the tablets in an Indian mound in 1877. "Holes in the top corners measure $3/8$-inch diameter and were used to hang the slate," McKusick says. Fell concedes this tablet may well have a fake figure of an Indian on it and came from Schmidt's Quarry, not far from the place where the tablets were found. The farm site now is occupied by the Thompson-Hayward Chemical Co., 2040 West River Drive.

"A dictionary and almanacs provided inspiration for the writing on the tablets," he said. "A janitor at the Academy admitted carving various Indian pipes, which also were found in the mound," McKusick said. "They were soaked in grease or rubbed with shoe black to make them look old." Two members of the academy were expelled in the ruckus that followed the claims of fraud but a curious sidelight to the controversy lies in the fact that none of the participants ever admitted in writing that they actually forged the tablets. All were under threat of libel at the time. The closest thing to a confession in McKusick's book is a statement by Judge James Bellinger made in 1947 to a Mr. Irving Hurlbut. In it, Bellinger tells of copying hieroglyphics out of old almanacs on slate he tore off the wall of the Old Slate House.

The story becomes suspect, however, when McKusick points out that Bellinger was only 9 years old at the time the tablets were found. "Whatever the judge may have said, he was nowhere near the scene of the events he so vividly describes," McKusick wrote.

"GULLIBLE PUBLIC"

In his report to *Science* McKusick says of the Fell book: "It is an unfortunate imposition upon a gullible public to have the Davenport frauds accepted as genuine and used to explain Egyptian explorations up the Mississippi 3,000 years ago.

"Fell, as a 'Harvard scholar,' has a scholarly responsibility to know the professional literature on subjects he is publishing theories about. His book, *America B.C.,* is irresponsible amateurism and is unfortunately but one example of a genre of speculation that is growing and sells well to the public."

"Modern technology may provide the means for resolving the issue of whether one or all of the tablets are fake," says Dr. Duane Anderson, who succeeded McKusick as state archeologist. "If the tablets could be submitted to a rigorous microscopic examination, it might be possible to determine that the writing is older than a mere 100 years," Anderson said. "Rock ages, and often a patina, or microscopic crust, develops on the surface. It might also be possible to detect traces of modern steel if the incisions were made with modern instruments," he said. Anderson continued, "But they might at least be able to reveal if the writing was done before 1877."

Anyone wishing to make such an examination will have to secure the cooperation of the Putnam Museum, which is the present custodian of the tablets. Museum Director Joseph Cartwright has steadfastly refused access to the tablets, saying they have "been removed from the museum collection.

"We are not anxious to dig up the whole controversy again," he said in a recent telephone interview. "It is not in the museum's interest to make them available. This is something the museum is not interested in." Asked if it might not be interesting for the public to put the tablets on display in view of the present renewal of the controversy, Cartwright replied, "It is our prerogative to decide, not yours."

HIEROGLYPHIC TABLETS IN MICHIGAN AND KENTUCKY

Evidence of writing and hieroglyphs has been found all over the country, attesting to widespread trade and wide-ranging cultural influences. Many examples have been found in Michigan, including the controversial Michigan tablets, which number in the thousands. Many more finds of writing have been discovered across the country, although many, like the Ten Commandments from Ohio and the Michigan and Illinois tablets, are still under hot dispute. Here are two finds from Michigan and Kentucky that appear genuine.

ANCIENT HIEROGLYPHICS AND WRITING ON A TABLET

DETROIT FREE PRESS, JUNE 14, 1894

The mounds on the south side of Crystal Lake, in Montcalm County, Michigan, have been opened and a prehistoric race unearthed. One contained five skeletons and the other three. In the first mound was an earthen tablet five inches long, four wide, and half as much thick. It was divided into four corners. On one of them were inscribed queer characters. The skeletons were arranged in the same relative positions, so far as the record is concerned.

In the other mound, there was a casket of earthen ware ten and one half inches long and three and a half inches wide. The cover bore various inscriptions. The characters found upon the tablet were also prominent on the casket. Upon opening the casket, a copper coin was revealed, together with several stone types, with which the inscriptions or casket had evidentially been made. There were also two pipes—one of stone, the other of pottery and apparently of the same material as the casket.

STRANGE ANCIENT WELSH MESSAGE WRITTEN ON A STONE?

PROCEEDINGS OF THE ANCIENT KENTUCKY HISTORICAL SOCIETY,
FEBRUARY 11, 1880

Craig Crecelius made a curious discovery in 1912, while plowing his field in Meade County, Kentucky. He had unearthed a limestone slab that had strange symbols chiseled onto the rock face. Knowing that he had made an important historical find, he sought information about the origins of the stone from the academics.

For over 50 years, Crecelius inquired of anyone with academic credentials about the significance of the carved symbols. Typical of the comments he received from the "experts" were like what one geologist in 1973 remarked that the rock was "geologic in origin" and "not an artifact." An archaeologist has said that the carvings were grooves created by shifting limestone pressures.

Disheartened and tired of being made fun of by the locals, Crecelius finally gave up his quest for finding out the rock's secrets. In the mid-1960s, he allowed Jon Whitfield, a former trustee of the Meade County, Kentucky, Library, to display the stone in the Brandenburg Library. This could very well have been the end of the story, had it not been for the observant Mr. Whitfield.

Whitfield attended a meeting of the Ancient Kentucky Historical Society (AKHS) and saw slides of other, similar-looking carved stones. He learned that the carvings were a script called Coelbren, used by the ancient Welsh. Whitfield was informed that similar stones had been widely found across the south-central part of the U.S. Pictures made of the Brandenburg Stone were submitted to two Welsh historians helping the AKHS in deciphering the scripts.

Alan Wilson and Baram Blackett, specialists in the study of the Coelbren script in Wales, immediately were able to read the script. The translation is intriguing; it appears that the stone may possibly have been a property or boundary marker: "Toward strength, divide the land we are spread over, purely between offspring in wisdom."

Wilson and Blackett place a connotation of the promotion of unity with the phrase "Toward strength" and a connotation of justice with the word "purely." The stone was on public display from 1999–2000 at the Falls of the Ohio State Park Interpretive Center in Clarksville, Indiana. The display has since been moved to the Charlestown Public Library, Clark County, Indiana.

ANCIENT COINS FOUND IN AMERICA

Scattered reports of ancient coins found buried around the country are usually dismissed as fraudulent by traditional archaeologists, but in the collection of stories that follow, one outlines a circumstance where the difficulty of creating a hoax belies that idea, while others tell of quite recent finds that have been authenticated by ancient coin experts.

The following first-person account of the discovery of two ancient coins is very instructive. The coins were found underneath the roots of a beech tree that had been blown up in order to clear a field. This is not something that could be done as a prank, as the entire operation would have been costly and pointless in the extreme.

The Natural and Aboriginal History of Tennessee, 1823
By Dr. John Haywood

A Copper Medal of King Richard III Found

Between the years of 1802 and 1809, in the state of Kentucky, Jefferson County, on Big Grass Creek, which runs into the Ohio River at Louisville, at the upper end of the falls, about ten miles above the mouth, near Middleton, Mr. Spear found under the roots of a beech tree, which had been blown up, two pieces of copper coin of the size of our old copper pence. On one side was represented an eagle with three heads united to one neck. The sovereign princes of Greece wore on their scepters the figure of a bird and often that of an eagle. Possibly this may have been a coin uttered in the time of the three Roman emperors.

Lately, a Cherokee Indian delivered to Mr. Dwyer, in the year 1822, who delivered to Mr. Earle, a copper medal, nearly or quite the size of a dollar. All around it, on both sides was a raised rim. On the one side is the robust figure of a man, apparently of the age of 40, with a crown upon his head, buttons upon his coat, and a garment flowing from a knot on his shoulder, toward and over the lower part of his breast, his hair short and curled; his face full; his nose aquiline, very prominent and long, the tip descending very considerably below the nostril; his mouth wide; the chin long, and the lower part very much curved, and projected outwards. Within the rim, which is on the margin, and just below it in Roman letters, are the words and figures: "Richardus III. DG. ANG. FR. Et HIB. Rex." The letters are none of them at all worn. Both the letters and figures protuberated from the surface. On the other side is a monument with a female figure reclined on it, her knees a little raised, with a crown upon them, and in her left hand a sharp pointed sword. Underneath the monument are the words: "Coronat 6 Jul. 1483." And under that line: "Mort 22 Aug. 1485."

Of Their Coins and Other Metals

About the year 1819, in digging a cellar at Mr. Norris's, in Fayetteville, on Elk river, which falls into Tennessee, and about two hundred yards from a creek, which empties into Elk, and not far from the ruins of a very ancient fortification on the creek, was found a small piece of silver coin of the size of a nine-penny piece.

On the one side of this coin is the image of an old man projected considerably from the superficies with a large Roman nose, his head covered apparently with a cap of curled hair; and on this side on the edge in old Roman letters, not so neat by far as on our modern coins, are the words: "Antoninus Aug: Pius. PP. RI. Ill cos."

On the other side the projected image of a young man, apparently 18 or 20 years of age; and on the edge: Juleiius Ceasar. AL/GP, 111.cos." It was coined in the third year of the reign of Antoninus, which was in the year of our Lord 137, and must in a few years afterwards have been deposited where it was lately found. The prominent images are not in the least impaired, nor in any way defaced, nor made dim or dull by rubbing with other money; neither are the letters on the edges. It must have lain in the place where lately found, 1500 or 1600 years.

For had it first circulated a century, before it was laid up, the worn-off parts of the letters and images would be observable. It was found five feet below the surface. The people living upon Elk River when it was brought into the country had some production of art, or of agriculture, for which this coin was brought to the place, to be exchanged. It could not have been brought by De Soto, for long before his time it would have been defaced and made smooth by circulation; and, besides, the crust of the earth would not have been increased to the depth of five feet in 177 years, the time elapsed since De Soto passed between the Alabama and the Tennessee, to the Mississippi.

Irrefutable Proof of Commerce by Sea

This coin furnishes irrefragable proof of one very important fact; namely, that there was an intercourse, either by sea or by land, between the ancient inhabitants of Elk River, and the Roman Empire in the time of Antoninus, or soon afterwards; or between the ancient Elkites, and some other nation, who had such intercourse with it. Had a Roman fleet been driven by a storm, in the time of Antoninus, on the American shores, the crews, even if they came to land all at the same place, would not have been able to penetrate to Elk river, nor would any discoverable motive have engaged them to do so.

And again: Roman vessels, the very largest in the Roman fleet of that day, were not of structure and strength sufficient to have lived in a storm of such violence and long continuance in the Atlantic ocean, as was necessary to have driven them from Europe to America. Nor are storms in such directions and of such continuance at all usual. Indeed, there is no instance of any such, which has occurred since the European settlements in America.

The people of Elk in ancient times did probably extend their commerce down the rivers that Elk communicated with; or if directly over land to the ocean, they were not impeded by small, independent tribes between them and the ocean but were part of an empire extended to it. A thick forest of trees, not more than 6 or 8 years ago, grew upon the surface where the coin was found, many of which could not be of more recent commencement than 300 or 400 years; a plain proof that the coin was not of Spanish or French importation.

Besides this coin impressed with the figures of Antoninus and Aurelius, another was also found in a gully washed by torrents about two and a half miles from Fayetteville, where the other coin was found. It was about four feet below the surface. The silver was very pure, as was also the silver of the other piece; evidently much more so than the silver coins of the present day.

The letters are rough. Some of them seem worn. On the one side is the image of a man, in high relief, apparently of the age of 25 or 30. And on the coin, near the edge were these words and letters: Commodus. The C is defaced, and hardly visible. AVG. HEREL, on the other side, f E. IMP. III. cos. H. PP. Oa rx. This latter side also is the figure of a woman, with a hoop in her right hand. She is seated in a square box; on the inside of which, touching each side, and resting on the ground, is a wheel. Her left arm, from the shoulder to the elbow, lies by her side, but from the elbow is raised a little above the top: and across a small distaff, proceeding from the hand, is a handle to which is added a trident with the teeth or prongs parallel to each other. It is supposed that Faustina, the mother of Commodus, who was defied after her death by her husband Marcus Aurelius, with the attributes of Venus, Juno, and Ceres, is represented by this figure.

The neck of Commodus is bare, with the upper part of his robes flowing in gatherings from the lower part of the neck. His head seemed to be covered with a cap of hair curled into many small knots, with a white fillet around it, near its edges, and the temples and forehead, with two ends falling some distance from the knot. Commodus reigned with his father, Marcus Aurelius, from the time he was 14 or 15 years of age, until the latter died, in the year of our Lord 180. From that time he reigned alone, until the 31st of December, 192, when he was put to death.

A HALF-SILVER-DOLLAR-SIZED SCENE OF HOUND AND DEER

Also from Haywood's book, here is a separate report from Lincoln, Tennessee, which is about eleven miles from the Fayetteville site, in which a silver medallion was discovered with the image of a deer being chased by a hound engraved on one side. More than thirty-five similar medallions were plowed up three miles from this site on a farm owned by a Mr. Oliver Williams.

The Natural and Aboriginal History of Tennessee, 1823

BY DR. JOHN HAYWOOD

Lincoln County, in West Tennessee, is eleven miles from Fayetteville, where the Roman coin above mentioned was found, and near to the mouth of Cold water creek, and about 600 yards distant from the river. The button is about the size of a half dollar in circumference and is of the intrinsic value of little more than 37.1 cents. The silver is very pure. The button is convex with the representation of a deer engraved on it and a hound in pursuit. The eye of the button appears to be as well soldered as though it had been effected by some of our modern silversmiths.

It was in the spring of 1819 when the first discovery of this button was made. On the opposite side of the river is an entrenchment, including a number of mounds. Mr. Oliver Williams lives within three miles of this place and says that during the year 1819 one dozen of the like buttons were ploughed up; and that for every year since, more or fewer of them have been found; the whole amounting to about three dozen. Upon all of them the device is that above stated. These buttons have been found promiscuously, at the depth to which the plough generally penetrates into the earth, or from 9 to 12 inches. The field in which the buttons were found contains from 60 to 70 acres of land. Trees lately grew upon it, before the land was cleared, from 4 to 5 feet in diameter. The country around is rather hilly than otherwise.

An Ancient Furnace Is Discovered

As to other metals found in Tennessee, there is this fact: In the month of June, in the year 1794, in the county of Davidson, on Manscoe's creek, at Manscoe's Lick, on the creek, which runs through the lick, a hole or well was dug by Mr. Cafftey, who, at the distance of 5 or 6 feet through black mud and loose rocks found the end of a bar of iron, which had been cut off by a cleaving iron, and had also been split lengthwise. A small distance from that, in yellow clay, 18 inches under the surface, was a furnace full of coals and ashes.

Another fact evinces most clearly, the residence of man in West Tennessee in very ancient times, who knew how to forge metals, make axes and other metallic tools and implements, and probably also the art of fusing ore and of making iron or hardened copper, such as have been long used in Chile by the natives. It also fixes such residence to a period long preceding that at which Columbus discovered America.

In the county of Bedford, in West Tennessee, northeast from Shelbyville, and seventeen miles from it, on the waters of the Garrison fork, one of the three forks of Duck river, on McBride's branch, in the year 1812, was cut down a poplar tree five feet some inches in diameter. It was felled by Samuel Pearse, Andrew Jones, and David Dobbs, who found within two or three inches of the heart, in the curve made by the ax cut into the tree, the old chop of an ax, which of course must have been made when the tree was a sapling not more than three inches in diameter.

Of 400 years of age when cut down, it must have been 70 when Columbus discovered America, and 118 when De Soto marched through Alabama. If the chop was made by an ax, which the natives obtained from him, it must have been made since the commencement of 282 years from this time; and a poplar sapling of three inches in diameter could not be more than 8 or 10 years of age; making the whole age of the tree, to the time it was cut down, about 300 years in which time a tree of that size could not probably have grown.

Brass Coin with Minerva on It

Two pieces of brass coin were found in the first part of the year 1823, two miles and a half from Murfreesborough, in an easterly direction from thence. Each of them had a hole near the edge. Their size was about that of a nine-penny silver piece of the present time. The rim projected beyond the circle, as if it had been intended to clip it.

On the obverse, was the figure in relief of a female, full faced, steady countenance, rather stern than otherwise; with a cap or helmet on the head, upon the top of which was a crescent extending from the forehead backwards. In the legend was the word Minerva; on the reverse was a slim female figure, with a ribbon in her left hand, which was tied to the neck of a slim, neatly formed dog that goes before her, and in the other a bow.

Amongst the letters of the legend in the reverse, are SL. After the ground, which covered this coin, had been for some years cleared and ploughed, it was enclosed in a garden on the summit of a small hill; and in digging there, these pieces were found eighteen inches under the surface.

A Brief History of Ancient Coinage

There are no Assyrian or Babylonian coins; nor is there any Phoenician one till 400 before Christ. Sidon and Tyre used weights. Coinage was unknown in Egypt in early times. The Lydian coins are the oldest. The Persian coins began 570 before Christ. The darics were issued by Darius Hystaspes 518 or 521 before Christ. Roman coins have been found in the Orkneys, and in the remotest parts of Europe. Romans have three heads upon the side, as that of Valerian and his two sons, Gallienus and Valerian.

On the Roman coins are figures of deities and personifications, which are commonly attended with their names; Minerva, for instance, with her helmet and name inscribed in the legend, sometimes a spear in her right hand, and shield, with Medusa's head, in the other, and an owl standing by her, and sometimes a cock and sometimes the olive. Diana is manifest by her crescent, by her bow and quiver on one side, and often by her hounds. The Roman brass coins have SC. for senatus consultam, till the time of Gallienus, about the year of our Lord 260. The small brass coins ceased to be issued for a time in the reign of Pertinax, 19 CE, and from thence to the time of Valerian. Small brass coins continued from the latter period till 640 CE. Some coins are found with holes pierced through them, and sometimes with small brass strings fastened.

Earliest Roman Coins Date Back to Antoninus

Such were worn as ornaments of the head, neck, and wrist, either by the ancients themselves, as bearing images of favorite deities, or in modern times when the Greek girls thus decorated themselves. From these criteria it may be determined, that these metals are not counters but coins. Of all the Roman coins that have been found in Tennessee and Kentucky, the earliest bears date in the time of Antoninus, the next in the time of Commodus, the next before the elevation of Pertinax, and the last in the time of Valerian. Coins prior or subsequent to the space embraced in these periods are not found; and from hence the conclusion seems to be furnished, that they were brought into America within one or two centuries at furthest, after the latter period, which is about the year of our Lord 354, and thence to 260; and by a people who had not afterwards any intercourse with the countries in which the Roman coins circulated.

One of these pieces was stained all over with a dark color resembling that of pale ink, which possibly is the verugo peculiar to that metal, which issued from it after lying in a dormant state for a great length of time, and which thus preserved it from decay. The legend on the reverse, on the lower part, below a line across are the letters "EL. SL. RECHP.—ENN."

The author, since writing the above, has seen another coin of the same metal precisely, which seems to be a mixture of silver and brass. Upon it, on one side, is the figure of a man's face; and in the legend,

LEOPOL. DG. IMP. On the other, under a mark or cross: EI. SL.; also, the sun at the top; and in the legend, only a contraction of those in the larger piece, namely, RL. C. PERNN.

This, then, is a German coin of modern date.

ROMAN COINS FOUND AT THE OHIO FALLS

In 1997, the Ohio Museum took possession of a cache of Roman coins that was originally discovered in 1963 by a construction engineer excavating on the north shore of the Ohio River during construction of the Sherman Minton Bridge. Coin experts have examined these Roman coins and declared them to be authentic.

Fig. 9.8. Claudius II (left), Maximinus II (right)
(courtesy of Troy McCormick)

The discoverer kept most of the hoard for himself but gave two of the coins to another engineer on the project. In 1997 the second engineer's widow brought these two to Troy McCormick, then manager of the new Falls of the Ohio State Park Interpretive Center in Clarksville, Indiana, not far from the find site. She donated them to the museum, where they remain today.

The larger coin has been identified by both Mark Lehman, president of Ancient Coins for Exploration, and Rev. Stephen A. Knapp, senior pastor at St. John Lutheran Church, Forest Park, Illinois, and a specialist in late Roman bronze coinage, as a follis of Maximinus II from 312 or 313 CE, despite McCormick's original identification of the coin as a 235 CE bronze of Maximinus I.

The coin of Claudius II is similar in type and period to the recently discovered Roman coins from Breathitt County, Kentucky, but is in a much better state of preservation. The latter coin makes this find several decades later than the Severian Period (193 to 235 CE), to which the Roman head from Calixtlahuaca, Mexico, has been attributed on stylistic grounds. Unfortunately, the discoverer moved south to work on another bridge shortly after the find, and the second engineer's widow could not remember his name, so the bulk of the hoard is lost.

For several years, the Falls of the Ohio State Park Interpretive Center had an exhibit about the find that displayed several casts of both sides of the two originals, so as to reflect the approximate number of coins originally in the hoard. The two original coins, depicted in fig. 9.8 (see page 272) are in storage and were not on public display. In February 2012, I was informed that the replicas were still on display, despite an earlier report to the contrary, in the Interpretive Center as part of the Myths and Legends exhibit, and that they will remain there at least into 2014.

Recently, three more heavily weathered Roman coins found in Breathitt County were examined hands-on by Norman Totten, professor of history, now professor emeritus, at Bentley College. Totten identified the two thinner coins as *antoniniani,* a type of bronze Roman coin minted between 238 and 305 CE. The obverses depict an unidentifiable emperor wearing the distinctive "solar crown" of the period. The reverse of one coin depicts two figures standing facing what apparently is a central altar, while that of the second coin depicts a female standing figure facing left with a cornucopia in her right hand.

These would originally have had a silver surface, which is long since gone. The third coin is thicker and depicts a bust facing right and wearing a laureate wreath rather than a crown. The reverse, according to Totten, is perhaps a figure of a centaur walking to the right and looking back. Its flan (the metal disk from which the coin is made) seems to be of a North African (Egyptian) or Middle Eastern type. This coin probably dates to a similar period to that of the two antoniniani (the singular of which is *antoninianus*).

10

EXTREMELY ANCIENT
RED-HAIRED MUMMIES

Mummies of ancient Caucasian giants with red hair have been found in startlingly diverse areas of the country, from Florida to Nevada. Along with these finds ample evidence of sophisticated culture, such as fine weavings, has also been found. Then there are the members of North Dakota's Mandan tribe, long known from the earliest days for their red hair and blue eyes. Perhaps the magnitude of the mystery they represent has been partially responsible for the lack of general knowledge about them, or has it been because of definite attempts at suppression of evidence that flouts all previous theories about origins?

GIANT MUMMIES OF SPIRIT CAVE

What do you think the international reaction would be to news that mummies were found in Egypt that predated the earliest ones ever discovered there by more than five thousand years? Surely it would be front-page news from one end of the planet to the other. Yet news that two 9,500-year-old mummies were found in America has elicited barely a whisper. You may think this is impossible or that I'm referring to some discredited rumor, but the truth could not be clearer or more convincing.

It turns out that the original discovery was made in 1940, and it has taken more than sixty years to come to light. Perhaps the only reason the public is now belatedly finding out about this earth-shattering discovery is the fact that the remains were not turned over to the Smithsonian, but kept instead by the Nevada State Museum. The original find in 1940 of two amazingly well-preserved mummies was made by Sydney and Georgia Wheeler, a husband and wife archaeological team working for the Nevada State Parks division, who were commissioned to study the archaeological effects that guano mining was having on any possible historical remains to be found in the arid caves scattered across the Nevada wastelands. (Bat guano is mined because it contains saltpeter, which is used to make fertilizer and is the main ingredient of gunpowder.)

The site was appropriately called Spirit Cave, and it is located thirteen miles east of Fallon, Nevada. In order to find the mummies and the sixty-seven related artifacts associated with the burial, the Wheelers had to dig through several feet of guano droppings that covered the base of the cave and preserved what lay underneath. The two human mummies were expertly wrapped in a highly sophisticated weaving made of tule matting that exhibited extremely fine knotting and hand weaving not thought to exist until thousands of years later. Because the mummies were sealed in bat guano the weavings are extremely well preserved, and they are arguably the greatest evidence of ancient weaving in the world, yet close to nothing is generally known about them.

THE SPIRIT CAVE MAN
AT THE MIDDLE OF ALL THE CONTROVERSY

The male mummy was in better condition and was found lying on a fur blanket, dressed in a twisted skin robe with leather moccasins on its feet and a twined mat sewn around its head and shoulders. A similar mat was wrapped around the lower portion of the body and bound under the feet. Skin remained on the back and shoulders as well as a small tuft of straight dark hair, which changed to reddish-brown when exposed to light and air. The age of the mummy was estimated at forty-five years and its height well in excess of six feet.

The original dig in 1940 was led by the Wheelers with the help of local residents, and the two mummies and sixty-seven related objects were taken to the Nevada State Museum, where they were examined and dated at between 1,500 and 2,000 years old. They were then transported to the museum's storage facility in Carson City and promptly forgotten about. In 1996 the mummies came to the attention of Erv Taylor, an anthropologist at the University of California, Riverside, who decided that new breakthroughs in mass spectrometry dating could reveal the true age of the mummies, especially in light of the extremely good condition of the tule diamond-plaited matte wrappings and the excellent preservation of the mummified bones and associated assorted relics.

One can only imagine Taylor's stunned reaction when the results came in. The mummies were dated to 9,400 before the present, in what is scientifically referred to as uncalibrated radio-carbon years before present (URCYP)—11.5 KYA.

Yet instead of this momentous news shattering the world of archaeology to its very roots, the Bureau of Land Management stepped into the breach and shut down all news of the discovery in 1997 when it ruled in favor of a claim by the Paiute-Shoshone tribe of Fallon, Nevada, that the bones belonged to them by rights of the Native American Graves Protection and Repatriation Act (NAGPRA).

Although no DNA testing was allowed at the time of Taylor's dating, the Paiute-Shoshone tribe's claim held until pressure from the academic community forced the courts to reconsider the claims of the Bureau of Land Management related to the Indian ancestral claims. In 2006, the courts overturned the findings of the bureau and the Paiute-Shoshone tribe and allowed DNA testing of the mummy by Douglas W.

Owsley, division head of Physical Anthropology at the Smithsonian's National Museum of Natural History, and Richard L. Jantz, an anthropology professor at the University of Tennessee, Knoxville. The tests revealed that the mummy was of a Caucasian origin, with a long face and cranium that most closely resembled either Nordic or Ainu ancestry and bore no ancestral relationship to either the Paiute or Shoshone tribes. Although these findings were made public and extensively covered by the local media, this groundbreaking news has received barely a glimmer of attention in the outside world.

In order to put this find in its proper context and understand the other related and equally amazing finds in this part of the western United States, it is imperative that we reconstruct the local topography of this area as it existed ten thousand years ago. Although this knowledge should be commonplace to most schoolchildren, the true map of ancient America remains a complete mystery to most all its citizens.

As it turns out, much like the Sahara region prior to 6000 BCE, the western United States prior to the gigantic Lassen volcanic explosion, posited at some time around 5000 BCE, was home to one of the biggest freshwater lakes in the world and contained a lush biodiversity that one geologist has characterized as abundant in every respect, perhaps the lushest in the world at that time, with every kind of plant and animal necessary for human life. The area of this ancient lake was immense, covering approximately 8,500 square miles in the northeast section of Nevada, bordering on California and Oregon.

Its name is Lake Lahonton, and at its peak around eleven thousand years ago it was almost one thousand feet deep in places and was fed by the Humboldt, Walker, Truckee, and Carson River systems. Remnants of the dried-out lake can be seen at Pyramid Lake, Lake Russell, and Lake Tahoe. At its peak the lake's resting waterline was at approximately 5,200 feet, and consequently many of the finds around its ancient shoreline are found at least at that height.

The Lenni Lenape Indians on the East Coast of America report that they originally lived in the West until their world was destroyed by fire and they were forced to migrate to the other side of the Mississippi River in search of food and shelter. When we understand that these desert regions were once home to abundant life, the other related prehistoric archaeological finds in this area become understandable and even expected, as we are no longer looking at isolated desert remains devoid of logic and contextual understanding.

Fig. 10.1. Ice age lakes in the Southwestern United States, with Red Rock Pass located on the north side of Lake Bonneville (courtesy of Ken Perry)

THE ANCIENT RED-HAIRED GIANTS OF LOVELOCK, NEVADA

In light of this, the equally amazing finds at Lovelock Cave, eighty miles east of Reno, should come as no surprise. Once again we are dealing with a guano-filled cave on the shoreline of Lake Lahonton, in an area called the Great Basin, only this time the original find was made in 1911 and involved considerably more bodies and artifacts that, because of their highly unusual nature, are routinely criticized and dismissed by mainstream archaeology to this day, although the related finds at Spirit Cave should change all of the doubters' minds, especially as the reality of Lake Lahonton's Great Basin culture becomes more well known and accepted.

Quite simply what we are dealing with here is what the popular press at the time called "red-haired giants," which immediately roused the hackles of mainstream academia and caused them to immediately sweep the whole unpleasant subject under the rug. Fortunately for us, the skeletons and artifacts were not sent to the Smithsonian, and although many of the pieces have disappeared from the historical record, some can still be found in local universities and museums in the area.

THE LEGEND OF THE SI-TE-CAH

The Paiute Indians have a legend about their ancestors and red-haired giants. These giants, known as the Si-Te-Cah, were a red-haired tribe of cannibals who lived near the Paiutes, often harassed them with constant war and occasionally captured victims to eat. Eventually the various Paiute groups had had enough and decided to band together to eradicate the Si-Te-Cah (translated as "tule eaters"). Legend has it that the Paiutes cornered the giants and forced them underground, into a cave system, piled brush over the entrance, and set it on fire with flaming arrows, extinguishing the Si-Te-Cah for good.

Modern historians and anthropologists have dismissed this legend as fantasy and allegorical myth, but others have claimed that archaeological finds indicate otherwise. Could there really have been a race of Caucasoid giants that inhabited North America before the Native Americans? Are the artifacts discovered in Lovelock Cave proof that history is wrong, or are they just another hoax?

Lovelock Cave first caught the attention of archaeologists in 1924, thirteen years after miners began harvesting the several-foot-thick layer of bat guano that had built up on the cave floor. The miners continued to dig until sifting out the ancient relics beneath the top layer of

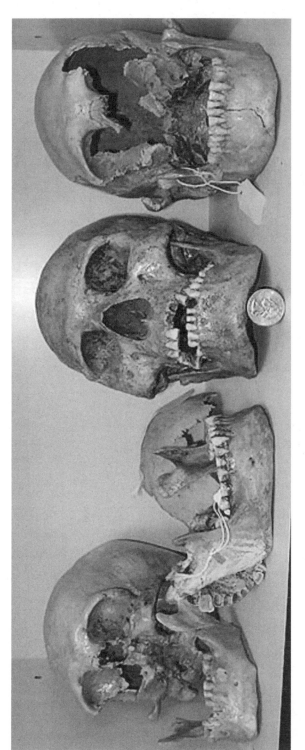

Fig. 10.2. These skulls were photographed at the Humboldt Museum in Winnemucca, Nevada.

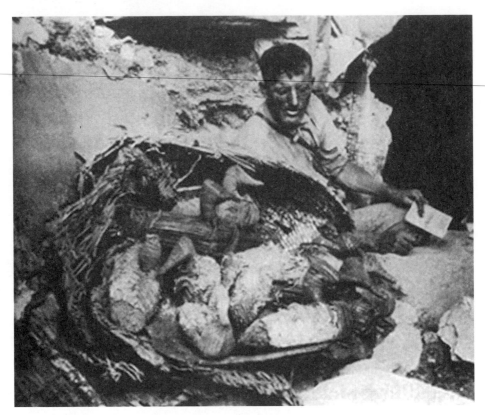

Fig. 10.3. L. L. Loud of the Paleontology Department of the University of California removes the famous duck decoys from Lovelock Cave.

bat guano became too much hassle. They notified the University of California about their finds, and the excavation began.

Among the artifacts found were woven cloth, tools, duck decoys (for hunting), inscribed stones, and supposedly, very tall red-haired mummies. Thousands of pieces were found discarded outside the cave after being separated from the guano. Most of the nonhuman artifacts can be found in local museums or at the University of California Museum of Paleontology in Berkeley, but the mysterious bones and mummies are not so easy to come by. The artifacts themselves prove that an advanced culture did indeed predate the Paiute Indians, but whether the legend of red-haired giants is historically accurate remains unknown.

What is significant to note is that the scientific community has

Fig. 10.4. A view from the mouth of Lovelock Cave

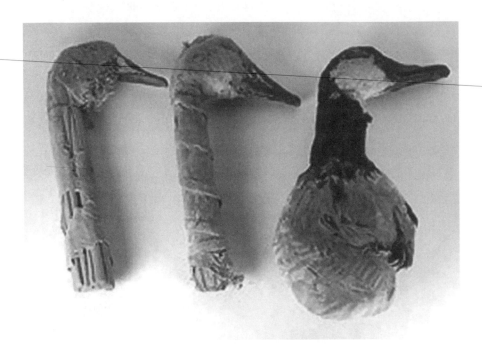

Fig. 10.5. Heads of the exquisite tule-wrapped duck decoys from Lovelock Cave

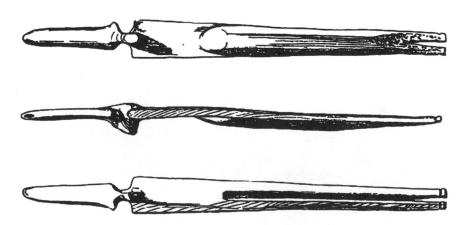

Fig. 10.6. Examples of the fine workmanship found in association with the Lovelock Cave burials

assiduously scrubbed all references to the six- to eight-foot-tall, red-haired skeletons found at the site. As will be seen, this repeated effort to clear the historical record of all references to a pre-Indian Caucasian culture in the United States can be seen as working in harmony with the NAGPRA policies of the federal government, which works on agendas based on political correctness and not objective science.

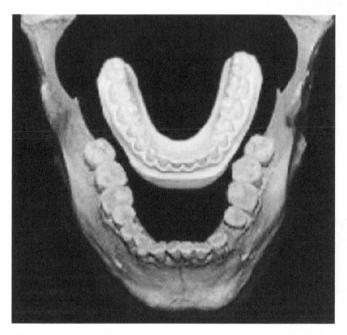

Fig. 10.7. Normal-size teeth compared with a giant jaw
from Lovelock Cave

Lovelock Cave, or Horseshoe Cave, as it was then known, was originally mined for fertilizer in 1911 by two miners named David Pugh and James Hart, who were hired to mine for bat guano from the cave, to be later used as gun powder and fertilizer. They removed a layer of guano estimated to be from three to six feet deep and weighing about 250 tons. The guano was dug up from the upper cave deposits, screened on the hillside outside the cave, and shipped to a fertilizer company in San Francisco. The miners had dumped the top layers into a heap outside of the cave. They were aware of the presence of some ancient artifacts, but only the most interesting specimens were saved. As the finds began to accumulate, L. L. Loud of the Paleontology Department at the University of California was contacted by the mining company, and in the spring of 1912 he arrived to recover any materials that remained from the guano mining of the previous year. Loud also excavated Lovelock Cave for five months and reportedly collected roughly ten thousand material remains. The majority of the finds were made in refuse pits inside and outside the cave, but the University of California alleges that no comprehensive lists of the skeletons and artifacts that were found were ever made, which is quite unusual and not in keeping with the protocol of the day.

What was reported at the time was that in addition to the thousands of artifacts, mummies similar to the ones found at Spirit Cave were, in fact, unearthed. The mummies were reported as being from six to eight feet tall with red hair and lying some four feet under the surface of the cave.

Twelve years after the first excavation, in the summer of 1924, Loud returned to Lovelock Cave with M. R. Harrington of the Museum of the American Indian. It was at this time that the most famous Lovelock artifacts were found, the amazing cache of eleven duck decoys that attests to the lake culture that predominated in this region. These amazing artifacts were made from bundled tule, which the Lake Lahonton culture used much like papyrus for clothing, boats, and artistic and religious objects. The decoys were painted and feathered, and despite their rich cultural and artistic importance, again, for unknown reasons, neither the Museum of the American Indian nor the Smithsonian nor the American Museum of Natural History accepted any of these objects into their collections.

It was not until 1984 that the duck decoys were properly studied in an academic environment. At that time, A. J. T. Tull of the University of Arizona, Tucson, conducted the dating of the specimens. Duck Decoy 13/4513 was dated at 2,080 + 330 BP, and Duck Decoy 13/4512B was

Fig. 10.8. This mummy wrap provides an example of the fine level of weaving achieved more than eight thousand years ago.

dated at 2,250 + 230 BCE. In addition to these duck decoys, a wide range of other materials has been recovered that includes slings, nets, sandals, tunics, and baskets. Not only are these items not on general public display, they also have never been tested as to their antiquity.

Since the scientific community refuses to acknowledge the reality of the skeletons found at Lovelock, the site has been dated by studying the coprolite droppings found in association with other artifacts on the accepted "surface floor" of the cave. Based on those findings it has been determined that the tule people had a diet rich in fish and game, and the earliest habitation of the cave has been dated to 2580 BCE. Since the remains of Spirit Cave were found in the same general area and on the shoreline of the same lake, this could mean that as the lake shrunk in size, the resident tule culture moved to recently exposed caves closer to the new shoreline, or more simply that the cave has never been properly studied and more extensive excavations could reveal continuous occupation going back at least five thousand more years to a date that corresponds to the similar cultural context of the findings at Spirit Cave.

Recently it has been confirmed that four of the ancient skulls unearthed at Lovelock Cave are, in fact, in the possession of the Humboldt Museum in Winnemucca, Nevada. According to Barbara Powell, who is director of the collection, the museum is prohibited by the state of Nevada from putting the skulls on public display because "the state does not recognize their legitimacy." They are instead kept in the storage room and shown to visitors from all over the world only by request. In addition, Powell said that additional bones and artifacts were transferred to the Phoebe A. Hearst Museum of Anthropology in Berkeley, California, where they are kept but also never put on display.

Whether the Lovelock Cave mummies ever really existed or were deliberately covered up, we may never know. The existing artifacts do seem to substantiate the Paiute legend, and evidence of gigantism has been discovered, and documented, in other places across the planet. The Lovelock Cave claim seems to have all the vital pieces, except for the giant mummies themselves. Were they hidden away in some

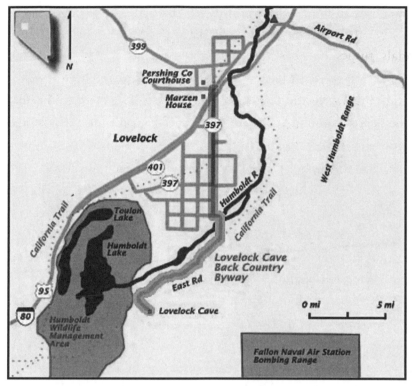

Fig. 10.9. The Lovelock Cave hugs the Humboldt River

Fig. 10.10. The entrance to Lovelock Cave can be seen in the upper
right-hand corner of the photograph.

warehouse, so humanity wouldn't see the errors of modern history? Or were they the imaginary compilation of an ancient legend and a few mysterious bones?

If you want to follow the trail and perhaps answer that question, you might begin with the PDF file of a document by Loud and Harrington titled "Lovelock Cave," published by the University of California in 1929. See appendices 3 and 4 for personal accounts of the legends of the cave. The investigators at the time did a very good job of analyzing what they could of the site. However, at that time knowledge of native U.S. archaeology and history was not what it is today, and they had so many interesting issues competing for their attention. I only wish the site and the legends could be reinvestigated today with open minds and that the original artifacts were still available.

Something to ponder in the meantime is provided by Sarah Winnemucca Hopkins, daughter of Paiute Chief Winnemucca, who related many stories about the Si-Te-Cah in her book *Life Among the Paiutes: Their Wrongs and Claims.*

My people say that the tribe we exterminated had reddish hair. I have some of their hair, which has been handed down from father to son. I have a dress, which has been in our family a great many years, trimmed with the reddish hair. I am going to wear it some time when I lecture. It is called a mourning dress, and no one has such a dress but my family.

GIANT SKELETON FOUND IN UTAH

THE NEW YORK SUN, AUGUST 27, 1891

The gigantic skeleton of a man, measuring 8 feet 6 inches in height, was found near the Jordan River just outside Salt Lake City, last week. The find was made by a workman who was digging an irrigation ditch. The skull was uncovered at a depth of eight feet from the surface of the ground and the skeleton was standing bolt upright. The workmen had to dig down nine feet in order to exhume it. The bones were much decayed and crumbled at the slightest touch. They were put together with great care and the skeleton was found to measure 8 feet 6 inches in height: the skull measured 11 inches in diameter and the feet 19 inches long. A copper chain, to which was attached three medallions covered with curious hieroglyphics, was found around the neck of the skeleton and near it were found a stone hammer, some pieces of pottery, an arrowhead, and some copper medals. Archaeologists believe that the original owner of the skeleton belonged to the race of mound builders.

THE FLORIDA BOG MUMMIES

Let's now turn our attention to the northeast coast of Florida and the case of the Florida bog mummies. The original finds were made in 1982 at Titusville, Florida, when real estate developers Jack Eckerd and Jim Swanson began building a road over the one-quarter-acre Windover Pond in Brevard County, about five miles from Cape Canaveral. When

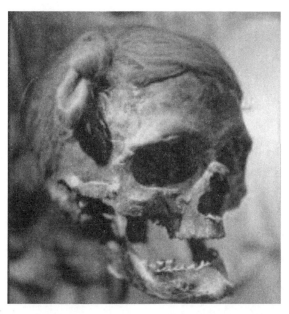

Fig. 10.11. This photo clearly shows the amazing preservation of the bog mummies' knotted red hair. Brain samples were also obtained, confirming a date of 7500 BCE (courtesy of Bullenwächer).

their backhoe operator uncovered several skulls, the developers immediately called in local archaeologists to have a look at the ancient stained bones that were being uncovered.

Despite the fact that the state of Florida has a responsibility to test finds of this nature, once the state determined that no current murder was involved, they refused to pay for proper radiocarbon dating of the bones. If not for the largesse and intellectual curiosity of Eckerd and Swanson, the age of what has been called "one of the most significant archaeological sites ever excavated" may never have been discovered at all.

Thankfully, Swanson and Eckerd paid for the radiocarbon dating out of their own pockets, and once the results came in, everyone was stunned by the findings.

Despite the fact that two anthropologists, Jerald T. Milanich of the University of Florida, Gainesville, and Glen Doran of Florida State University, were both apprised of the spectacular findings, no monies were allocated to drain the bog pond to see what else was waiting to be discovered under several feet of water. In order to facilitate a proper excavation, the two developers changed their construction plans and even donated $60,000 worth of pumping equipment to see that the pond was properly drained. Once again, no state or federal funds were forthcoming, and Doran had to spend the next two years securing private donations to facilitate the drainage of the pond.

In 1984, work finally got under way to drain the pond of its six to ten feet of water in order to gain access to the bones that were found under six feet of peat. All told, the workers had to dig 160 wells, which drained more than ten thousand gallons of water a minute, in order to finally drain the pond down to its peat base. Once it was drained, workers then used picks and shovels to dig into the peat until the ritual burials were discovered at the level of six feet under the surface of the pond's bottom bed. One of the head archaeologists on the excavation compared digging out the peat to trying to scoop up chocolate pudding while bobbing underwater. Due to finances, only half the pond was eventually excavated, but what was found was historic.

All told, the bones of 168 individuals were recovered, ranging in age from infants to adults in excess of sixty years of age. That this was an official cemetery there can be no doubt, as the heads of all the individuals were held down by ritual stakes and the bodies were all laid on their left sides with their heads pointing to the west. The oldest skeletons were found to be in excess of 8,280 years old, and there was evidence of continual use of the burial site for more than one thousand years.

Around 8000 BCE the oceans were about three hundred feet lower than they are today, and the weather was cooler and less humid than at present. Food was plentiful in this heavily forested region of Florida, making life good for the people who buried their dead in a shallow pond near what is now Titusville. In the shadow of today's Disney World, they hunted white-tailed deer and bobcat among the pine and oak trees and fished for bass and sunfish or scooped up turtles, frogs, and snakes.

"They enjoyed a good lifestyle," said Doran, the Florida State University anthropologist who oversaw the Windover Pond excavation, which lasted from 1984 to 1986. "Life was a little easier than it even may have been a few thousand years later. You had a lot of different resources packed pretty densely into this area within a few kilometers walk in any direction. Clearly, this was a good place to be."

Even more incredible was the state of preservation of the skeletons due to being sealed in the acid-neutral peat. In over ninety of the skeletons actual brain matter was preserved. This allowed the scientists the unprecedented opportunity to test the intact skulls with X-rays, computed tomography (CT) scans, and magnetic resonance imaging (MRI). The average height of the inhabitants was between 5'2" and 5'8", and the bodies were buried within twenty-four to forty-eight hours after death, based on the DNA and tissue that was examined. DNA testing on the bodies was conducted by Joe Lorenz, and as was the case with the skeletons at Spirit Cave in Nevada, the genomes were found to contain Haplogroup X, which is a distinct DNA marker, only found in Caucasians of generally northern European origin. That these were

Fig. 10.12. This bog mummy from Wales illustrates the remarkable state of preservation possible in a bog burial (courtesy of Carlos Muñoz-Yagüe).

what are called "water burials" is evidenced by the tight textile wrapping of the body and the ritual wooden stakes that were used to secure the heads and keep the skeletons from floating to the surface. The only other evidence for this type of water burial is found in northern Europe and most specifically the British Isles.

In addition, the textiles found at this site exhibit a high degree of weaving sophistication, and like the textiles found at Spirit Cave, they fly in face of the general understanding of the weaving techniques at that distant date. "To put this into context," Doran said, "these people had already been dead for three thousand or four thousand years before the first stones were laid for the Egyptian pyramids!"

Fig. 10.13. Col. Bill Royal began diving in the Warm Springs sinkhole in the 1950s and almost immediately began finding human skeletal remains.

Despite the problems associated with gaining the finances to excavate this site, they pale in comparison with the problems that have been encountered since the passage in 1990 of the NAGPRA federal laws, now enforced arbitrarily in defense of Native American tribes' sensibilities regarding extremely ancient skeletons. One of the major reasons the discoveries at this site are not better known and the results of the Haplogroup X DNA tests are not general knowledge can be laid at the door of the NAGPRA restrictions regarding discussion or exhibition of any of these ancient finds, as it would be considered sacrilege by the local Indian tribes of the area.

The irony about this slavish obedience to local American Indian sensibilities is that at both the Spirit and Lovelock Caves in Nevada and the now numerous bog sites in Florida, the Indians' own native lore speaks of the original inhabitants of the area as being white-skinned, red-haired giants.

The vast number of finds at Windover Pond caused archaeologists to reappraise other bog and water burial sites found in that area of Florida, and what they have found is even more astonishing in terms of dating in relation to the original inhabitants. The other Florida bog burial sites that are now officially recognized as being from the same general era date, incredibly in some cases, to 12,000 BCE and before. The first of these burial sites is located on the western coast of Florida, a little over midway down the coast, in Little Salt Springs on U.S. Route 41 in North Port, Florida, which is located in Sarasota County. In the 1950s, scuba divers in the area discovered that this seemingly small freshwater pond was actually a sinkhole or cenote that extended more than two hundred feet down to its peat moss base. Later underwater mapping revealed that the lake was actually forty-five feet deep, and an inverted cone shaft dropped vertically from the bottom another 245 feet, and that its general shape resembled similar cenotes found in the Yucatan peninsula. During unofficial dives in the 1960s and 1970s, bones and other human and animal remains were discovered, both in the peat moss base and along the sides of the shaft, and in 1979 the pond was added to the National Register of Historic Places and in 1982 was officially gifted to the University of Miami so that it could be preserved and catalogued in proper academic fashion.

Although bone, wood, stone, and charcoal objects dating from 4000 to 12,000 BC have been found there, it is the hundreds of human burials dating from 3000 to 6000 BCE that are causing controversy at the site. Although the site has been in the possession of the University of Miami since 1982, it has not been under the supervision of anyone from the archaeology department, but instead has been overseen by Associate Professor John Gifford of the university's Rosenstiel School of Marine and Atmospheric Science, and it was not until 2009 that the William and Marie Selby Foundation donated $100,000 to support studying the remains found in the spring in a more comprehensive manner, in conjunction with John Francis, vice president of research, conservation, and exploration at *National Geographic*. Although a majority of the hundreds of burials have been recovered with brain tissue intact, as was the case with the Windover Pond mummies, the university alleges that no definitive DNA Haplogroup evidence has been obtained so far, which is ridiculous and, if true, argues very badly for the scientific reputation of the university.

Finds similar to those found at Windover Pond and Little Salt Springs have also been reported at Bay West in Collier County near Naples, on the west coast of Florida, south of Little Salt Springs. The bones at this site have been dated to between 4000 and 6000 BCE, and despite the fact that the site has been known about for more than thirty years, no other information regarding DNA status has so far been released. Similar finds in Republic Grove in Hardee County have also been found to date between 5,500 and 6,500 years ago.

In terms of human dating the most spectacular finds in Florida so far are those made at Warm Springs, another sinkhole found in the city of North Port, on the western coast of Florida.

Unfortunately for history, the Warm Springs sinkhole was virtually stripped bare by amateur divers before the city of North Port in Sarasota County finally bought it for $5.5 million at the end of 2010. The sinkhole

Fig. 10.14. This drawing gives you an idea of the different levels of the spring. Warm Springs was originally thought to be about thirty to forty feet deep.

is an hour-glass-shaped structure approximately 250 feet deep with a peat moss base like its sister sinkhole in Little Salt Springs, which is also in the city of North Port. Scuba divers led by Col. Bill Royal began diving in the sinkhole in the 1950s and almost immediately began finding human and animal remains, including the skeletons of giant ground sloths, saber-toothed tigers, horses, and camelids dating up to twelve thousand years old. Unfortunately the site was turned into a health spa in the 1960s, and guests were encouraged to dive the site and take home any artifacts they found while they were exploring underwater.

In 1972 Wilburn Cockrell of Florida State University became aware of the importance of the site and explored there from 1972 to 1975 and again from 1984 to 1986. During that time he reported finding twenty skeletons with their skulls held in place with ritual wooden stakes, all resting on their left sides with their heads turned to the west in the exact same manner as the skeletons found at the adjacent sinkholes in Little Salt Springs and Windover Pond. Also consistent with the other finds, intact brain matter was also recovered, and radiocarbon dating placed the oldest of the skeletons at 9000 BCE. The skeletons on average were between 5'6" and 6'2" tall. Cockrell also found a variety of grave goods and artifacts and is convinced that this was a major burial ground that at one time probably contained thousands of burials and artifacts, which were stripped from the site during its history as a recreational diving hole. Although intact brain matter has been recovered from the site, Florida State University has never released any DNA testing on the Haplogroup status of the skeletons in question, but since the burial methods are identical to those found at Windover Pond, one can safely assume that they are also of Haplogroup X.

THE LOST KINGDOM OF THE RED-HAIRED, BLUE-EYED INDIANS

The Mandan Indians are generally found in North Dakota, and since their first contact with French explorers in 1738, this blond- and red-haired, blue-eyed tribe has been the source of intense speculation as to their European origins. In 1796, the Mandans were visited by the Welsh explorer John Evans, who was hoping to find proof that their language contained Welsh words. Evans had arrived in St. Louis two years prior, and after being imprisoned for a year, was hired by Spanish authorities to lead an expedition to chart the upper Missouri. Evans spent the winter of 1796–1797 with the Mandans but found no evidence of any Welsh influence. In July 1797 he wrote to Dr. Samuel Jones, "Thus having explored and charted the Missurie for 1,800 miles and by my Communications with the Indians this side of the Pacific Ocean from 35 to 49 degrees of Latitude, I am able to inform you that there is no such People as the Welsh Indians." In 1804, Lewis and Clark spent time visiting with the tribe, and it was here that they met Sacagawea, who later aided them as a scout and translator. Then, even later, in 1833, Western artist George Catlin, who was also convinced of their European roots, lived with the tribe and painted their village life and religious ceremonies. Although traditional archaeologists reject outright any European heritage for this mysterious tribe, no definitive Haplogroup X testing has ever been done on any of the surviving tribe members, and until scientific blood work is performed, all theories as to their original origins are purely based on superstition, academic bias, and ill-founded opinions.

THE MANDANS AND REPORTS OF RED-HAIRED, BLUE-EYED INDIANS— LEWIS AND CLARK JOURNALS

The following section regarding the Mandans is from James P. Ronda's book *Lewis and Clark among the Indians,* a modern telling of Lewis and Clark's explorations that uses their journals to focus on their interactions with the various Indian tribes they encountered.

From *Lewis and Clark among the Indians*

BY JAMES P. RONDA

The center of a Mandan village was the sacred cedar post and the open plaza around it. The cedar post represented Lone Man, the primary Mandan culture hero. On the north edge of the plaza was the large medicine or Okipa lodge. Hanging on poles outside the Okipa lodge were effigies representing various spirits. The Mandan villages seen by Lewis and Clark consisted of about forty to fifty domestic lodges arranged around the plaza. The social position of each household determined the location of lodges. Those families with important ceremonial responsibilities and those who owned powerful bundles lived near the plaza while less prominent households occupied lodges farther away. Mandan and Hidatsa earth lodges were usually occupied for anywhere between seven to twelve years. Each lodge housed from five to sixteen persons with the average number in a Mandan lodge being ten persons. At the time of Lewis and Clark, Mandan and Hidatsa villages were defended by log palisades.

These villages, so familiar from the descriptions of explorers and traders like Lewis and Clark and Alexander Henry the Younger and nineteenth-century artists like George Catlin and Karl Bodmer, were in fact only part of the settled experience of the Upper Missouri villagers. They divided their time between large, permanent summer lodge towns and smaller winter camps. The winter lodges, built in wooded bottoms to escape the harsh winter storms, were neither large nor especially well constructed. Lewis and Clark did not comment on these winter camps, and it is possible that fear of Sioux attack kept many Mandans and Hidatsas within the protection of the more substantial summer villages. Looking down on the towns from a high riverbank, David Thompson was reminded of "so many large hives clustered together." And so must they have seemed to Lewis and Clark seven years later.

Lewis and Clark were not the first white men to see the Mandan and Hidatsa villages and their surrounding fields of corn, beans, squash, and sunflowers. The first recorded European visit to the villages had occurred on the afternoon of December 3, 1738, when Pierre Gaultier de Varennes de La Vérendrye, accompanied by French traders and Assiniboin guides, entered a Mandan "fort" near the Heart River. Attracted by tales of fair-skinned, red-haired natives who lived in large towns and possessed precious metals, La Vérendrye had made the long journey from Fort La Reine on the Assiniboine River to see those mysterious people. Although La Vérendrye did not find the fabled white Indians, he did record the first European impressions of the Mandan lifeway. That record, taken along with evidence preserved from the 1742–43 visit of La Vérendrye's sons to the region, offers the picture of prosperous earth lodge people living along the Missouri River near the Heart and already enjoying French and Spanish goods.

11

MEGALITHIC CATALINA

The Blond-Haired Children of the Nine-Feet-Tall Kings

The most amazing discoveries in California were eventually found on Catalina Island. In the 1920s, the island of Catalina was owned by the Wrigley Chewing Gum family, who hired Professor Ralph Glidden, curator of the Catalina Museum, to conduct a series of digs on the island under the direction of the museum. What they found made headlines around the world, only to be written out of the history books less than ten years later. In short, Glidden and his team exhumed the remains of 3,781 skeletons of a race of blond-haired giants. The tallest was believed to be a king who measured nine feet, two inches tall and the average height of the skeletons was reported to be around seven feet. In addition, the team found the remains of a megalithic "Stonehenge-era" temple.

The selected articles below from 1928 to 1930 detail the discoveries and demonstrate the excitement about them at the time.

HOW OUR WHITE INDIANS ARE RISING OUT OF LEGEND INTO FACT

FOUND: THE MYSTERIOUS ROYAL BURYING GROUND OF BLOND CHILDREN FATHERED BY A RACE OF GIANTS THREE THOUSAND YEARS AGO ON CATALINA ISLAND

OGDEN, UTAH, NOVEMBER 10, 1929

That a race of magnificent, tall, white Indians once roamed the Americas long before the first European sailor crossed the Atlantic has been a subject for mild, almost bantering debate among archaeologists. None of them took the thing very seriously; it was regarded as picturesque legend. But now amazing new discoveries have confirmed beyond question that white men had already lived in America for centuries when Columbus landed.

THESE FINDS ARE THE MOST IMPORTANT IN YEARS

New finds on Catalina Island, off the California coast, overshadow in richness and significance most of the archaeological finds of recent years. Digging on an outlying part of the island, long the favorite location for movie directors, Professor Ralph Glidden, curator of the Catalina Museum, has uncovered overwhelming truth that a fair-skinned, tow-headed, highly intelligent race once lived in the West.

A VAST CACHE OF SKELETONS

Glidden's discovery of a vast cache of skeletons, urns, heads, wampum, and domestic utensils, is no ordinary Indian relic find. Not only does it reveal the existence of a white race of Indians living in Catalina at least 3000 years ago, but it poses a tragic mystery.

Professor Glidden's first startling find was a huge funeral urn carved out of stone and containing the skeleton of a young girl, crouched in an upright position within, the finger-bones of her little hand clenched over the wampum-inlaid brim. In a circle surrounding the urn were interred the bodies of 64 little children in tiers four deep, their little heads placed close together.

Some five feet below the children, was the skeleton of a gigantic man: a man measuring seven feet eight inches from the top of the skull to the ankle bone. A spear blade was imbedded in the ribs of the left side.

There was conclusive evidence—including strands of hair—that all these people were blondes. At first these white Indians were thought to be albinos. But careful examination proved that they were not, although they did possess some albino characteristics.

One of the curator's chief problems was to dry the skulls, which he found buried in damp sand near the water's edge. Great care had to be taken that

Fig. 11.1. Just one of many nationally syndicated articles on the incredible finds at Catalina Island (*Ogden Standard Examiner*, November 10, 1929)

they did not crumble when exposed to the air. In the daytime he would place them in rows in front of his tent. At night he covered them with tarpaulin to keep out the dampness.

A GIFT TO CHEW ON: 187 GIANT SKULLS PRESENTED TO WRIGLEY HEIR, ALSO 187 ARTIFACTS FOUND

One evening, Philip K. Wrigley of Chicago, whose father, William Wrigley Jr., owns Catalina Island, visited the expedition's leader. Wrigley had been on a strenuous wild mountain goat hunt and stopped by to ask how Professor Glidden was getting on.

"Fine," replied the Professor and pulled away the tarpaulin. The revelation was startling: 187 human skulls, staring grimly at Wrigley in the moonlight.

AT RIGHT
This Skeleton of a Man Who was 7 Feet 8 Inches Tall Reposed Below the Tomb in Which the Remains of 64 Children Were Found.

During the expedition to the interior of Catalina Professor Glidden collected the skeletons of 3,781 Indians. The largest he found was of a man 9 feet 2 inches tall. Practically all the male adults were of gigantic stature, averaging around 7 feet in height.

Fig. 11.2. During the dig on Catalina Island, Professor Glidden collected the skeletons of 3,781 "Indians." The largest he found was a man nine feet, two inches tall. Practically all the male adults were of gigantic stature, averaging around seven feet in height.

Fig. 11.3. Professor Ralph Glidden, curator of the Catalina Museum, 1929

GIANTS, TEMPLES AND MISSING SKELETONS
ON THE WEST COAST

A GIANT'S TEMPLE TO THE SUN GOD FOUND ON CATALINA ISLAND

BY LYLE ABBOTT

TYRONE DAILY HERALD, JANUARY 6, 1930

A trail of human sacrifices leading to the temple of the sun god of the ancient Channel Island Indians was followed today by Professor Ralph Glidden, archaeologist. Three of the four gates of the supposed temple of Chinigchinich, that bloody deity of the long ago, have been unearthed. A rich reward of relic treasures awaits the third expedition in search of the east gate. Glidden is Curator of the Catalina Museum.

At the north temple gate, Glidden found a large funeral urn containing the skeleton of a girl. He believes the girl, a princess from the riches of her ornament, was a human sacrifice. The small

Fig. 11.4. Photograph of artifact from Catalina Island, California, 1932 (courtesy of Southwest Museum of the American Indian collection)

hands of the sacrifice were clutching the rim of the urn. Beneath the urn lay the skeletons of 64 children, the heads forming a circle.

SEVEN-FOOT, SIX-INCH GIANT UNCOVERED IN CATALINA

Still deeper in the soil, Glidden found the bones of a man who in life measured seven feet, six inches, in height. He had been killed by a spear thrust. The first spear head was still imbedded in the chest. Pearl pendants, carved eagle claws, little boxes of clam-shell trinkets of carved bone and stone, and a jasper knife blade were found with the skeletons.

IN 1542 AND 1602 SPANISH HISTORIANS REPORTED ON THE SUN TEMPLE

Two Spanish historians who accompanied the expeditions of Don Juan Cabrillo and Don Viscaino to Catalina Island in 1542 and 1602, have left vivid word-pictures of the Indians they found there. Both Father Torquemada and Father Geronimo de Zarate Zalmeron saw the Temple of Chinigchinich.

At that early time the Temple consisted of a large circle of upright stones, similar to the Druid temple at Stonehenge, England. The stones were believed to point to the sun at midday. The circle of upright monoliths enclosed the hideous idol of the Sun God. This idol bore some resemblance to the images found by the Spaniards in the Aztec temples of Mexico. Thousands of artifacts have been unearthed by Glidden. "They show," he says, "a high state of barbaric progress on the island."

Glidden's work is sponsored by William Wrigley, Jr., owner of the island.

The following account of the Catalina temple appeared less than two years prior to the preceding story. This syndicated story provides additional details, like the discovery of an ancient map and the machine-like details of the 134-pound urn, which indicate the high degree of masonry and machining skills of the extremely ancient settlers of California.

CHILD SACRIFICES AT THE CATALINA SUN GOD TEMPLE

APPLETON POST-CRESCENT, NOVEMBER 19, 1928

An attempt to follow ancient trails to the long lost ancient island temple of Chinigchinich, the Sun God, has resulted instead in the discovery of a burial space of a small Indian princess some 3000 years ago, and evidence indicating that child sacrifices were made in wholesale fashion by tribes of the Channel Islands, off the coast of California. Within a stone urn, weighing some 134 pounds and fashioned as skillfully as though by modern tools instead of primitive instruments was found the skeleton of an Indian girl between five and seven years. Her small hands had clutched the rim of the urn whose rich ornamentation bespeaks her royal lineage. In a circle with the urn as a center were counted by Professor Ralph Glidden, curator of the Catalina museum of the Channel Island Indians, the skeletons of 64 children buried in tiers four deep, with small heads touching each other. Beneath them was the skeleton of a seven-foot man. A spear blade was still fixed in the ribs. The sand within the funeral urn had the appearance of ground crystal—apparently, according to the discoverer, a sacred sand used in the burial of Indian royalty—and was far different from that which had sifted over the graves of the other children.

These finds, as well as a wealth of obsidian knives, spear points, and arrow heads and hundreds of other articles of wampum-inlaid stone and bone have provided material over which Glidden has puzzled since he has discovered them.

A MAP TO MORE ANCIENT BURIAL SITES

One thin piece of slate he believes to be a stone map, holes having been drilled to indicate trails to the four main burying grounds on Santa Catalina Island. Wampum-inlaid in four broken circles on the rim of the urn with "gates" leading to the four points of the compass led Glidden to believe that the burial place may be near the site of the temple of Chinigchinich.

Fig. 11.5. Photograph of shell artifacts from Catalina Island, California, early to mid-1900s (courtesy of Southwest Museum of the American Indian Collection)

REWRITING THE HISTORY OF THE WHITE RACE

"The whole significance of the finds now related has not yet been worked out by anthropologists. But the establishment as fact of the old story of a fair race of giants in America is causing a new leaf to be written in the textbooks. It may result finally in a revision of our ideas as to where the white race originated—and as to how the primeval races reached what is called the New World," naively concluded a reporter for the *Examiner* in 1929.

187 ARTIFACTS, ALSO 187 SKULLS RECOVERED

EXAMINER, 1929

Buried in the pit with the skeletons were 187 artifacts. These, fashioned of shell, bone and stone, included treasure boxes made of two large clam shells cemented together with asphaltum and containing abalone pearl pendants, carved stone beads, small stone rings, and other trinkets. There were also small paint pots, bone needles, carved heating stones, pipes, stone toys, and miniature canoes.

Later radiocarbon dating revealed that some of the skeletons unearthed were seven thousand years old. For more than fifty years the proofs pertaining to these discoveries were vigorously denied by the University of California and the Smithsonian, but in 2011 it was finally admitted that the evidence for these finds had been locked away from the public in the restricted-access evidence rooms of the Smithsonian, along with detailed field reports and hundreds of photos, as can be seen from the following inventory chart:

RALPH GLIDDEN NEGATIVES, 1919–1923	
Creator	Glidden, R. (Ralph)
Title	Ralph Glidden negatives, 1919–1923.
Phy. Description	536 acetate negatives: black and white; 5 × 7 inches.
Bio/His Notes	Ralph Glidden was an archaeologist and curator at the Catalina Museum of the Channel Islands in the 1930s. He also worked for the Museum of the American Indian/Heye Foundation.
Summary	This collection contains 536 black-and-white acetate negatives taken by Ralph Glidden between 1919–1923. Most of the images depict scenic views and archaeological excavations on Catalina Island, San Miguel Island, San Nicolas Island and San Clemente Island, California. Also included are approximately 88 images of objects excavated by Glidden; these objects are now in the collections of the National Museum of the American Indian.

RALPH GLIDDEN NEGATIVES, 1919–1923	
Organization	Organized in individual sleeves; arranged by image number.
Cite as	Ralph Glidden negatives, National Museum of the American Indian Archives, Smithsonian Institution (negative, slide or catalog number).
Restrictions	Access is by appointment only, Monday–Friday, 9:30 am–4:30 pm. Please contact the archives to make an appointment.
Copyright	National Museum of the American Indian. Some images are restricted due to cultural sensitivity. Please contact the archivist for further information.
Subject–Topical	Excavations (Archaeology)–California
	Indians of North America–California
Subject–Geographical	California–Antiquities
	San Clemente Island (Calif.)
	San Miguel Island (Calif.)
	San Nicolas Island (Calif.)
	Santa Catalina Island (Calif.)
Form/Genre	Black-and-white negatives
Repository Loc	National Museum of the American Indian Archives, Cultural Resources Center, 4220 Silver Hill Road, Suitland, Maryland 20746. (tel: 301-238-1400, fax: 301-238-3038, email: nmaiarchives@si.edu).

DOCUMENTS DISCOVERED BY MUSEUM CURATOR REVEAL CATALINA ISLAND'S EARLIEST HISTORY

ART DAILY, THURSDAY, APRIL 12, 2012

He was a colorful character whose research into many of North America's earliest human settlements was both groundbreaking and highly controversial, which made all the more remarkable the announcement this past week that a large cache of original papers and photographs had been discovered documenting the earliest excavations of Catalina Island by the amateur archaeologist Ralph Glidden. Details of the discovery were first reported in a front-page article published in the *Los Angeles Times.* The article describes how a curator at the Catalina Island Museum discovered numerous journals, personal letters, albums, newspaper articles, and, most significantly, hundreds of photographs that Glidden had compiled during his years of research on the island.

"The sheer scale of this discovery is immense," stated John Boraggina, the curator who discovered the collection and who has been on the job for less than a year. "One scholar from UCLA looked at all the documents and claimed that it represented 20 years of research."

The archive of material provides the kind of documentation of Glidden's excavations that many scholars believed either did not exist or had been lost. Found in two modestly sized boxes in the museum's research center, the entire archive is related to the hundreds of sites Glidden excavated on the island between 1919 and 1928. Many of the oldest settlements known are located on Catalina Island and date back at least 8,000 years. Glidden was the first archaeologist granted permission to excavate the island's interior

by William Wrigley, Jr.—the chewing gum magnate—who virtually bought the island in 1919.

Glidden uncovered thousands of artifacts, including mortars and pestles used for preparing food, knives of bone and stone, cooking stones for boiling soup in baskets, flutes made of bone, beads used as currency, arrowheads, war clubs, and fishhooks made of shell and weighted with stone. The artifacts reside today in the permanent collection of the Catalina Island Museum, a museum that William Wrigley, Jr.'s son, Philip K. Wrigley, helped to establish in 1953. Glidden's digs uncovered human remains often, and perhaps his greatest discovery was an enormous ancient cemetery with hundreds of burial sites. The archive of documents recently discovered has been described as a "missing link" that provides written and visual documentation of the thousands of skeletons and artifacts uncovered by Glidden during his nearly 10 years of excavating Santa Catalina.

"The insight that the photographs alone lend into Glidden's work is remarkable," Boraggina stated recently. "We had previously thought that Glidden paid little regard to any type of scientific method when working with human remains. But these photographs are evidence of his attempt to document human remains during the earliest stages of their excavation. We see a large number of undisturbed skeletons, the majority of which have been buried in what seems to be the fetal position. We've never before had this amount of evidence related to Glidden's work."

"None of the Glidden archive had ever been exhibited," Dr. Michael De Marsche, Executive Director of the museum recently stated while standing before a display case now dedicated to material from the discovery. "I assumed my position less than two years ago, and we now know that some 20 years ago research took place on the collection, but then it was all put in boxes and placed on a shelf. I know scholars from other museums have asked if it might exist. But our records were so poor that we didn't know. We have no central catalog listing all the material in our archive. The boxes John discovered were simply marked 'Glidden.' We're in the midst of updating and organizing everything, but this won't be fully accomplished for years."

In 1924 Glidden opened the first "museum" on Catalina Island: the Museum of the American Indian on the Channel Islands. It certainly lived up to Glidden's expectation that it be "unlike anything else anywhere in this country." He based its interior on a chapel on the island of Malta, whose walls were decorated with motifs formed from the bones of monks. Many of the recently dis-

covered photographs provide views of the museum and Glidden's use of skeletal remains as a macabre form of decoration. But the photographs also reveal that the unsettling interior of his museum was a popular stop for tourists. In one photograph, Glidden holds a skull while talking to two women dressed in their Sunday best.

"I think this archive lends a more complex portrait of the man," Boraggina said while scanning the photographs. "You have to acknowledge that Glidden exploited Native American remains in the most insensitive manner imaginable. He certainly did not honor the sanctity of these remains when he organized his museum. He resorted to crass sensationalism when trying to sell tickets. On the other hand, we now know that while excavating he attempted, at times, to subscribe to a standard of archaeology prevalent during his day."

Glidden's museum closed in 1950, and in 1952, Philip Wrigley purchased Glidden's entire collection of remains, documents, and artifacts and donated them to the Catalina Island Museum. The Native American Graves Protection and Repatriation Act of 1990 granted Native Americans the right to reclaim the remains of their ancestors and other sacred objects. Today, museums in the United States no longer exhibit Native American remains. "We're in the midst of building a new museum, which will allow us to store and study this collection with the respect it deserves," De Marsche said. "I hope to exhibit as much of our archival material and artifacts as possible. It's exciting to think that the day our new building opens, the Catalina Island Museum becomes a respected center of scholarship in this incredibly important area of our history."

The Catalina Island Museum is Avalon's sole institution devoted to art, culture and the rich history of Santa Catalina Island.

Notice how they have studiously avoided mention of the giants and the true extent of the thousands of burials?

Fig. 11.6. Avalon, California: Photograph of artifacts from Catalina Island, California, circa 1937 by Carl Hegner (courtesy of Southwest Museum of the American Indian Collection)

BONES FLESH OUT AN ISLAND'S HISTORY

FILES OF MAN WHO DUG UP INDIAN SKELETONS COULD CHANGE VIEWS OF EARLY CATALINA LIFE

By Louis Sahagun

LOS ANGELES TIMES, APRIL 2, 2012

The curator of the Catalina Island Museum opened the door to a musty backroom a few weeks ago hoping to find material for an upcoming exhibit on the World War II era. Closing the door behind him, he trudged down a narrow aisle lined with storage boxes and bins filled with gray photocopies of old letters, civic records, celebrity kitsch, and dust.

"No luck," curator John Boraggina muttered.

But as he made his way to a back corner, he noticed another row of boxes. He carried the largest to a table, blew off the dust and lifted the lid.

Inside were leather-bound journals and yellowing photographs showing freshly unearthed skeletons lying on their backs or sides, or curled as if in sleep. Many were surrounded by grinding stones, pots and beadwork.

Several photos showed a man in soiled clothes standing tall with spade in hand beside chaotic jumbles of bones. Boraggina recognized him: Ralph Glidden.

The images, Boraggina soon realized, came from a time 90 years ago that many on Santa Catalina Island had forgotten—or tried to forget. The photos were of the work of a pseudo-scientist—some say a huckster—who made a living unearthing Native American artifacts and human remains for sale and trade. Glidden had ruined much of Catalina's Native American cultural heritage, but in the process he also made discoveries thought lost in the passage of time.

Boraggina closed the big box and called the museum's executive director, Michael De Marsche. "Michael, hurry over. I discovered something amazing," he said. "I found Glidden's archives."

Minutes later, De Marsche was taking stock of enough historical photographs and handwritten documents to fill a gallery in the 60-year-old museum.

In the weeks since, the contents of the boxes have grown in importance. Researchers and scholars of California history—especially at UCLA's Fowler Museum, where some 200 of Glidden's skeletons are housed—say the discovery will probably change the understanding of early life here and could eventually ease the anger of Native Americans outraged by the grave-robbing of the last century.

It is not often that a small-town curator unearths modern-day clues to a prehistoric past, but scientists believe that's what happened here.

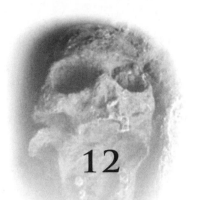

12

INSIGHTS INTO ORIGINS

THE SCYTHIAN CONNECTION

In many of the reports I came across there was conjecture as to the roots of the mound-builder race. The two top contenders posited by various authors seem to be the ancient Cretans and the ancient Scythians. In the following excerpt from Haywood's history of Tennessee, he cites the Scythian's large stature, burial practices involving barrows, and custom of scalping enemies as examples of their influence.

The Natural and Aboriginal History of Tennessee, 1823

By Dr. John Haywood

When we reflect that the Scythian nations between the Danube and the Tanais, as late as within one century of the Christian era were of a size which astonished the southern inhabitants of Europe and Asia; that they scalped their enemy; that they buried their dead in heaps of earth thrown over them with such articles as were deemed by the deceased most valuable in his lifetime; and that their tumuli, or barrows, are yet to be seen in the plains towards the upper part of the Irish and Jenesee and from the banks of the Volga to the lake Baikal; we cannot refrain from the conclusion, that this skeleton belonged to a human body of the same race, education, and notions with those who lived on the Volga, Tanais, and Obey.

The same unknown cause, which, in the course of 2000 years, has reduced the size of the ancient Scythians and their tribes, the Gauls and Germans and Sarmatians has produced the same effects here. The descendants of these giants, both in the old and new world, agree with each other in bulk, as their ancestors did with each other, which proves a uniform cause operating equally both in the old and new world. The decrease in bulk seems to have kept pace everywhere with the increase of warm temperature and with the abbreviation of longevity.

The giants of Hebron and Gath and those of Laconia and Italy, whose large skeletons to this day attest that there they formerly dwelt, compared with those now found in West Tennessee, demonstrate that a change of climate or of some other cause has worked a remarkable change in the human system; and with respect to the mammoth, the megalonyx, and other animals, has either extinguished or driven them into other and far distant latitudes. Nature, as it grows in age, is less vigorous than at the beginning, and its productions correspond with its debility, and the time must come, when she, like all her productions, will give up the ghost and work no more. But the principal use we have to make of the skeleton before us is to discover first that he came from a cold or northern climate and not from the south, as the primitive aborigines did, for men of large stature were never found within the tropics.

Second, that he must have come from the north of Europe or Asia, because of the similarity of customs already remarked. Third, that he probably belonged to those northern tribes, which some centuries ago exterminated the nations that had come from the south and were settled upon the Cumberland and its waters.

With this skeleton was found another of nearly the same size, with the top of his head flat, and his eyes placed apparently in the upper part of his forehead. The Aztecs or Mexicans represent their principal divinities, as their hieroglyphical manuscripts prove, with a head much more flattened than any that have been seen amongst the Caribs, and they never disfigured the heads of their children.

Concerning the Unnatural Practice of Child-Boarding Skulls

But many of the southern tribes have adopted the barbarous custom of pressing the heads of their children between two boards, in imitation, no doubt, of the Mexican form, which, in their estimation was beautiful, or in some way advantageous. And here it may not be amiss to mention, that the Chileans, who lived as far to the south of the equator, as formerly did the Scythians, Goths, Vandals, Gauls, and Germans—on the other side of it—were men of large stature.

One remark may be of some use in the drawing of inferences from the preceding facts. The skeletons, we find, are entirely under conical mounds or, in part, consumed by fire, and under such mounds, or entirely in shallow graves with flat rocks placed on the edges, at the sides, and at the head and feet. They may also be entirely above the common surface and in the conical mounds enclosed in rocks that are placed together in the form of a box. The skeletons may stand erect in such boxes, with the head some depth below the surface.

To burn and cover with a mound, is Hinduic or Grecian, and belonging to the ancient countries of Asia Minor, and probably belonged to the aborigines of America. To cover the entire body is Scythic. To bury in graves or in boxes is Ethiopic, Egyptian, and in part Hebraic, the Hebrews having learned it during their residence in Egypt, though they did not generally adopt it.

It may be concluded that the mounds over entire bodies are Scythic; graves and boxes are Hebraic; boxes in the mounds are Hebraic and Scythic; and the unconsumed skeletons we see here are either pure Scythians or Hebrew Scythians, whilst all others are Hinduic, or in other words aboriginal. The large men of the world have always been found in the north, and they have often invaded and broken up the people of the south. They have never been found in the south; nor have the people of the south ever broken up their settlements there and marched upon those of the north to expel them from their possessions in order to make room for themselves.

The men who deposited the skeletons we are now contemplating were of northern growth, and they came to the south to drive away the inhabitants whom they found there and to seat themselves in their possessions.

The Giants' Love for Martial Music

About 18 miles east from Rogersville in the county of Hawkins in East Tennessee was ploughed up a stone trumpet. It tapers on the outside from either end to the middle and is there surrounded by two rings of raised stone. The inside at each end is a hollow, of an inch and a quarter in diameter; but at one end the orifice is not as large as at the other. Probably the sound is shrill and sharp when blown from one end, and more full and sonorous when blown from the other.

The hollow continues throughout, from the one end to the other, and in the middle, under the rings, it is not as wide as at the ends. It seems to have been made of hard soapstone; and when blown through, makes a sound which may be heard perhaps two miles. It is very smooth on the outside, but rough within.

An Ancient Hunting Horn

Probably it was used for similar purposes to those for which the trumpet of the Israelites was used, namely to convene assemblies and to regulate the movements of the army. On days of rejoicing it was used to make a part of the musical sounds with which the people were entertained. From it, perhaps, these deductions may be made. There were no large hollow horns in the country, which could have been used for the same purpose, and more effectually, too, as large steer horns are now used by hunters. But a more important question is: Whence could those who made the trumpet have known its properties and use? They could not have attained that knowledge by blowing through the large horns of animals because there were none such here, or they never would have made this stone trumpet.

"Prior to the Departure of the Israelites from Egypt, There Is No Scriptural or Other Account of Trumpets"

Most evidently, it was conceived to be of great value; otherwise so much time, as must necessarily have been consumed in fashioning and hollowing it, would not have been spent for such purpose. The makers must have learnt its use from some nation that employed the trumpet in sounding charges, or for giving directions to march, or to stop the pursuit of an enemy. Prior to the departure of the Israelites from Egypt, there is no scriptural or other account of trumpets.

In Egypt, Pharaoh followed the army of the Israelites with chariots and horsemen, but the trumpet is not spoken of. It was sounded on Mount Sinai, where God delivered the law to Moses; and it is intimated that the people had never before heard the sound of the trumpet. "The voice of the trumpet was exceedingly loud, so that all the people that were in the camp trembled. And all the people saw the thundering and the lightning and the noise of the trumpet and the mountains smoking; and when the people saw it, they removed and stood afar off." Afterwards it was directed that two trumpets should be made for convening the elders and for giving signals for the marching of the tribes.

Some were to march at one signal, and some at another. A signal was appointed for convening the whole congregation. Sometime afterward, the Israelites made use of trumpets for various other purposes; but being separated by their natural institutions and religion from all the other people of the world, soon communicated to them the use of this instrument (Exodus, ch. 14, v. 6, 7, ch. 19, v. 13, 16, ch. 20, v. 18).

When Bacchus overran India with an army from the west, the use of the trumpet was not known. In the time of the Trojan War, neither Greeks nor Trojans used the trumpet. The Trojans had in their camp the sound of flutes and of pipes. Stentor, a man of mighty voice, proclaimed to the army the orders which were given by the general. In the year 14 before Christ, when Darius the Mede crossed the Danube and invaded the Scythians, on his return, finding the bridge broken down, which he had left, he caused an Egyptian, remarkable for the loudness of his voice, to pronounce with all his strength, the name of the admiral of the fleet, who immediately answered and came to him, and made a new bridge of boats, for his transportation. A trumpet could have been much more effectually used, and could have sent the appointed signal to a much greater distance.

When Xerxes invaded Greece, 478 years before Christ, no trumpet was then used; the signal for battle was given by torchbearers. In aftertimes it was given by drum or trumpet. Signals also announcing any important occurrence were given by holding up a torch of fire. Soon after the invasion of Greece by the Persians, trumpets were used in Greece for many purposes, as well as those relative to the motions of their armies. The Greeks probably learned it from the Phoenicians. The dispersed Israelites, either those carried into captivity by the Assyrians or those of the Chaldean captivity have imparted the knowledge of the trumpet and its uses, to the people from whom it came, mediately or immediately, to the Americans who made the trumpet in question. The communication must have been made in or subsequent to the sixth century before the Christian era, possibly several centuries afterwards. But still it furnishes an additional and strong evidence of the fact inferred, namely: that the trumpet and its uses came either mediately or immediately from the countries of the east, where the trumpet was first used.

Thence they may have obtained the knowledge of it through various nations; or possibly were the descendants of the very Israelites, who were removed by the Assyrians to the east and north of the Caspian sea and of the Euxine; and who built on the east of the former, the city of Charazen, named after a city of the same name on the east of the river Jordan and the city of Samarsand, originally, before the name was corrupted, called Samaria, after the city of that name from which the ten tribes were carried into captivity.

Near to this mound is a cave, which contained, at the time of the first settlements by the whites, a great number of human skulls without any other appearance of human bones near them. Baal and Ashteroth, spoken of in scripture, were the sun and moon. The latter being a female, was also called the Queen of Heaven, Venus, Urania, Succoth-bemoth, Diana, Hecate, Lucena, Celestes and was represented with breasts, sometimes all over, to signify that she is the supplier of the juices that are essential to animal and vegetable existence. Mr. Earle has lately made another and more scrutinizing examination of this mound, by which have been brought to light several particulars of great consequence in this discussion.

Situated near Sulphur Springs—Mining in the Area

His report follows: This mound is situated in a plain and is surrounded by hills, which enclose from 75 to 80 acres of flat land, with three fine sulphur springs, and at the junction of four roads leading to different parts of the state, and considerably traveled, and about two miles from Cragfont, the residence of General Winchester. This is the place where Spencer and his friend Mr. Brake spent the winter of 1779 and 1780.

The trunk of the tree, which they inhabited during this hard winter, is just visible above the ground. The diameter is 13 feet. The mound measures, beginning at the northwest corner, running east, four and a half poles to the northeast corner; then the horizontal projection from the principal mound, north one pole; then east 11 poles, to the southeast corner; then west 11 poles, to the original mound; thence with the original mound west 4 poles; thence north 4 poles, to the northwest corner before mentioned.

The elevation to the top of the chief mound is 2 poles; its diameter 2 poles, in the center, and from three to four feet. The declivity of the mound is an angle of about 45 degrees. A tree of considerable size is yet growing on the mound, and a decayed stump of 2 feet in diameter, but too much decayed to count the annual rings or circles in it.

An entrenchment and circumvallation encloses 40 acres and encircles this mound and others of lesser size. There is also a circumvallatory parapet, five feet high. On the parapet are small tumuli like watch-towers, about 95 feet distant from one to the other. In the line of circumvallation, and from each fifth tumulus, there is an average distance of 45 or from thence to 180 feet to the next one. It thus continues around the whole breastwork.

Mr. Earle dug into the parapet in several places, from two to three feet in depth, and found ashes, pottery ware, flint, mussel shells, coal, and so forth. On the outside of the entrenchment are a number of graves. In several different places, flat stones are set up edge-wise, enclosing skeletons buried from 12 to 18 inches under the surface.

Three hundred yards distant from the great mound, on the southwest side of the entrenchment, is a mound of 50 yards in circumference, and six in height. In the opposite direction, from this to the northeast stands another smaller mound, and of the same dimensions as the one last mentioned. So that the three stand upon a line, from northeast to southwest, in the same order as the trimurti arc placed even to this day in the temple of Juggernaut.

The next (in size) principal mound was within the intrenchment in a southeast course from the great mound and about 170 yards distant, circumference 90 yards, elevation 100 feet. Thirty-five yards distant, in a southwest course, is a small tumulus, two thirds as large as the one last mentioned. At the same distance, on the northeast corner of the great mound, is another of the same size as that last mentioned. Each of these tumuli hath a small one of about half its size in the center between them and the great mound. The earth in which this mound was constructed, appears to have been taken, not from one place, leaving a cavity in the earth, but evenly fixing all the surface around the mound.

Mounds are spaced by intervals of five. In about 200 yards distant, extending from the mound, the soil has been taken off to a considerable depth. The corn, which is planted within this place, yields but a small increase. The tumuli upon the parapet project beyond it, both inwards and outwards: the summit of these being 15 feet above the summit of the parapet, and 5 feet above the surface of the common earth. They are 10 or 12 feet in diameter at the base.

Between every fifth tumulus and the next tumulus, which is the first of the next five, there is a large interstice. One of the intervals to the north, is 180 feet wide. The next toward the west, is 145 feet. The summit of each tumulus diverges from the base toward a point but at the top is flat and wide enough for two or three men to stand on. The common distance between the tumuli is 95 feet, without any variation. The entrenchment is on the inside of the parapet all around. From it the parapet has been made.

Alternating Levels of Ash and Earth

Mr. Earle commenced his excavation on the north side of the principal mound, ten feet above the common surface of the earth, and penetrated to the center of the mound in a cavity of about 7 feet in breadth. Two feet from the summit was found a stratum of ashes 14 inches through to a stratum of earth. On the east side of the cavity the sania stratum of ashes was oily from three to four inches in depth. The diggers then came to the common earth, which was only two feet through to the same substance, ashes. Then again commenced the layers of ashes from one to two inches through to the earth; then again to ashes; and so the layers continued alternately, as far as they proceeded. The layers of ashes were counted as far as the excavation descended, and amounted to 28.

The earth between the layers of ashes was of a peculiar description: yellow and grey. The ashes were of a blackish color. The yellow earth was of a saponaceous and flexible nature. The grey was of a similar kind to that of the common earth.

At eight feet from the top of the mound, they came to a grave, which had the appearance of having once been an ancient sepulcher. The earth caved in as the diggers sunk the cavity. The cause of this was soon ascertained to be the skeleton of a child in quite a decayed state, but sufficiently preserved to ascertain the size. Doctor Green and Doctor Saunders of Cairo examined the bones and pronounced them to be the bones of a child. This skeleton was lying on three cedar piles, five feet and a half in length, and considerably decayed but sound at the heart.

The head of the child lay towards the east, facing the west, with a jug made of sandstone, lying at its feet. This jug or bottle was of the ordinary size of modern gallon bottles, such as are commonly manufactured at Pittsburgh, with the exception that the neck is longer, and there is an indentation upon its side, indicating that a strap was used to carry it.

The grave was on the east side of the cavity, eight feet from the center of the mound north. The excavation from the top of the mound; perpendicularly into the earth was 13 feet. At the time they found the grave as above mentioned, they also found other graves, and small pieces of decayed human bones, and bones of animals, amongst which was the jaw bone with the tusk attached to it, of some unknown animal. The jaw bone is about a foot long, having at the extremity a tusk one inch and a half in length. The tusk is in the same form as that of Cuvier's mastodon, but has more curvature.

Having been accidentally broken, it was found to be hollow. The jaw bone has in it at this time, two grinders, like those of ruminating animals, with an empty socket for one other of the same size, and one large single tooth. Towards the extremity of the jaw and near to the tusk, is another small socket, calculated for a tooth of minor magnitude. This jaw bone was found at the depth of 18 feet from the surface of the earth. They also found the bones of birds, arrow points of flint, pottery ware, some of which was glazed, mussel shells and trinkets, coal, isinglass (mica), burnt corncobs.

The further they penetrated downwards, the greater were the quantities of flat stone, found all standing edgewise, promiscuously placed, with the appearance of once having underwent the action of fire, and finding at every few inches, a thin stratum of ashes and small pieces of human bones. At 19 feet they dug up part of a corncob, and small pieces of cedar completely rotted.

MOUND BUILT PRECISELY TO THE CARDINAL POINTS

Despite the fact that astronomical and geographic alignments have been studied at major mound sites like Cahokia, similar studies on lesser-known mound sites have never been performed. That is why this account is so interesting. In it Haywood notes, "This mound was built precisely to the cardinal points, as were the mounds of Mexico, the pyramids of Egypt, and the Chaldean tower of Babel. Like them, its top was flattened. The image, which once stood on its top, was similar to that of Ashtoreth, or the moon." This mention of an Ashtoreth-like moon image that was found on top of the mound is tantalizing, to say the least. Now let's return to Haywood's narrative.

> We will now make a few remarks. This mound was built precisely to the cardinal points, as were the mounds of Mexico, the pyramids of Egypt, and the Chaldean tower of Babel. Like them, its top was flattened. The image, which once stood on its top, was similar to that of Ashtoreth, or the moon. Those who worshipped stood on the east of the image on the platform and held their heads towards her. The ditch was probably dug with metallic tools. That and the parapet perhaps represented the year. The five tumuli represented the five days into which the Mexicans divided time. The interstices, the four quarters into which each Mexican month was divided. The whole composing the 72 quintals that made up the year, or 360 days. The wider passages to the north and south, east and west, like the Hindu temple of Seringham, which is heretofore described represented the four quarters or seasons of the year. The walls around the ancient temples of India are passed by passages precisely to the cardinal points.

The three mounds in a line, the larger being in the middle, represent the trimurti, or three great deities of India, upon all three of which idols were probably once placed, as they are now placed in the temple of Juggernaut and are intended to represent EOA, or Ye-Ho-Wah: whence in every country in Asia, including the Hebrews, came the sacred reverence for the number three, which is so apparent in all their solemnities. Part of this name, the A and O, or the alpha and omega, yet signify with us, the beginning and end of all things with three attributes, which is, which was, and which is to come. This was a part of the description, which belonged to the triune great one whom idolatry caused mankind to lose sight of, whilst those who only worshipped a spiritual God, preserved it in its original purity. But in every country, whether corrupted by idolatry or not, proceeds from the great, original, and uncorrupted religion, which emanated immediately and directly from EOA or the great good spirit.

It cannot be conceived for a moment, that here was a fortification for military purposes. For when did ever any such work have so many passages, so regularly and equally placed. The worshippers of the heavenly hosts were the greatest cultivators of astronomy, whilst the only religion of the world opposed to them, the Vatican raged the contemplation of those objects of her heathenish adoration. They involved in the circle of their adorables, all the constellations and planets.

THE MOUNDS REPRESENT THE PLEIADES

Modern readers are familiar with the sensation that was caused when Robert Bauval likened the arrangement of the Great Pyramid complex to Orion's belt. In this account, which is almost two hundred years old, Haywood notes a similar stellar arrangement in the placement of the mounds he is examining in Tennessee, only this time in relation to the Pleiades.

In some places we see a mound and five or six smaller ones around, which seem to represent the Pleiades, and sometimes other luminaries seem to be represented. These layers of ashes are unlike those in the time of the Trojan War over which were raised mounds of earth, after the bodies of Patroclus and Hector were consumed in them, and their bones taken away and put into an urn.

SIGNS OF HUMAN SACRIFICE

Many of the bodies that have been exhumed from mounds across the country show signs that they were ritually burned before being covered in layers of dirt and ash. In other bodies from mounds, notes Haywood, evidence of decapitation and flaying have also been found.

But the strata of ashes, at intervals from top to bottom, with human bones intermixed, show that there were human victims committed to the flames, after decapitation and removal of the skull to the neighboring cave, where it was laid up in darkness for the use of the deity. The black ashes denote the consumption of tobacco, the only incense in America, which they could offer, in which also was consumed the consecrated victim. A heated fire of solid wood would have consumed bone and all.

The great number of graves on the outside, show that the people neither usually buried in rounds, nor usually consumed dead bodies on the funeral pile. The skeleton of the child found within shows that it was a privilege peculiar to his family to be buried there, whilst the other ranks of men were buried without the circumvallation. He was very probably one of the children of the sun.

The earth taken from the surface, within the circumvallation, was holy and consecrated; it was earth impregnated by the beams of the sun, and must have been removed by a great number of hands, compelled by despotic power to obedience. When placed on the expiring embers of sacrificial fire, the enclosures of all such mounds are circular, or for the most part are meant to represent possibly the course of the revolving year, and to make upon them the divisions of time that the sun describes in his progress. It is easy to compare what he found in this mound and about it, with the collection of scriptural passages, before stated, and to see how far there is accordance between them or not. And therefore it is needless for the writer any further to pursue the subject.

BLOND-HAIRED SKELETON BURIED IN CAVE

This account by Haywood of a skeleton of a blond-haired girl found in a cave near Carthage is but one of many similar accounts I discovered in reports from across the United States. In this case, the girl's hair was covered by a mantle of feathers.

The section upon the literal inscriptions of Tennessee gives one instance of a skeleton in a cave near Carthage, the hair of which was yellow. The hair of the female covered with the curious mantle of feathers in the section of manufactures, which was found in a cave in White county, was of a yellow cast, and very fine. It is evident, that these did not belong to Indians of the same races with those of the present day.

SECRET ROOM IN A CAVE IS DISCOVERED

Haywood says that in a cave that was found about eleven miles north of Cairo, Tennessee, workmen had to open two secret passages before they discovered a twenty-five-feet-square room that contained the bodies of a man, a woman, and a child. They were said to be auburn-haired and blue-eyed and of normal height, and the man was covered by fourteen deerskin blankets. The bodies were enclosed in pyramidal baskets.

Near the confines of Smith and Wilson counties, on the south side of Cumberland river about 11 miles above Cairo, on the waters of

Smith's Fork of Cany Fork, is a cave, the aperture into which is very small.

The workmen in the cave enlarged the entrance and went in; and digging in the apartment, next to the entrance, after removing the dirt and using it, they came, upon the same level with the entrance, to another small aperture, which also they entered and went through, when they came into a narrow room, 25 feet square. Everything here was neat and smooth. The room seemed to have been carefully preserved for the reception and keeping of the dead.

In this room, near about the center, were found sitting in baskets made of cane three human bodies; the flesh entire, but a little shriveled, and not much so. The bodies were those of a man, a female, and a small child. The complexion of all was very fair and white, without any intermixture of the copper color. Their eyes were blue; their hair auburn, and fine. The teeth were very white; their stature was delicate, about the size of the whites of the present day. The man was wrapped in 14 dressed deer skins. The 14 deer skins were wrapped in what those present called blankets. They were made of bark, like those found in the cave in White county. The form of the baskets, which enclosed them, was pyramidal, being larger at the bottom, and declining to the top. The heads of the skeletons from the neck were above the summits of the blankets.

THE WELL SHOWS SIGNS OF ENGINEERING

The walled water tanks found in association with the mounds described in the next extract showed signs of advanced engineering, which Haywood attributes to Hindu, Mesopotamian, or Judean influence.

The remarks, which offer themselves upon these mounds, are not only that the doctrine of triplicity here is very prominent, but also that the well, or tank, for holding of water must have been constructed with peculiar art probably upon the plan that the Hindu tanks were, and those of Mesopotamia and Judea were in ancient times. But the most material consideration is the uses to which the waters of the tank were applied. Is it probable that the inhabitants of the country lived upon this consecrated ground, upon which stood their temples and gods? If not, the waters of the tank were for sacred uses; for ablutions and purifications; another great symptom of the Hindu ritual. It is a remarkable truth that the same law of defilement and ablutions has actually existed amongst the Hindus from times of the remotest antiquity, which Moses delivered to the Hebrews. What the Mosaic law was is stated in various scriptural passages and retains only such rites observed by the Hindus and Egyptians as were proper for the Hebrews in the new countries and climates in which they were about to settle.

A STANDING STONE MARKS A BURIAL

Standing stones mark many mound-builder burial sites. In this report by Haywood from Cany Fork, about fourteen miles from Sparta, a standing stone marked the burials of several skeletons that were said to be about six and a half feet in height, with bones that were thicker than normal and with longer teeth and larger skulls than is considered normal.

On the Cany Fork of Cumberland, 13 or 14 miles from Sparta in a southwesterly direction, Mr. Tilford observed a stone standing erect, the top being about a foot above the ground, the width a foot, and extending to a depth of a foot in the ground. He moved it from its position and dug in, and discovered, about twelve inches under the surface, some bones of a human skeleton. He took up several.

They were larger than those of men of common stature, indicating that the whole skeleton would be six feet three or four inches in length. They were thicker than bones of the same denomination ordinarily are. The teeth were in a state of preservation as far as the enamel reached, but those parts which entered the socket were in a state of decay. The teeth were longer than those of an ordinary man. The skull was larger in the same proportion, and by the operations of time had become thinner than skulls usually are.

Hence was inferred the great antiquity of the grave; though, perhaps, as correct an inference would be, the northern formation and growth of the skull, far from the vertical rays of the sun, which usually thicken the skull when not defended by hats or bonnets or mitres. A vast number of periwinkles lay near the grave and around it, spread over two or three acres ground. They are supposed to have been brought from the Cany Fork, which is about half a mile from the spot, but they are of much larger size than any that are found at this time on that river.

The thigh bone, when there was an attempt to move it, fell into dust.

EVIDENCE FOR GREAT ANTIQUITY

A vast majority of the mounds examined in Haywood's report had trees growing out of them that were already hundreds of years old. In addition, when workers unearthed bodies, the bones often fell to dust the minute they were exposed to the open air.

These latter circumstances are taken as concurrent evidences of great antiquity. The grave was on the summit of a high bluff, rising from the river to the spot. The trees near it were of such large size as any in the adjacent forest, and at a small distance were some mounds on which the timber was of equal size. A part of the skull, when exposed to the air, was quickly dissolved into dust.

In this grave Mr. Tilford found, near where the neck of the skeleton was, a great number of beads, some of them adhering closely together in a circular shape, which showed that they once encircled the neck. Others were separated. He took up 260 of them and left a considerable number more, which he did not remove.

EVIDENCE OF IVORY WORK AND FINE DRILLS

As noted by Haywood, one of the skeletons unearthed at this burial site had a necklace around his neck made from finely worked ivory beads that were drilled lengthwise through the center in order to accommodate a rope or chain to thread the beads into a necklace. Two hundred and sixty of these ivory beads were used to make this one necklace alone.

> One was larger than all the rest, in the shape of a barrel, bored through the center from one end to the other, one half of an inch in length and about one half that length in diameter, supposed to have been placed on a string which connected the whole, at the lower part, so as to divide one half of the beads above, from the other half above. This bead, when cut on the surface, is very smooth, of a whitish color, inclining by a small shade towards a pale yellow, and very much resembles ivory.

> Fine longitudinal veins are visible on the surface, and it is the opinion of good judges, that they are made of a species of ivory. The other beads are circular, all of the like materials that compose the large bead. Some of them are of greater diameter than the others and some of greater width from the one side to the other. The diameter of the larger ones is about one fourth of an inch; the width of the exterior of the circle, about a third of the length of the diameter. The side of the one adjoining the side of its neighbor, when connected by a string, appears to have been made smoother by friction than when first formed.

> It is as smooth and ungranulated as an ivory comb; in some instances, however, showing the unevenness of the cut made by the tool, which originally separated the bead from the mass it was taken from. In some instances the bead, from the hole in the center to the exterior of the circle, appears by friction to have removed the width of the exterior from one side to the other, so as to make it unequal to

the opposite exterior of the circle; whence is inferred the long time it had been used before the death of the wearer.

MADE OF THE FINEST AND BEST QUALITY IVORY

The ivory used to make these beads was thought to come from mastodon or alligator teeth. Haywood reported that the beads were examined by Dr. Throchmorlin of Sparta and were declared to be of the "finest and best quality."

The materials of which they are composed are probably not the product of Tennessee; though it is possible, they may have been taken from the tooth of the mastodon or alligator.

This writer, with the cordon of beads before him, in order to avoid the possibility of mistake caused them to be submitted to the inspection of Dr. Throchmorlin of Sparta, whose uncommon intelligence makes him particularly well qualified to decide upon the question of whether the materials be of stone or some other substance.

His decision: that unquestionably they are of ivory of the finest and best quality. The dingy coating, which obscured the beads, was cleared by his experiments, from one of them, and it then appeared to be a beautiful white, with the degree of shade, which characterizes and softens the ivory color. The whole chain thus brightened, must have formerly exhibited a very superb appearance.

From Whence Came This Giant?

Upon the contemplation of this discovery, the inquisitive mind is impelled irresistibly to ask from whence came this gigantic skeleton, the chain of which he wore and the ivory beads that compose it? His size and the thinness of his skull prove that he was from the north and probably of that race of huge stature which, in the time of the Roman Empire, so much excited the wonder of their writers;

and which, in the decline of the empire, spread desolation, ruin, and darkness over its whole extent.

Of the Religion of the Aborigines of Tennessee

Let us first take a view of the aboriginal religion of Tennessee, so far as it is to be collected from the ancient signs, which have been left us, and which are fairly referable to this topic. These are suns and moons painted upon rocks; marks or tokens of triplicity; the cross; mounds; images; human sacrifices; the lingam; the dress of the images; conch shells; and vestiges of the sanctity of the number seven.

Of the Sun and Moon Painted upon Rocks

About two miles below the road, which crosses Harpeth River, from Nashville to Charlotte, is a bend of the river, and in the bend is a large mound, 30 or 40 feet high, and a number of smaller ones near it, which will be particularly described here-after.

About six miles from it is a large rock, on the side of the river, with a perpendicular face of 70 or 80 feet altitude. On it, below the top some distance, and on the side, are painted the sun and moon in yellow colors, which have not faded since the white people first knew it.

The figure of the sun is six feet in diameter: that of the moon is of the old moon. The sun and moon are also painted on a high rock on the side of the Cumberland River in a spot where several ladders placed upon each other could not reach; and which is also inaccessible except by ropes let down the summit of the rock to the place where the painting was performed. This is near the residence of Mr. Dozun; and it is affirmed by a person of good credit, that by climbing from tree to tree, he once got near enough to take a near view of this painting, and that with it, on the rock, were literal characters, which did not belong to the Roman alphabet; but at this time, 1822, for he looked again lately, the paint has so-far faded as to make the form of these characters indistinguishable.

The sun is also painted on a high rock, on the side of the Cumberland River, six or seven miles below Clarksville; and it is said to be painted also at the junction of the Holstein and Frenchbroad rivers, above Knoxville, in East Tennessee. Also on Duck River, below the bend called the Devil's Elbow, on the west side of the river, on a bluff: and on a perpendicular flat rock facing the river, 20 feet below the top of the bluff, and 60 feet above the water out of which the rock rises, is the painted representation of the sun in red and yellow colors, six feet in circumference, yellow on the upper side and a yellowish red on the lower.

The colors are very fresh and unfaded. The rays both yellow and red are represented as darting from the center. It has been spoken of ever since the river was navigated, and has been there from time immemorial. No one has been able since the white people knew it to approach the circle either from above or below. The circle is a perfect one.

Neat, Elegant, Inaccessible Paintings

The painting is done in the most neat and elegant style. It can be seen at the distance of half a mile. The painting on Big Harpeth, before spoken of is more than 80 feet from the water, and 30 or 40 below the summit. All these paintings are in unfading colors, and on parts of the rock inaccessible to animals of every description except the fowls of the air.

The painting is neatly executed and was performed at an immense hazard of the operator. It must have been for a sacred purpose and as an object of adoration. What other motive was capable of inciting to a work so perilous, laborious, and expensive as those paintings must have been? From whence came the unfading dyes and the skilled artist capable to execute the work? By what means was he let down and placed near enough to operate? And for what reward did he undertake so dangerous a work? When executed, of what use could it be to any one, unless to see and to worship?

Taken in connection with the mounds, which are in the vicinity, the high places upon which, in the old world, the worshippers of the sun performed their devotional exercises, there can be but little difficulty in perceiving that these paintings had some relation to the adoration of that luminary, the god of the Egyptians, Hindus, and Phoenicians, and the great god of the Mexicans and Natchez, and of the ancient inhabitants west of the Mississippi.

Of Triplicity

In White county, in West Tennessee, was dug up a few years ago, in an open temple, situated on the Cany Fork of Cumberland river, a flagon designed into the shape of three distinct and hollow heads, joined to the central neck of the vessel, by short thick tubes, leading from each respective occupant. It was made of a light, yellow and compact clay, intimately intermixed with small broken fragments, and dust of powdered carbon of lime, and in a state of crystallization.

The Use of Quart Measurements from Extreme Antiquity

This vessel held a quart. Its workmanship is well executed. The heads are perfectly natural and display a striking resemblance of the Asiatic countenance. None of the minor parts have been attended to, though a small oval prominence somewhat towards the top of each head is probably meant to represent a knot of hair.

Ancient Heads of Different Races and Classes

In other respects they appear bold. Each face is painted in a different manner, and strongly resembles the modes by which the Hindus designate their different castes. One of the faces is slightly covered all over with red ochre, having deep blotches of the same paint on the central part of each cheek. The second face has a broad streak of brown ochre across the forehead, and another running parallel with the same, enveloping the eyes, and extending as far as the ears. The third face has a streak of yellow ochre, which

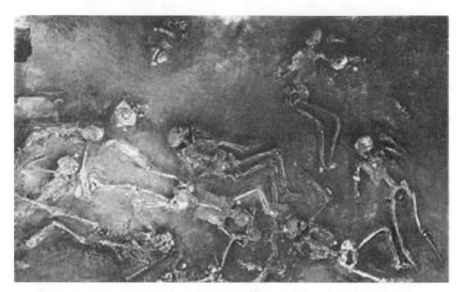

Fig.12.1. These are the purported remains of radioactive skeletons of
Mohenjo-daro, Pakistan, dating to around 2000 to 2500 BCE.

surrounds and extends across the eyes, running from the center
at right angles, down the nose to the upper lip; whilst another
broad streak passes from each ear, along the lower jaw and chin.

A PROPOSED CONNECTION WITH
THE HINDU RELIGION

In White County, Tennessee, face jugs were discovered that "display a
striking resemblance of the Asiatic countenance." Haywood noted face
painting and lines on the cheeks and forehead that bear a striking similarity to caste marks used by the Hindu religion to mark social standing
and religious status. It is interesting that face jugs of extreme antiquity
were discovered in this area, as it is common to this day in this part of
the South to throw face jugs that can still be bought in this area's pottery shops.

Upon this image the following remarks suggest themselves: The Hindus have various marks, by which they paint their faces to designate the different casts and to distinguish amongst the same castes those who are the peculiar votaries of certain gods. Mr. Dubois says they use only three colors, red, black, and yellow.

"Probably the face, which now seems to be covered with brown ochre, was originally black," says Mr. Clifford. "If it was a metallic paint, as the other colors certainly are, the black, having an admixture of iron, would certainly change from the lapse of time, and become what to all appearance it now is: a dark brown ochre. The other two colors, being native minerals usually found in the earth, are not subject to change. If so, these colors were originally the same as those used in Hindustan." Mr. Dubois mentions that the Hindus draw three or four horizontal lines between the eyebrows, whilst others describe a perpendicular line from the top of the forehead to the root of the nose. Some northern Brahmans apply the marks to either jaw, meaning probably the same sort of line above described in the face painted with yellow ochre, as extending from the ears, along the lower jaw, to the chin. He says further, that the Brahmans draw a horizontal line around the forehead to denote that they have bathed and are pure. The vessel described, Mr. Clifford thought, was intended for sacred uses. It being found within one of the circumvallatory temples is evidence in favor of this supposition. It would certainly not have been a convenient vessel for any domestic purpose. The angular position of the heads; with respect to the neck of the flagon, must have prevented its being emptied of any liquid, by other means than a complete inversion.

The contents of two of the heads might be discharged by an inclined position with some difficulty and much gargling. But to empty the other, the neck must become vertical. The ancients were unacquainted with goblets, pitchers, and decanters, as intermediate vessels. They used large jars or vases to hold their liquors for safe keeping or carriage, and poured the contents into bowls or horns, from which they drank.

Our aborigines were hardly more refined. And whilst the small size of the flagon precludes the idea of its being a vessel for deposits of liquids, its shape plainly indicates that it could not have been used for a drinking vessel. As the ancients always completely inverted the vessel from which they poured their libations, it is reasonable to suppose that this flagon was intended for the same purpose; and that the three heads, with the different marks of castes might designate the various orders of men for which such libations were made.

If so, the evidence is most directly connected to the identity of religion professed by the Hindus and the aborigines of Tennessee. No fabulous circumstance or train of thought, could have occasioned such striking similarity in the paints and modes of applying them, in order to distinguish the different orders of men in their respective nations. If, however, the flagon is not a vessel of libation, the fact of its having three heads, possessing Asiatic features, and painted as before stated, is certainly a strong evidence of Asiatic origination. Brahma, one of the three principal gods of the Hindus, was represented with a triple head. From the remotest antiquity it is proved from his colossal statue in the cave of Elephanta. Numerous Hindu idols on the island of Java have three heads. This character in the image of their gods was very common as is proved by a number of them delineated by Mr. Raffle, in the second volume of his history.

Hebrew Cherubim with Three Faces,
Also Baal Shalisha Has Three Faces

Some of the Hebrew cherubim are represented with three faces. Baal Shalisha, or the god of triplicity—or the deity whose image is divided into three distinctions, yet remaining combined in one whole—was a common emblem, and still maintains itself in India.

INDIANS OF CAROLINA KNEW
THE WORLD WAS ROUND

Engraved on one of the medallions found in association with a mound-builder burial in North Carolina is an image of a triple-headed goddess holding a round globe of the world in one of her hands. In the following extract, John Haywood posits this as proof of contact with Asia, as well as proof that these ancient explorers had knowledge that the earth was round.

In the same temple of Elephanta before mentioned is another triple-formed divinity, with three faces, and three arms; in one hand holding a globe; a proof that the ancients of India, as well as the Indians of Carolina, knew that the world was round.

On a medal of Syracuse, is a figure with three heads, extremely like the symbols adopted by the Hindus, and resembling much the Indian figures. The famous Siberian medal hath three heads, and three pair of arms. The resemblance of the heads, to the deities of India, leaves no doubt of the origin of the emblem. It is seated on a tower. The heads hold various symbolic articles, among which the ring is clearly distinguishable.

The Hindus celebrate the first day of the year for three days. At the winter solstice they keep a festival for three days. Three prostrations are made in presence of distinguished persons. When a child is named by the Brahmans, and the mantras or prayers are made, the father calls him three times by the name he has received. The Brahmans wear a cord over the shoulders, of three thick twists of cotton, called the triple cord. The threads are not twisted together, but are separate from one another. On the third day of the ceremonies for investing with the triple cord, the young Brahman, his father and mother seat themselves upon three little stools.

When carrying a body to the funeral pile, they stop with it three times on the way. The chief of the funeral goes three times around the funeral pile; and when the body is consumed, the four attending

Brahmans go around it three times. When a minyam is made, he takes with him three articles; a cane of a bamboo with seven knots, a gourd filled with water, and an antelope's skin. He drinks of the water in the pitcher. The sacredness of this number was recognized in Chaldea, for the Hebrew children were to be instructed three years. Daniel kneeled upon his knees three times a day. Amongst the Hebrews themselves, it was received, and had as firmly grown into a custom with them, as it was established in India.

The Cross and Its Ancient Association with the Cosmic Bird of Cygnus

It is not recollected that the cross has been found in Tennessee except upon the small vessels buried with the pigmy skeletons in White county. The ring or cross in ancient Persian medals was represented as sacred symbols, and had a commemorative intention. In one place the circle is surrounded by 19 points resembling jewels, and it unites in a cross. There are creatures cut on rocks at Persepolis, of Baal and Moloch, on horseback. Moloch has a club in his left hand, holding a large ring in his right hand. The ring, in this instance, is the symbol of unity. Amorsea, Baal, and Moloch, reconciled, united. The family of Isaiah was early divided into two parties; one called of the sun, the other of the moon. They boasted of their divinity each to the other; and to prove their superiority, each fought the other's divinity. This shows their reconciliation. These are the most ancient idols.

A medal of Demetrius the second, dated in the 168th year of the Leleucida, has on it the representation of a goddess, a Tyrian and Sidonian Venus, standing giving directions. Her right hand and arm extended; in her left, she holds a cross with a long stem to it. These without any further multiplication of instances prove sufficiently that in ancient time in Asia Minor, Persia, and India, the ring was symbolic of union, and the cross a sacred symbol.

CONCLUSION

Now that you have reviewed the evidence for a former race of giants in North America, I invite you to consider both their legends and their reality. There are legends of giants in many cultures, such as the Titans of Greece or Goliath in the Bible. In fact, the Bible has several references to giants, known as the Rephaim, Anakim, Zuzim, Sepherim, and Nephilim, as in the following quote from Numbers 13:32–33: "The land, through which we have gone to search it, is a land that eateth up the inhabitants thereof; and all the people that we saw in it are men of a great stature. And there we saw the giants, the sons of Anak, which come of the giants: and we were in our own sight as grasshoppers, and so we were in their sight."

Could it truly be that all these cultural legends are mere legends—with no basis in fact? Are these legends just the result of a human need to create something "larger than ourselves"? I think not. In these pages and pages of documentation we have now seen the American giants' widespread presence, their sophisticated cultures, their royal status, their Caucasian genetic links, and signs of cultural links to other areas of the globe long before Columbus.

The fact that almost no one is aware of these giants today is a telling comment on the role played by the Smithsonian Institution and other institutions of higher learning, on which we rely to explore, preserve, and offer insights into our heritage, perhaps most especially those aspects that hint at broader horizons. What do the roles these institutions have played in this matter teach us about the role of bias in all studies of a supposedly academic or scientific nature? What would be the reason for not keeping this information in the public eye?

And what have we lost by losing our collective memory of these early, extraordinary inhabitants of America? What insights into not only American but also global prehistory might their existence offer us?

It is natural to want to point fingers in a situation like this, but the reality is that no one who is presently at the Smithsonian probably has the faintest idea about the history of the giants presented here. In fact, if their academic indoctrination has been rigorous enough, they will probably still remain unmoved by the overwhelming evidence presented in this book.

This should come as no surprise to those who are aware of the 1,200-ton stones in Baalbek, the advanced mathematics and engineering of the Great Pyramids, or the stories of Atlantis, as related by Plato. We live in an age where we are hypnotized by our own ignorance, acting as if atomic energy and digital electronics are the heights of human achievement, patting ourselves on the back that we are the best and the brightest. One might call it hubris; wiser minds would call it cultural myopia and adolescent grandstanding.

The stories of myth and antiquity are real. There were other ages as great as, or greater than, our own, and whatever we have accomplished was built on the shoulders of giants.

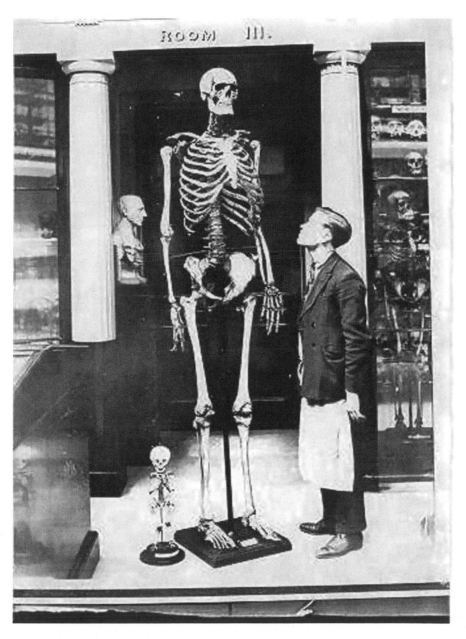

Fig. C.1. "There were giants upon the earth in those days"—Genesis 6:4.
The skeletons of Charles Byrne (1761–1783), "The Irish Giant,"
and Caroline Crachami (ca. 1815–1824), "The Sicillian Dwarf," from
The Strand Magazine, published in 1896.

BIBLIOGRAPHY

Adovasio, James M. *The First Americans: In Pursuit of Archaeology's Greatest Mystery.* New York: Random House, 2002.

Davis, Edwin, and Ephraim Squier. *Ancient Monuments of the Mississippi Valley: Comprising the Results of Extensive Original Surveys and Explorations.* Washington, D.C.: Smithsonian Institution, 1848.

Drier, Roy Ward, and Octave Joseph DuTemple. *Prehistoric Copper Mining in the Lake Superior Region.* Published privately by the authors, 1961.

Fell, Barry, *America B.C.: Ancient Settlers in the New World.* New York: Pocket Books, 1989.

Haywood, John. *The Natural and Aboriginal History of Tennessee: Up to the First Settlements Therein by the White People, in the Year 1768.* Nashville, Tenn.: George Wilson, 1823.

Heckewelder, John Gottlieb Ernestus. *An Account of the History, Manners, and Customs of the Indian Nations Who Once Inhabited Pennsylvania and the Neighboring States 1819.* New York: Arno Press, 1971, copyright 1876.

Hopkins, Sarah Winnemucca. *Life among the Paiutes: Their Wrongs and Claims.* Boston: Cupples, Upham, and Co.; New York: G. P. Putnam's Sons, 1883.

Howe, Henry. *Historical Collection of Ohio.* Cincinnati, Ohio: E. Morgan and Co., 1847.

Howley, J. P. *The Beothucks or Red Indians.* Cambridge: Cambridge University Press, 1915.

Kohl, Johann Georg. *Reisen im Nordwesten der Vereinigten Staaten* [Travels in Northwestern Parts of the United States]. New York: D. Appleton & Co., 1857.

Lee, Bourke. *Death Valley Men*. New York: Macmillan Co., 1932.

McKusick, Marshall. *The Davenport Conspiracy*. Iowa City: University of Iowa Press, 1970.

Moore, Clarence B. *Some Aboriginal Sites on Red River*. Philadelphia, Pa.: P. C. Stockhausen, 1912.

Ronda, James P. *Lewis and Clark among the Indians*. Lincoln: University of Nebraska Press, 2002.

Schoolcraft, Henry Rowe, *Narrative Journal of Travels through the Northwestern Regions of the United States*. Albany, N.Y.: E. & E. Hosford, 1821.

Scott, Joseph. *Geographical Description of Pennsylvania*. Philadelphia, Pa.: Robert Cochran, 1806.

INDEX

Page numbers in *italics* refer to figures.

BOOKS OF RELATED INTEREST

Ancient Giants
History, Myth, and Scientific Evidence from around the World
by Xaviant Haze

Denisovan Origins
Hybrid Humans, Gobekli Tepe, and the Genesis
of the Giants of Ancient America
by Andrew Collins and Gregory L. Little, Ed.D.

Lost Race of the Giants
The Mystery of Their Culture, Influence,
and Decline throughout the World
by Patrick Chouinard

There Were Giants Upon the Earth
Gods, Demigods, and Human Ancestry: The Evidence of Alien DNA
by Zecharia Sitchin

Advanced Civilizations of Prehistoric America
The Lost Kingdoms of the Adena, Hopewell, Mississippians, and Anasazi
by Frank Joseph

The Suppressed History of America
The Murder of Meriwether Lewis and the Mysterious Discoveries
of the Lewis and Clark Expedition
by Paul Schrag and Xaviant Haze

Secrets of Ancient America
Archaeoastronomy and the Legacy of the Phoenicians,
Celts, and Other Forgotten Explorers
by Carl Lehrburger

Lost Knowledge of the Ancients
A Graham Hancock Reader
Edited by Glenn Kreisberg

Inner Traditions • Bear & Company
P.O. Box 388
Rochester, VT 05767
1-800-246-8648
www.InnerTraditions.com

Or contact your local bookseller